PRAISE FOR *About My Sisters*

"Poignant. . . . Debra Ginsberg takes a bighearted look at the ties that bind and the bonds that break and mend again."
—*Elle* magazine

"Warm, funny, and true."   —*Booklist*

"Ginsberg's thinking-out-loud style makes you laugh, sigh, even blink back tears. . . . You can't help but stop reading somewhere, mid-sentence, and marvel at how much she is teaching you about those most-important relationships in our lives."
—*San Diego Union-Tribune*

"This witty, entertaining account of a loving, intergenerational, and eccentric family will appeal to those encountering Ginsberg for the first time as well as those already familiar with her writing."   —*Library Journal*

"With eloquence, deep feeling and altruism, Ginsberg depicts the life of her family through a year of celebrations and crises . . . as entertaining as a novel."   —*Publishers Weekly*

"A rich celebration of life with three sisters. In this clear-eyed but always loving description of her family, memoirist Ginsberg explores the differing ways her siblings relate to each other, ways familiar to all who have sisters. . . . Loving and candid, as the best family stories are."   —*Kirkus Reviews*

"A lovely book. Painfully honest, dryly funny, heartbreakingly real. You might just fall in love with this strange, wonderful family. *About My Sisters* turned my life-long desire for a sister into an active ache. Debra Ginsberg manages to write about the complex and mysterious dynamics of sisterhood with both candor and love—a very neat trick."

—Patricia Gaffney, author of *Flight Lessons* and *The Saving Graces*

"Like all family relationships, the bond that entwines sisters unites and separates, brings comfort and causes friction. . . . Ginsberg details the imperfect love she shares with her three sisters."

—*USA Weekend*

"*About My Sisters* . . . delves into the eccentricities that come with sisterly and familial relationships."   —*Dallas Observer*

"Debra Ginsberg mines the rich vein of sororal relations in *About My Sisters*."

—*East Bay Express*

PRAISE FOR *Waiting*

"Ginsberg . . . has told an attractive story about coping with a life that has been different than what she expected."

—*New York Times Book Review*

"[Ginsberg's] poignant, gently written stories of waitressing are metaphors for life."   —*Dallas Morning News*

"[Ginsberg] tells the story with enough honesty and wry humor to connect with other people—especially women."

—*Detroit Free Press*

"Written with the consciousness and conscience of a novelist, Debra Ginsberg's *Raising Blaze* is a memoir without the 'me,' and in place of the me is a 'thou,' her son, Blaze. It is he whom Ginsberg, like every mother of a brilliant, square-peg child, disabled only by society's inabilities to serve him, considers a holy innocent. Her story is tough, unsentimental and moving, achieving, as only a few others do, a selfless grace."
—Jacquelyn Mitchard, author of *The Theory of Relativity*

"This is the poignant and compelling story of raising a child with an undefinable disability centering on emotional/behavioral issues. . . . This mother and son's tale not only reveals the beauty and strength in struggle but also acts as a supportive text for parents and guardians of disabled children. Highly recommended." —*Library Journal* (starred review)

"[*Raising Blaze*] is a journey . . . filled with humor and horror and above all, honesty. Ginsberg . . . is a gifted writer. . . .With an expertise learned from sheer necessity, she teaches all of us to fight, whatever our battles are, and she teaches us why that fight is important." —*San Diego Union-Tribune*

"A stirring record of a mother's battle fought with zest, humor, and love." —*Kirkus Reviews*

"[Ginsberg] not only reveals what it means to be the mother of an exceptional child but also shares a tale in which all mothers can see themselves." —*Washington Post Book World*

Ron Perry

About the Author

DEBRA GINSBERG is the author of *Waiting: The True
Confessions of a Waitress* and *Raising Blaze: Bringing
Up an Extraordinary Son in an Ordinary World*. She
is a graduate of Reed College and a contributor to
NPR's "All Things Considered" and the *San Diego
Union-Tribune* Books section.

ALSO BY DEBRA GINSBERG

Waiting
Raising Blaze

About

My

Sisters

D E B R A   G I N S B E R G

Perennial
An Imprint of HarperCollins*Publishers*

Grateful acknowledgment is made to Ron Perry for permission to reprint the photographs on pages 8 and 292. All other photographs courtesy of the author.

A hardcover edition of this book was published in 2004 by HarperCollins Publishers.

HarperCollins books may be purchased for educational, business, or sales promotional use. For information please write: Special Markets Department, HarperCollins Publishers Inc., 10 East 53rd Street, New York, NY 10022.

FIRST PERENNIAL EDITION PUBLISHED 2005.

Designed by Sarah Maya Gubkin

The Library of Congress has catalogued the hardcover edition as follows:

Ginsberg, Debra.
   About my sisters / Debra Ginsberg.— 1st ed.
      p. cm.
ISBN 0-06-052202-X
   1. Ginsberg, Debra. 2. Sisters—United States—Biography. 3. Sisters—Family relationships.   I. Title.

CT275.G435A3 2004
920.72'0973—dc21

2003050945

ISBN 0-06-052203-8 (pbk.)

05 06 07 08 09 ❖/RRD   10 9 8 7 6 5 4 3 2 1

With the exception of members of the author's immediate family, all names and identifying characteristics of individuals discussed in this book have been changed to protect their privacy.

For my sisters,

and for our mother

Contents

Our mother and her sister.

Prologue

It's a week after Valentine's Day. Winter, such as it is here in southern California, is effectively over. The air is warm and dry enough to crackle with static electricity. I've had twelve long-stemmed red roses sitting on my coffee table since last week and they are still fresh. They are huge and beautiful and look as if they might live forever.

In South Africa, on the other side of the world, my mother's sister is dying.

My aunt, who has been fighting cancer for the last few years, is not an old woman. She has been ill for some time, it is true, but, until recently, it seemed as if she might have beaten her disease. It is only now, in the last month, that her death has become imminent. My mother spoke to her sister a few weeks ago in what turned out to be their last conversation. They discussed my aunt's illness but not her death. Now my aunt is in the hospital and no longer conscious. And my mother waits for a phone call.

Among us, my family has experienced few premature deaths. In this way, we have been very fortunate. My parents have also spent most of their adult lives physically separated from their families of origin. We have always been removed, by many miles, from the deaths of our relatives. I am almost forty years old and I have never been to a funeral.

Although she was a presence in my life and despite the fact that I saw her fairly regularly over the years, I have never been very close to my aunt. The constant geographical distance between us prevented the formation of a strong bond and it is impossible to know now whether or not one might have been created had we lived in closer proximity. I have spent more time thinking about her in the last few days than in the last several years combined. I grieve for my cousins, her children, although I can't truly imagine how they must be feeling. It is for my own mother, however, that I feel the greatest sadness. She is losing her sister. And the loss of a sister is one, in the selfishness of my sorrow, I can't envision.

I can remember a time before I was a mother. And, with some difficulty, I can picture a future when I am no longer a daughter. But I can neither remember nor imagine my life without sisters. As the eldest of five children, four of them girls and one of them our only brother, my role as sister will always be an inextricable part of my personal identity. All four of us maintain an exceptionally intimate bond with each other. We all live within ten minutes of each other and speak every day. This is not a recent phenomenon. My sisters and I have been close our entire lives. The four of us are hardly ever in unanimous agreement and our very different personalities prevent us from ever thinking with one mind. Yet, in our relationships, our work, the face we present to the world, in every day of our lives, each one of us carries some part of her sisters with her. I can't imagine my life without any one of them. Nor do I want to try.

In keeping with our disparate viewpoints, my sisters and I have been responding to our mother's grief in different ways. But we are united now in the desire to comfort her. This is why we are gathering to take her out for lunch and shopping today. Despite the frequency with which we see each other, we are seldom together at the same place and time and never go shopping as a group, so this is an extraordinary circumstance.

We assemble at my mother's house and, after some debate, decide to ride in one car. My mother seems subdued but not depressed. I've made her a mixed CD of all the songs that have been going through my head over the last couple of weeks. They are songs that were always playing in our house when I was growing up. There's a bit of Leon Russell; a little Sly and the Family Stone, some Beatles, Neil Young, Aretha Franklin, and the Staple Singers. We listen to it in the car, and my mother says, "This is lovely."

Nobody talks about my aunt, although she's there, in the air among us.

I am impressed by how well my mother seems to be managing emotionally. She is sad, yes, but not in a morbid way. I've been talking to her every day lately, after she receives updates on her sister's condition. Although she has clearly come to an acceptance of what is happening, she still expresses some surprise at the inevitable trajectory of this illness.

"She's a very strong woman," my mother says. "She always has been. She didn't have to die this way. She's had a lifetime of bad advice, all of which she's taken as the gospel."

For the most part, though, my mother seems philosophical and resigned, willing and able to let her sister go. I have begun to believe that my mother will get through what is euphemistically called "this difficult time" with heartache that will at least be bearable. My mother can be cagey about certain things, but I've never known her to hide her emotions. What she projects is almost always what she feels. Still, I expect to see a crack in this calmness of hers. I anticipate a visceral expression of impending loss. I wait for tears.

That rupture comes now, before we can hit the freeway. One of us asks her whether we should go to Ikea or Nordstrom, and my mother leans her head against the window, hand to her mouth, and sobs.

The inside of the car rings with a chorus of "What? What is it?"

"I hate to think of her there, dying," my mother weeps. "Alone. She's all alone."

My sister Maya says, "She isn't alone. All of her children and her grandchildren are there with her."

My sister Lavander says, "Don't feel bad because you aren't there. There isn't anything you can do other than what you are doing."

My sister Déja says, "In the end, you have to go alone. There isn't any other way."

I say nothing. Alone without her sister. This is what my mother means.

"Do you want to skip this outing?" Lavander asks her. "We don't have to go if you're not up for it."

"Or we can just go to my house for tea," Maya says.

"What do you think, Mumsie?" says Déja.

"I'm all right," my mother says, wiping her eyes. "I'll be okay. It just hit me now. That's all."

"Then you still want to go?" I ask her.

"The living must live," she says. "And how often do I get to spend time with all my beautiful daughters?"

"All the time, actually," Déja says.

"I mean *together*," my mother says.

There is an uncharacteristic quiet in the car for a while after this, as we each shift around in our seats, wondering what to say or whether to say anything at all. And then, as if her memory has opened in a slide show before her, my mother says, "When I was a girl, I had this friend Shirley who was an artist. We must have been about eighteen or so and she had a project she had to do for a class, a lino cut. She asked me to write a poem and she'd make the print to go with it. So I wrote this poem, 'Four Thin Girls.' Shirley did a Modigliani thing with these four figures and she displayed it with the poem on one side." She pauses as she looks at the print in her mind's eye.

"Do you remember the poem?" I ask her, and she recites it easily.

> *"Four thin girls standing in the rain.*
> *'Are we living or are we dead?'*
> *Four weary souls, they complain,*
> *'We are dissatisfied, we are well-bred.' "*

"Not a happy poem," I say.

"It's not *un*happy," she protests.

"What does it mean?" says Lavander.

"It's all of you," my mother says. "I just remembered it and realized that the poem is about you. I didn't know then, of course, but those four girls are you. I saw all of you way back then. Four sisters. My girls."

Less than a week after our shopping trip, my mother gets the phone call. And then she calls me.

"My sister died," she says.

"Are you all right?" I ask her.

"Yes," she says. "I'm okay."

We don't talk about it again in any detail. We still speak on the phone every day, but there are no more updates. She is no longer waiting to hear. What is left now is to sift and sort through

the layers of emotion. My mother will do this on her own. As for
me, I have been spending my time thinking about my own sisters and our relationships. I have been thinking about the nature
and the quiet strength of sisterhood. My sisters and I are unique
in our particulars. There is a fifteen-year span between the first
and last, for example, and because of this, we have grown up in
different generations. We share the same parents, but not the
same parenting. Our family lives closer and spends more time
together than most. But in our generalities, we are much like sisters everywhere. With personalities shaped by birth order, we are
the keepers of each other's secrets and protectors of each other's
childhood memories. We are givers and receivers of female wisdom and are constantly learning from each other. We are each
other's harshest critics and strongest supporters. As sisters, we
mirror and define ourselves as women through each other's eyes.

It is this relationship, I decide now, that I want to write about.

After I make this decision, but before I really embark on the
journey, I put the proposal to my sisters. I have written two mem-
oirs in the last two years. The first, *Waiting*, is an account of the
twenty years I spent as a waitress. The second, *Raising Blaze*, is
about my son, an exceptional child with undiagnosable learning
differences, and the journey the two of us have made through the
public education system. My sisters have appeared in both books,
but as supporting players. This time the focus will be sharpened
on them. I am not asking their permission, but I want—no, I *need*
to have their approval. Characteristically, my sisters don't ask me
why I want to write about them. They have long since come to an
acceptance of my position as family chronicler. Maya tells me to
go ahead, that she's got nothing to hide. Lavander assures me that
I will do a great job, but asks me, please, not to ruin her career.
Déja says she thinks this will be the easiest book I'll ever write
because what else, *who* else, am I more familiar with?

It is true, my sisters are as constant and familiar as fixed stars in the night sky. They are my geography. But it is also true that any landscape can change depending on the lens and angle through which it is viewed. This is what I think about as I start writing. I rely on the familiar, but I expect to find some new scenery here in the territory of my sisters.

Debra, Maya, Lavander, and Déja.

1

Four Elements, One Pattern

march

Maya stands in our kitchen wielding a spatula.

"I'm making dinner," she says. This brief sentence of hers tells me much more than it would seem. It doesn't just mean that she is whipping up something for the two of us. If that were the case, she'd ask me, "What do you feel like eating?" and then we'd go around for twenty minutes with neither one of us able to decide what culinary ethnicity we'd prefer:

"What about Greek? You want Greek?"

"Too much garlic. How about Chinese?"

"Too much work. Pasta?"

"Boring. Want to have Thai for a change?"

"I can't eat Thai, too much peanut sauce in everything."

And then, ultimately, we'd grow weary of the debate to the

point where nothing seemed worth eating and settle for a couple of frozen pizzas, or toast (my default meal), or prepackaged stir-fry (hers).

But when she says, "I'm making dinner," it means she's already decided; that we will be having penne with fresh juli-enned vegetables, or orzo with feta and tomatoes, or tofu Milanese with roasted corn and mashed potatoes. It also means that we will be having a big family gathering. Just how big remains to be determined. Our parents will be here for certain. Our brother probably won't show up. Our other two sisters prob-ably will. And there is always the possibility that various signifi-cant others might appear. Everybody will arrive at a different time, despite the fact that Maya has designated a specific hour for the meal. There will almost definitely be an argument about that. There may be other arguments as well. There might be a couple of scenes or more than one furious exit. There might be a lively debate over whatever turns out to be the topic of the day and it might even be amicable, but it certainly won't be calm and quiet. Calm and quiet is not something my family does when they're all together. However, the exact tenor of the meal will be determined by who shows up this time and by what well-established patterns we choose to tread. And my sisters and I are adept—no, *brilliant*—at maintaining our patterns of behavior.

I am trying to remember when it was, exactly, that Maya started making these dinners or how our house got to be the des-ignated destination of almost every family gathering. It may have been about fifteen years ago when our family owned Peppy's, a little pizza parlor in Oregon, and Maya became the chief cook (in reality the *only* person who could actually make a pizza). But I think her position as family chef has its origins much earlier. Although I had my turns with crescent rolls and apple pies when we were growing up, Maya was the one who really developed an affinity for and understanding of pastry and cakes. Where I found cooking for large groups of people (our family, in other words) overwhelming, Maya was always able to put together a big meal with whatever was in the house. I got very tired of using the same ingredients in the same way (there's nothing more depressing to me than a pot of boiling potatoes), but Maya was always able to replicate her dishes effortlessly. For Maya, cooking was not only easy but a source of pride. I always preferred to clean up afterward.

Maya and I moved in together in 1987 and our house (or apartment—there have been five different places since then) gradually became the place to go whenever there was a meal attached to a birthday, a celebration, Sunday brunch, Mother's Day, a New Year's Eve party, or anything that could be seen as an *occasion*. For a while, we were all eating a meal together at least once a week. There was a period, too, when dinner at our house became the testing ground for new friends and lovers. The theory behind this being that it is less threatening to introduce someone to your whole family when it's your *sister's* house as opposed to your parents. And between the two of us, we've got a couple of important bases covered. Maya cooks, providing nourishment, and I do the astrological birth charts and subsequent interpretations for the potential mates. I can always tell that there's a new romantic interest in the offing when one of my sisters (or my brother, for that matter) calls me up and says, "Hey, can you run a quick chart for me?"

When a friend or lover becomes a long-term relationship, Maya will even fix up a to-go container if that person can't quite make it to dinner, but sends a message that he just loves Maya's cooking so much and is so sorry that he can't be there in person and will miss it so much. . . . And the Tupperware comes out. Like I said, it's a source of pride for her.

"Who's coming?" I ask her now. I need to be prepared.

"Everybody, I think."

"What do you mean, everybody?"

"Lavander, Déja, Mom, Dad . . ."

Well, that covers the parents and the sisters at least. "What about Bo?" I ask, referring to our brother, who doesn't attend these gatherings regularly.

"He's coming, too."

"Really? And Danny?" Danny, Déja's boyfriend, has lately been a fixture at these family dinners.

"Yes, Danny's coming, too."

Full house, I think, and am mentally adjusting when another thought crosses.

"Tony's not coming, is he?"

Maya says nothing just long enough for me to know that Tony, Lavander's current boyfriend, might actually be attending. "I don't know," she says, finally.

"What do you mean, you don't know?" I ask her. "Didn't we all decide that it was a *bad idea* to have that guy over for dinner? Or anywhere, for that matter?"

By "we" I don't just mean the two of us. This has been a family conclusion that's been bubbling to the surface for the last few weeks. Lavander started seeing Tony in December. He was here, at our house, on Christmas Day when we all gathered for a family brunch. As I recall, we all liked him and welcomed him with open arms at that point. Somewhere in the last three months, things started to go south between the two of them and, therefore, between him and the rest of us.

"Well, what do you want me to do?" Maya says with exasperation as if we've already been arguing about this for hours. "I can't *not* invite him. I can't tell her not to bring him, can I? Well, can I?"

"Why not?" I ask her. "He's not exactly popular at the moment. Why would we have him over for dinner? Why would we act like he's part of the family? Why?"

"Because he's her boyfriend, that's why."

I know she's right, that to specifically eliminate Tony would spark a war the likes of which nobody even cares to contemplate. And Lavander is so good at setting us up this way, using our dislike of her boyfriend (a dislike I believe she has fostered herself) as a reason to act wounded, misunderstood, and angry. So what if he's a loser/sponge/poser or any of the other epithets that she, herself, has slung his way lately? He's her boyfriend—the Boyfriend of Damocles, hanging precariously over all of our heads.

"I really don't want him here," I say.

"Yes, well, maybe she'll have the good sense not to bring him," Maya says.

"If she had any good sense, she wouldn't be seeing him in the first place," I say.

"Well, we *know* that."

We sigh in tandem, and then I ask her, "What are you making?"

This is the other Rubicon to cross where dinner is concerned. Everybody has at least one favorite dish and one that they can't stand. Lately, too, several members of my family have developed special dietary rules (aside from vegetarianism, which we've all had in common for twenty-five years) that must be adhered to. For example, my mother is "off" pasta this week. Last month, she wouldn't eat any cheese. Now she doesn't want bread either and is asking for raw food. My father has rules against "fruit and nuts in food." No raisins on the salad, in other words. Nothing even approaching say, pears, in a main course. He's only just accepted capers into his culinary pantheon, previously dismissing them as "too exotic." Danny, on the other hand, won't eat tomatoes. His plate can always be identified by a bright red ring of picked-out pieces around the rim. Lavander will most likely arrive saying she's "not very hungry" because she "had a big lunch," which will set Maya off ("Why come to dinner then? That's what we do at dinner—we *eat*") and then she'll pick from the serving dishes until she's eaten the equivalent of a full plate.

Ironically, my son, Blaze, who is always thrilled when we have these get-togethers, won't be eating with us at all, having an intense aversion to most foods and their odors. He only joins the table for dessert, of which he always partakes. And I must admit, I have my own dietary peculiarities. I have issues with both garlic and onions, two foods that *nobody* else has a problem with. But even Maya, who claims open-mindedness about everything, has a few items she won't touch. No avocado. No mushrooms.

Admittedly, these restrictions tend to make dinner more interesting. Maya is very sensitive about her cooking, as well as being proud of her abilities with food, so if someone dares to say something snide about bell peppers, for example, she takes it very personally. So, naturally, during the course of any given dinner, someone is bound to say something snide about something. Tonight will doubtless be no different.

"Well?" I ask Maya a second time. "What are you making?"

She shoots me a somewhat sardonic look and says, "Macaroni and cheese."

"Trying to start a revolution?" I ask her. Surely this dish, containing onion, garlic, cheese, pasta, *and* tomato, is guaranteed to commit dietary offenses for just about everyone.

"I can't do anything about it," she says, "there are too many people to make anything else and I can't keep up with what people are eating or not eating this week. Besides, there's a salad."

"Yes, well, just be prepared," I tell her. "Salad or no. So what time do the festivities begin?"

"I told everyone six o'clock. We'll see who manages to get here on time." I glance over at the clock. An hour and a half. I wonder if there is anything I can clean while I'm waiting.

The macaroni and cheese is in the oven and Maya is in the shower when I hear the clickety-click of high heels on the walkway outside our front door. Lavander walks in, half hobbling and slightly bowlegged, as if she's just gotten off a horse. She's wearing a tiny black sweater with faux leopard trim and tight black Capri pants, neither of which contains a single natural fiber. Tony, I am relieved to discover, is nowhere in sight.

"Ugh," she says by way of greeting, "I just had a Brazilian wax. I'm in such pain."

"Brazilian . . ." I venture. "That means, what, everything? Almost everything?"

"They leave a little bit," she says patiently. "It's called a landing strip."

"You're kidding, right?"

"Want to see? Look," she says, and starts pulling down her pants.

"Oh no, please. Oh, hell no," I gasp, shielding my eyes with my hand. I'm not squeamish, not in the least. I can deal with open wounds, projectile vomiting, bleeding, and injections. But this is too much even for me.

"You know, there's a *reason* we have hair there," I tell Lavander when she's covered up and I can safely look at her again. "What you've done—I don't know, it's like self-mutilation or something."

"It is not," she says indignantly. "It looks so much better like this."

"To *whom*?" I ask.

"Oh, come on," she says.

"Why would a man want a woman to be hairless?" I ask. "Think about it, you're making yourself look like a child. I think that's really weird, don't you? I couldn't look at my*self* if I had that done. And the pain! Like the bikini line isn't bad enough."

"Debra," she says slowly, as if speaking to a child, "I don't think you understand. But it's okay. Women *your age* like to have a nice little triangle there. And that's what men *your age* like."

I cross my arms in the ancient posture of self-defense. "My age?"

"You know," she says, "over thirty-five. This is for women in their twenties. Times change, you know."

"You're not in your twenties."

"I'm only thirty."

It's true, she's only thirty, but looking at her now, I am reminded once again of Grandma, our father's mother. Lavander has always had a fair bit of Grandma coming through her, in fact. Historically, Lavander hasn't enjoyed that distinction, although my father once pointed out that, "You know, in her time, my mother was considered a beautiful woman."

"By whom?" my mother asked wryly. "Like Daryl Zanuck spotted her somewhere and thought she was a beauty?"

"Among her group," my father said testily. "Those who knew her. Lavander has that same kind of beauty."

"Whatever," Lavander said.

None of us knew Grandma "in her time," and there are no photos of her in her youth, so it is impossible to say exactly what she looked like then. But more than a similarity of actual features, Lavander has inherited from Grandma a certain mode, a collection of mannerisms. There are the fingernails, for one thing. Grandma always had the most immaculately polished and shaped nails. Lavander's are the same. Every nail parlor within a twenty-mile radius has an intimate knowledge of the state of her cuticles. Her nails, in fact, are one of her business expenses. And differences in clothing styles aside, Lavander dresses very much as Grandma used to. Grandma was one of the most "put-together" women I've ever known. Everything matched, from pants and tops to jackets and purses, and she had a belt to go with everything. Grandma could wear anything and somehow make it look stylish, from macramé to gold chain. She even looked good in white vinyl. Lavander is the only other woman in the world who can wear white vinyl and not seem like she's going to a 1960s revival party. In fact, like Grandma, Lavander can pull off just about any bizarre cut or poly blend while simultaneously matching it with an accessory or two.

There was a certain quirkiness to Grandma that I see reflected in Lavander, as well as what I can only describe as an orderly, precise kind of sadness. Lavander had just turned four when Grandma had her sixtieth birthday and she remembers nothing of that day, but for me, it stands out in sharp relief. Grandma wasn't particularly thrilled to be turning sixty in the first place and didn't seem very jovial, but she went through the motions of having a birthday celebration convincingly enough. It was the only time we would ever celebrate her birthday together; before and after that year we would always be living in different places when it came around.

That afternoon, Grandma was wearing a cream-colored sweater set, belted at the waist, and matching slacks. Sometime around four or so, she took her cigarettes and went into the large walk-in closet off the living room where we kept the stereo. She sat there in the dark for a long time, smoking and listening to Billie Holliday as one tear followed another in wet tracks down her face. She let them go, let her cheeks soak with them. All the time, her only movement was the lift of a cigarette to her lips. I watched the glowing coal between her pearl-painted fingertips as it went back and forth and down to the ashtray. At thirteen, it was the first time I really felt the silent weight of adult sorrow. Grandma had been dealt some difficult cards in her lifetime. She'd lost her first child, a daughter, to pneumonia. Her husband had died young, leaving her a widow in her forties. She never remarried. These were the events I knew about, but I sensed that there were more under the surface. She could have been crying about any one of them. What struck me even more than the intimacy of grief, though, was the utter *femaleness* of it.

It was something always present in Grandma, but never as much displayed as it was that day. Lavander has none of the same life experiences as Grandma at this point, yet I can see it in her, that same kind of controlled female pain.

Lavander is looking at me now, asking me something, drawing me out of my reverie.

"What?" I ask dimly.

"I said, you should try it. Why not?"

"The waxing thing? Never. I'm still mad at you for convincing me to wax my upper lip. I can't stand it, it's the most painful thing and now I have to keep doing it every few weeks because it keeps growing in."

"Oh no, you really had to do it. You had a mustache, a thick one."

"I did not," I whine, instinctively touching my upper lip. "I just allowed you to talk me into it because I'm insecure."

"Didn't you *finally* start seeing someone after you got rid of that 'stache?"

"Two years later," I tell her. "You know, I think you have a problem with hair."

And it's not over, this hair/no hair debate, not by a long shot, because now Maya has reappeared in the kitchen and Lavander is in there after her, going through the same maneuvers, attempting to bring her over to the side of the hairless.

"Oh no," I hear Maya say. "No, please don't show—oh no, that's awful."

"Sisters!" Déja bursts through the door with her customary greeting. (Nobody knocks when they come here, they just immediately turn the door handle. If it's not locked, they stride right in. If it's locked, there's a second or two of angry pounding as if to say, "You *knew* we were coming over, so why is this door locked?").

"Déja!" Maya exclaims in response.

"Hey, Déja, come look at this," Lavander says, "I got a Brazil-ian."

"Where's Danny?" I ask.

"He's coming with Bo, because I have to leave early," Déja says, giving me a kiss on the cheek. Déja has been the most physically affectionate sister since her earliest infancy. As a baby, she was constantly smothered with kisses and hugs of which she could never get enough. She's the same way now; at twenty-four she's unable to enter a family room without a kiss and a hug for every-one present. When she exits, it's the same, except she always com-bines the kisses with an I-love-you, something she never leaves out of her phone conversations either. Lavander is big on saying "I love you" also, will do a nice job of air-kissing from time to time, and isn't above the occasional embrace, but it's not a priority like it is with Déja. Maya is very affectionate with Déja and sometimes with Lavander, but I can't remember the last time she and I exchanged either a hug or a kiss. Even when we were very little, Maya and I weren't very physically demonstrative with each other. We were just too close. Kissing her is like kissing myself. And the number of times we have *said* we love each other in our lifetimes can probably be counted on the fingers of one hand. But not Déja, who seems to need these expressions of love and who soaks them up like a sponge. We indulge her, this baby of the family who, at five feet seven, towers over her sisters who are between five feet and five feet two. She moves among us now, bestowing kisses, laughing at Lavander's wax obsession, and proclaiming that she is "absolutely starving."

For a few minutes, we four sisters are by ourselves. Although we speak to each other every day and see each other almost as often, it is a rare occurrence for all of us to be in the same room without the rest of our family. It's an unstable combination, this quartet. Astrologically, we have all the elements covered: fire

(Déja, the Sagittarius), earth (Lavander, the Virgo), air (me, the Gemini), and water (Maya, the Pisces). Conventional astrological wisdom would assume a balance in this combination, a flow of disparate but complementary energies. But most often we form a tight square when we are together, each one of us protecting her own corner, holding fast to a pattern shaped by birth order, personality, and the gravity of inertia. When there are only two or even three of us together, we are able, with some effort, to reach out past our positions, but when we are four, our combined elements are often more like oil and water, salt and sugar, or gunpowder and spark. Predictably volatile, in other words. The only question is what will be the trigger.

Lavander is still going on about her waxing. This time, she's cornered Déja whose friend Katie is the one who performed the actual tearing out of hair.

"How can she do that?" Lavander wants to know. "How can she get all over people's crotches without getting sick? And she's totally cool about it, says it doesn't bother her at all."

"Well, it *is* her job," Déja says. "But, you know, I'm angry at her and I don't want to talk about how great she is because she has *not* been a good friend to me lately."

"Well, can you please make up with her?" Lavander says testily.

This is something of a hallmark of my sisters' and my relationship with the rest of the world. If one of us is happy with a hairstylist, doctor, or beautician, the rest of us will usually patronize that person as well. Business from one of us almost always translates to business from us all. Conversely, if one of us has a bad experience with any of the above, there is pressure for all of us to drop out. Katie is proving to be a sticky exception. Déja has known Katie since high school (and she's shared many family meals with us), but their friendship has always been a bit erratic. They're on the outs now, but Lavander and Maya have become so enthralled with her skills as a beautician that they've even offered to go in on a portable wax pot for her so that she can make house calls.

"I'm not going to stop going to her," Lavander says now with a touch of stridency creeping into her voice, "so I hope you can work it out."

"Do what you like," Déja says. "I don't care."

But of course she *does* care and Lavander knows it. If the current tiff isn't worked out, Lavander, who is fiercely loyal, especially to her *baby* sister, will have to find someone else. This is always the bottom line.

"Where's Blaze?" Déja says.

"In his room," I answer. This is Blaze's usual pattern when everyone comes over here. He stays in his room and lets everybody come to him, one by one. Individually, he has a completely different relationship with each one of my sisters, and seeing them one at a time allows him to control the conversation more easily than when they are in a group. Blaze is no fool; he wised up to the "Who's your favorite auntie?" question when he was still a baby. "You are," he'd say. "But don't tell the others."

"Well, I'm going to go say hello to him," Déja says and disappears down the hall.

There is a too-brief silence before Maya says, "I'm making macaroni and cheese, I hope you can handle it." She turns to Lavander. "Don't tell me you're not hungry."

"Why? Do I have to leave if I'm not hungry? Will you throw me out?"

A preemptive strike and a counterpunch. Should be an interesting evening.

"I'm just saying, I've made a lot of food here," Maya backpedals, "and I want it to get eaten. Because you know what it's like living with Debra. She never eats anything. Doesn't believe in meals."

A brilliant deflection. Now I'm in the fray, too.

"It's true," Lavander says, turning to me. "I never see you eat. You have food issues."

"Oh, please," I sigh. "I do not. I just can't eat continuously or think about eating all the time. Three meals a day is too many for me."

"That isn't normal," Lavander says. "Those are not normal eating habits."

"Oh, like yours are normal," I tell her. I cast a glance over her tiny little frame, her birdlike ankles and wrists. Lavander and I are the same height, but she's a full size smaller than I am and I am fairly light at the moment. She's been losing too much weight lately, on the verge of trading trim for gaunt. "You don't eat properly either," I tell her.

I am hoping against hope that this discussion doesn't go any further because then we'll surely get into the topic of smoking, at which point Lavander will accuse me of doing what she does, smoking on the sly. There are many ex and secret smokers in my family, but Lavander and I are the only two who have smoked to keep our weight down. When she told me recently that the most effective diet she knew of involved a few bottles of water and a pack of cigarettes, I had to tell her that I'd already discovered it many years ago. "Throw in a heartbreak," I added, "and Bob's your uncle. Skinny in no time." Maya and Déja don't share this neurosis, although both of them, like every woman I have ever known, occasionally complain about their bodies. Not one of us is completely free of insecurity when it comes to the way we look and we will often make "suggestions" as to how our sisters can improve their hair, clothing, or makeup ("You know, you should probably wear something different. Those pants don't really *do* anything for you") as well as soliciting their opinions on the same topics.

But on the issue of weight, there is an unspoken agreement

between all of us. When we argue with each other, there is a Maginot Line that may never be crossed. Every one of us is adept at cursing and have been known to call each other some choice names. But we never, *ever* use the F word. We have a silent understanding that, even in the heat of battle, the word *fat* must never be hurled. We can insult each other's intelligence, life choices, or emotional development, but never the amount of flesh we are carrying. In the array of insults, even the vilest of all possible slurs is trumped by *fat*. Fat is like a nuclear bomb—there is no turning back once it is dropped and the devastation would be irrevocable. Were I or any of my sisters ever to use this word, the ensuing rift would be unbridgeable. But too thin, now, there's a topic that just begs to be broached because somewhere in that indictment there is a twisted compliment, a slightly sick sense of accomplishment. And that's where I go with Lavander right now.

"You're starting to look too skinny," I tell her. "You should be careful."

"Hmm," she says, inspecting the amount of give in her waistband. "I don't think so."

I wonder how much of Lavander's current weight loss and desire to remove as much body hair as possible has to do with Tony, who, by her own account, is obsessed with appearances. Although none of us can understand how, he seems to have convinced Lavander (or she's convinced herself) that he is some sort of Adonis and totally irresistible to women. I find him a bit closer to Narcissus, if we're going for a Greek mythological counterpart, although I think this might give Tony a bit too much credit. At any rate, Lavander's general mood has been on a downswing since the two of them have been together. This, to put a point on it, is what really bothers me and everybody else about their relationship. And it is also something I can't talk to her about, not while she's got that familiar jittery, combative energy coming off her like little lightning bolts.

Déja reappears from Blaze's room.

"He said he'd come sit at the table with us tonight," she says. "I asked him."

"He won't," I say. "There's salad. He can't stand the smell."

"You know, Debra, he should sit with his family when we're all having dinner. You should insist on it. I don't see why he can't."

"Oh no," I say, looking up at my little sister. "You're not going to do this, are you? You're not going to start? Please."

Déja looks at me through her big, round blue eyes that have changed not one bit since she was an infant. Occasionally, I'll allow her to give me parenting advice because I know that the bond she shares with Blaze is a special one and that he will tell her things he won't share with anyone else. But tonight it's just not going to happen.

"I just think—" she starts, but I cut her off.

"And please, Déja, take off those giant shoes. You're just too damn tall in them."

"Not my fault you're a short person," she says, but she concedes. On both counts.

The front door is flung open once more and my parents stride in. "We're here!" my father exclaims. "Let's eat!"

"And only fifteen minutes late," Maya says, but in sotto voce.

I feel the shift occur somewhere in my midsection. Subtly and silently, my sisters and I adjust to the presence of our mother and father. The pattern holds, hardening its shape.

Our brother is next, lumbering through the still-open door with Danny. "Where's the grub at?" he says, and Danny laughs, closing the door. Now it's really a party.

There is much shuffling of chairs as everyone struggles to find a seat. A central irony of the fact that family dinners are most often here is that we only have four dining chairs and a round table that doesn't really seat more than five comfortably. Somehow we manage, plates balanced precariously on the edge of the table, elbows bumping, and folding chairs creaking under too much weight, to accommodate however many people show up. It's a particularly full table tonight because Bo and Danny take up a lot more space than my little sisters. Maya sets a giant steaming bowl of gourmet macaroni and cheese in the center of the table with a great flourish.

"Here you go," she says.

Ah," my father says, "*mac*-aroni and cheese."

"What?" Maya says. "What's wrong with macaroni and cheese?"

"Nothing," my father says. "Nothing at all. Did I say there was anything wrong with it?"

"You implied—"

"Pity about the pasta," my mother adds.

"You know, I can't keep up with all the different diets," Maya says. "This isn't a restaurant. In fact, even if it *were* a restaurant, you probably couldn't get all these special requests. Danny, I'm sorry, but maybe you can just pick the tomatoes out. I didn't put any in the salad."

"Hey, I'm fine," Danny says. "This is great, really."

"Maya, if you're going to invite people to dinner, you can't have such a bad attitude about feeding them," my father says. "You can make people physically ill with an attitude like that."

My mother and I stare at each other across the table. I mouth the words, "Same argument every time," and my mother mouths back, "Without fail."

Déja says, "Why are you giving Maya a hard time, Daddy? She made this lovely meal—"

"Yes, but there are always restrictions," Lavander pipes in. "There are always rules for Maya's dinners."

"What is *with* you?" Maya says, turning to Lavander. "Why do you always have to chime in against me."

"Nobody's against you," my father says. "Don't be paranoid."

"You're always defending her," Maya says.

"We have *neighbors*, you know," I say. The decibel level has gone up considerably in the last few seconds. We're on the verge of no return here. I see that my mother already has her head in her hands and, any second now, she's going to interject with a slightly hysterical admonishment that will exacerbate all tensions and solve nothing. My brother looks as if he's getting ready to flee, his usual mode when arguing starts, but Danny eats gamely, soldiering on. He and Déja have been together for two years now and he's seen quite a few of these dinners.

"*Anyway,*" I cut in, "what were we talking about? I believe it was me, wasn't it?" I am guaranteed to get myself in trouble with this question, but it's all that I can think of on the spur of the moment. Call it the verbal equivalent of a sacrifice fly.

"Oh yes," my father says, "let's talk about you. We haven't talked about you for at least ten minutes. What's happening in your world?"

"No, let's talk about me," Déja says. Another sacrifice. I smile to myself. We do tend to look out for each other from time to time.

"Yes, let's," my mother says. "Let's talk about Déja's play."

Between my sisters and me, we've got most of the arts covered. I am the writer, Maya is the musician, and Déja is the actress. Lavander, in real estate, is the only one whose chosen profession is outside the entertainment field. For this, she has earned the distinction of being the only "closer" in the family. For example, when my mother had an opening at a local art gallery recently (she's the visual artist in the family), Maya played her violin at the reception. Next to my mother's business cards were two stacks of postcards: one advertising the opening of Déja's play and the other announcing the publication of my new book. Lavander, on the other hand, brought in some wealthy clients who immediately bought two of my mother's paintings.

The play Déja is rehearsing for now is her first in two years and it's as if she's had new life breathed into her. When Déja is performing, she is like a lighted torch. The last two years have been fallow for her, creatively speaking, and her natural sense of drama, brilliant onstage, was starting to warp into moodiness.

"Yes, let's talk about my play," Déja says. "It's opening next week. I don't want anyone to show up on opening night, please. I want to make sure we have it right before you all see it. And you are all coming, of course. And just a warning, it's a farce, but it's very sexual. And I'm playing a very sexual character, so I want you all to be prepared. It is called *Down South*, so you can take it from there." She's speaking to all of us, but she's looking at Danny. Word is, he's a bit disturbed by the sexual content of the play.

"What do you mean, *Down South?*" my mother says. "Where does it take place?"

"It takes place *down south*," Déja says. "Get it?"

"Yes, but where is it set?" my mother presses on.

"Philadelphia," Déja says, sighing.

"Speaking of down south," Lavander says, "I'd like to get some opinions on the Brazilian wax."

"Oh come on," I tell her. "Do we really have to talk about this *again?*"

"Nobody minds, do they?" she says. "I just want to know what some men think of this whole thing."

"You can't ask *these* men," Maya says.

"Yes, I can. Daddy, what do you think?" Lavander leans over to my father, hand under her chin, sweet as you please.

"Do not answer her," my mother warns my father. "I am telling you, say nothing."

"Wha—?" my father gets out.

"Come on, Lavander, you know the only reason you're at all interested in this is because Tony likes it," Déja says.

"All men my age like it," Lavander says and this sets off a

round-robin cacophony of voices: yes, they do; no, they don't; it looks good; it looks weird; beauty should come from within; and does Katie wax hairy backs? In the middle of all of this, Déja says, "The only reason Tony likes that look is because he watches so much porn."

"Porn?" snaps Lavander. "Who said porn?"

Déja raises her hand and laughs.

"How do you know he watches porn?" Lavander says.

"You tol—um, I mean, uh, *somebody* told me," Déja finishes lamely, but can't stop herself from giggling.

"This guy just keeps getting better and better," Maya mutters under her breath.

"Who watches porn?" my father says.

"You watch porn?" Danny asks him, completely confused.

"It's okay, Dan, I'd just stay out of this one if I were you," I tell him.

"Yeah, I think I'm going to have some more salad," Danny says.

Lavander turns from my father to my brother. "You're a man," she says, "what do you think?"

My brother waits half a beat before throwing propriety to the winds and making an obscene gesture with his tongue. It's clearly all he can think to do and it's so ridiculous, so childish, and yet so deeply amusing that every one of his sisters starts laughing uncontrollably. We can't stop; Lavander with her high-pitched shriek, Maya slapping the table and gasping, Déja with her deep chuckle, and me, silently convulsed. We laugh until each one of us has tears streaming down our cheeks and then we laugh some more. It is the first time I can remember that my brother has made all four of us laugh at the same time and he is clearly both astonished and very pleased with his efforts.

"We used to fight when we all got together for dinner," Bo says. "Now we're talking about porn. What's happened to us?"

The laughfest diffuses the tension at the table and soon all the food is gone as well. We break up; Maya to the kitchen to do the dishes (I feel only the slightest twinge of guilt that she has cooked *and* cleaned—after all, this dinner was her idea), Déja, Danny, and Bo to Blaze's room, and the rest of us to the living room. This post–dinner hour can also be a little dicey, a time when the angry exits occur if they're going to happen at all.

"I have an announcement," Lavander says, settling into the couch. "There is going to be an addition to the family."

We stare at her blankly, knowing that she's not talking about a baby, a news item that could not possibly be announced with such nonchalance.

"I'm getting a dog," she says.

"Don't be ridiculous," my father says immediately.

"Sure, a dog, that's all you need," my mother adds.

"I know what you're all going to say," Lavander cuts in, "because I know how *this family* is about these kinds of things. But I'm telling you all right now that I'm meeting with a breeder on Tuesday and I'm going to buy a dog. A Jack Russell, I think."

My parents are not pet people. In Lavander's lifetime, we've never had so much as a parakeet in the house. What she can't possibly remember is that, a year before she was born, we had two cats, Marlon and Greta (after Brando and Garbo), and a hamster (Hampstead, after the Heath in London, which is where we were living at the time). Marlon was a wild fat tabby and black Greta liked to perch on the bathtub and scratch anyone who tried to show her any affection. Maya and I both played with the cats, although neither one of them was particularly cuddly, but I adored that hamster. I thought his little face was the cutest, most darling thing in the world. I was in charge of his cage, which I kept very clean and Maya kept his water bottle filled. Both of us spent many hours playing with him.

One evening, we all returned home from a party (there were a lot of adult parties happening in those days and Maya and I almost always went with) to find an empty cage upset on the floor and Marlon lying next to it with a Hampstead-size lump in his belly. We searched the flat up and down, but it was apparent that we weren't going to find any semblance of a living hamster. I was inconsolable, weeping hysterically and insisting that my mother throw the cat out on the heath to punish him for his savagery. My parents took a much more philosophical approach. They described the circle of life and how it was a cat's nature to eat a rodent and that the cat was compelled, by his blood, to kill. Sara, a friend of my parents, was living with us then, too, and she chimed in as well, telling me about karma, speculating what kind of creature Hampstead would come back as, and expressing awe at the sheer murderous majesty of the cat. I was not impressed. I cried over that hamster for days and avoided both cats until we gave them to Sara when we moved to New York less than a year later. After this episode, my parents never even entertained the idea of owning another pet.

"You don't know anything about dogs," I tell Lavander now. "You don't even like dogs. Why a dog all of a sudden?"

"Lavander, you can't keep a dog cooped up in your place all day. What's going to happen to it when you go to work?" my father says, wondering, I am sure, if the task of caring for this imagined creature will fall to him.

"I'll take it with me," she says, "it can ride in the car with me."

"I really don't think you've thought this through," I tell her. "You can't keep a dog in a hot car all day long. Unless you want to be one of those freaks who carries a tiny little rat-dog around in her purse. In diapers."

"My friend Allison and I are going to co-parent the dog, so you don't have to worry."

"You know," I say, "you've got a lot of good catch phrases here, like 'meeting with a breeder' and 'co-parent,' but, honestly, I don't think you have any idea of what the reality of caring for an animal is like."

"That's right," my father says, startling me, since he rarely agrees with me in general family discussions.

"Well, would you rather I had a *baby*?" Lavander says, pointedly. "Because that's what I'm going to do if I don't get a dog."

So now we've gotten to the bottom of what this gesture is all about.

"Is that a threat?" my mother asks.

Maya walks in from the kitchen, where she's been listening to this conversation. "You know what you're overlooking here?" she says. "A dog is incredibly expensive. Especially if you buy one from a breeder. And then there are vet bills and food."

"I'm certainly not worried about food," Lavander says.

"You're going to start shopping at the Tack and Feed now?" my father says.

"Hey, that's a good idea," Maya says, "you can pick up a riding crop for Tony while you're there."

"That's very funny," Lavander spits. "At least *my* boyfriend doesn't look like a chipmunk."

"I don't have a boyfriend," Maya says very quietly, her face flushing deep red.

"Then your ex-chipmunk-boyfriend," Lavander says.

"I can't believe you," Maya says, her voice rising. "Everyone's been talking trash about Tony all night, with the porn and everything, and you say nothing. I make one comment—and it was a joke, by the way—and you lash out at me. I mean, there are all kinds of things I could say, like the fact that your wonderful boyfriend is a cross-dresser, for example, but I don't. So I don't know why it is that you always attack me."

We're way into the deep end now. Our love lives are where everything breaks down. Here, we handle each other with kid gloves over iron fists; we try and we fail, we have contempt, compassion, joy, and despair for each other's choices. And it is here that we can never seem to help each other. For all our differences, and the fact that we are spread out over fifteen years, my sisters and I have some key similarities. None of us are married. Among us, we have produced only one child, Blaze. My romantic past, as well as Lavander's, is littered with emotional wreckage. Maya presents her romantic life as if it were a wounded bear: don't look at it, don't talk, and certainly do not attempt to touch it. Déja is the only one with a successful track record in this area, but this is because Danny is her first and only boyfriend. Before him, her love life was a tabula rasa.

Lavander and Maya glare at each other for a moment and then Maya folds. "You know what, forget it," she says. "Get a dog, do whatever. I don't want to talk about this anymore."

"I'm sorry," Lavander says, "I didn't mean to attack you. It's just that I expect my family, especially my *sisters*," she shoots a meaningful glance in my direction, "to be supportive of the choices I make."

"We are supportive," Maya says. "That's why we offer our opinions, to help you in the choices you make."

"Well, I don't really want any advice right now," Lavander says. "I just want support."

"It doesn't work that way," I say, but before Lavander can respond, Déja reappears with Bo and Danny in tow.

"I've got to go," Déja says. "Sorry I can't stay for tea."

"We're off, too," Bo says.

It takes a few minutes and a flurry of activity for the three of them to get out the door, as it always does. Déja needs to make a plan with Maya to go swimming in the morning and then she can't find her big shoes. Danny rummages around for his keys, which are too similar to the other sets he's put them next to, and Bo seems to have misplaced his sweatshirt. Soon, however, they are gone, and with them, most of the energy in the room.

"I'm leaving, too," Lavander says. "Thanks for dinner, Maya. I'll call you tomorrow."

"I think it's time for us to go also," my mother says as the click of Lavander's heels fades. "Unless there's tea and cookies happening," she adds hopefully.

"Not tonight," Maya and I say in unison.

"That's not very nice," my mother says.

"They stick together, these two," my father says to my mother. "See how clannish they are? All right, girls, we're leaving."

"You don't have to go," Maya says. "It's just that we don't have any dessert. We can do some karaoke if you want."

"There's no way," I tell her.

"No, really, it's okay," my father says. "I'm tired anyway."

"Party poopers," my mother says.

Our parents say good-bye to Blaze, who has not come out of his room once tonight, and then they, too, are gone. Maya and I each select a couch and fall into the pillows. Both of us spend a few minutes listening to the ambient hum of the white noise in our living room.

Maya says, "Really, a dog. Can you see her walking a dog in those heels of hers?"

"She won't do it," I say.

"She will, you know. Meeting with a breeder . . ."

"She won't do it."

"And Tony?"

"I know."

"At least Déja . . ."

"I know."

I wait for a moment before I add, "And we're 'clannish.'"

"I know," she says. "That's sort of the point, isn't it?"

There's no need to answer and so I don't. Our postmortem is concluded. Now it's just the two of us again, spinning back to the space and pattern where we started. And where we always return.

Maya and Debra.

2

The Mariannas

april

I have a dream that I am dying. The dream isn't clear about why I am dying, only that I am gradually but surely fading away. I stand mute in my dreamscape, wondering if there's been some kind of mistake because nothing hurts. And it seems to me that dying should involve more pain. Then I see my son and Maya walking ahead of me. A wave of terrible guilt and sadness washes over me when I realize that I'm leaving my child behind. He needs me, I think, and I'm deserting him. I am failing in my responsibility to take care of him. But then I see Maya put her arm around him and I am completely relieved. I know she will take care of him as well as I ever could. With her, he will be fine and I don't have to worry. But now the real emotion of the dream hits me so hard that my eyes hurt from sudden, ferocious tears. It is Maya who I can't bear to leave. I find my voice and I call out to my sister, "Won't you miss me?" But I am already dead in the dream and she can't hear me. I try one more time. "If you were gone," I cry out, "I would miss you so much." And then I realize that I already do. Now, finally, there is the agonizing pain of separation. How can I go so far away without her? What will I do if she's not there? Who will I tell?

For all practical purposes, there was never a time before I had a sister. *Technically*, of course, I was an only child for two years and nine months, but that was more of an obligatory waiting period than anything else. I was more than ready for Maya by the time she was born.

"Can she talk?" I asked my mother when she called from the hospital to tell me that I had a new sister. "Does she have purple eyes?" Of course, her ability to communicate was of the utmost importance. The purple eyes, an afterthought really, would have been an added bonus. But my new sister had sleepy blue eyes, which were disappointingly shut most of the time. My mother has often said that Maya was born tired and that she slept through most of the first two years of her life.

"Not like you," my mother tells me now. "You *never* slept. I'd put you down for a nap and come in to check on you and there you'd be, standing up in your crib, eyes wide open, staring at me. You never cried, mind you," she adds, "but it was a little strange how you just stood there, waiting."

Waiting, I remind my mother, is something I've been doing since the day I was born and perhaps before. My earliest memories are of waiting (with increasing impatience as time went by) for Maya to talk and for her to exit her infancy and play with me. Naturally, given her propensity for it, much of that time involved watching her sleep. Maya's ability to luxuriate in slumber was a gift she shared with my mother and one I never possessed.

We were living in London, where Maya and I were both born, in a large flat in Belsize Park. I remember, with the precision of someone who has witnessed the same scene a thousand times, how, at naptime, my mother put *Songs of Leonard Cohen* on the turntable and lay, still as a corpse, with her arm over her eyes. Maya curled up beside her, lost to sleep, intermittently sucking her fingers. I lay awake, impatient, and fidgeting at the foot of the bed until my mother, moving nothing but her lips, sharply insisted I stop. Leonard wailed on about tea and oranges that came all the way from China and I tried to lie as still as possible. I counted all the square-shaped objects in the room. I counted the knotted tassels on the bedspread. I counted Maya's breaths and matched them with my mother's. Occasionally, I tried to fall asleep, but it never worked. I just ended up staring at the shifting shades of gray sky outside the big bay windows of our flat.

My mother was a big believer in early bedtimes as well as frequent naps. Maya and I were in bed by 6:00 P.M. every night but Tuesday when we were allowed to stay up for an extra hour to watch *Top of the Pops* on television. Maya was predictably crashed out within minutes even when it was still light outside. Many nights I crept out of bed and sidled down the hall to the living room.

"I can't sleep," I told my mother. "My eyes won't shut."

"All right," she said, "you can come in for five minutes and tell me a story." She sat at her typewriter, smoking a Players cigarette, composing beautiful poetry I didn't understand on thin sheets of peach-colored onionskin. When I came in, she took out lined paper and a green felt-tip pen and wrote down the stories I dictated. There were always dragons in these stories and they were always eating me or my dolls (they found good girls especially tasty). My mother copied them faithfully and tucked them away with her own orderly typewritten pages. Always too soon, it was time for me to go back to bed, where I lay next to my sleeping sister watching the shadows turn into dancing dragons on the ceiling.

I admit, I was sometimes so sleepless that I pestered my sister in an effort to get her to talk to me. She made a few valiant attempts to stay up, gurgling nonsense as her eyes closed. Sometimes I simply talked *at* her, trying to involve her in a story I was composing as I went along.

"Maya, what if elephants wore ballet slippers?" I asked her. "What would it sound like? Maya? Are you awake?"

Sometimes, frustrated beyond belief at her lack of alertness, I actually poked her or threw dolls at her bed (softly, of course, because I never wanted to actually hurt her). But this almost never worked. When I *could* rouse her, she woke up frightened and called for our mother, which invariably got me into trouble.

"Leave her alone!" my mother admonished. "It's cruel not to let a person sleep."

So I learned how to entertain myself during the time I spent waiting for Maya. I started reading and I often practiced by reading aloud to her. When my mother finally stopped insisting that I take a nap, I became very good at passing the hours with a box of crayons, a book, or a pen and some paper. I enjoyed the things I did alone and very early developed ways to sustain myself in solitude that would serve me well right into adulthood.

But I needed my sister in order to feel complete. With her I was one of two, half of a set, and somehow whole.

Sibling rivalry was a concept that never entered into my relationship with Maya. When we were together, there was never a need to compete for parental attention. We had each other's attention and that was enough. We were also born with a sense of complicity. If we disagreed or even argued, neither one of us ever went complaining to our parents. If one of us got in trouble, the other would sit close by and wait until the storm passed.

Whatever possessions we had were better when pooled together. If I got a new dress or a new book, I wanted Maya to have one, as well or my enjoyment of it was severely diluted. This worked in reverse, too. If Maya got a new doll, I needed to have one, too. We had several dolls and each belonged to either Maya or me but it was the community of the dolls that was important to us. We never played with them individually.

At about four or five years of age, Maya was finally able to stay awake through an entire day and had caught up enough conversationally that I figured she was ready for some quality play. For some time she'd been looking at me expectantly with those marine blue eyes as if to say, "What are we going to do next? You decide."

So I invented the Mariannas, two characters in a perfect game that Maya and I would play, uninterrupted, for years.

The name probably came from listening to Leonard Cohen wail "So long, Marianne" through all those naptimes, but I can't be sure. At any rate, it was a lovely name with lots of syllables and I thought it sounded grand. The Mariannas needed nothing, no props, no play space, not even a house. We could play this game anywhere from airplane and boat to train and car. In fact, it was a game that was often made better by a change in venue. It went something like this:

Maya and I were both grown-ups (or "ladies" as we called ourselves—never "girls" and never "women"). My name was Marianna and so was Maya's ("How funny!" the Mariannas exclaimed when they met each other for the first time. "Both of us have the same name!"). The Mariannas were both married and both husbands were named Harry. The Harrys were never "home" when the Mariannas got together and neither Maya nor I ever invented specific jobs for the Harrys—somehow, this was a detail that never seemed important. It was enough to imagine that my Harry (and so Maya's, too) was always out doing something incredibly important or dangerous or noble. From the start, though, Maya's Harry was considerably more laid-back than mine. I needed my Harry to be an excellent husband, a dragon slayer even, and a constant source of love, support, and comfort. It was a fairly tall order, even for an imagined man, and so I was occasionally frustrated and complained to Marianna about his failings. Maya, on the other hand, was content to let her Harry just exist on the periphery of our game.

The Harrys often hung out with each other when the Mariannas got together and generally had as much fun as their wives, although Maya and I would occasionally invent disputes between the two of them:

"You know, Marianna, your Harry said something bad to my Harry and now he's upset."

"Well my Harry said *your* Harry said something to *him*."

"Really? What was it?"

"I don't know, he didn't tell me."

When the Mariannas (or Ma's as we started calling them) got together, it was always for tea. Maya and I were both literally weaned on hot tea with milk. Our mother filled our baby bottles with it. And as soon as I was tall enough to reach the stove, I was putting on the kettle and making tea myself. The Mariannas liked their tea strong and something sweet to go with it. McVitie's chocolate digestive biscuits were always popular but in the absence of those, we were happy to eat toast fingers with butter and Marmite, and speculate on what we might do in the future. Part of this future involved children and we added them as we got older and the game continued. I was the first to imagine a baby (Little Marianna) and then Maya had one (another Little Marianna). We followed the girls with a Harry Jr. each. Like the Harrys, our children existed off the set of our game. It would have been unthinkable to approximate babies with dolls, for example. To do so would destroy the illusion of reality we were so careful to create.

Over our cups and saucers, we discussed where we had been and where we might go. Often, there was little need to exaggerate or embellish because there was no shortage of real life adventures for the Mariannas.

When we went to Spain for weekend trips, for example, the Ma's came with. We slept in a windmill on the island of Ibiza and the Mariannas were delighted ("I *always* stay in windmills when I come to Spain, don't you, Ma'?").

When we sat in a plane on a runway in Rome, waiting for a strike to be resolved so that we could fly to California, the Mariannas became sophisticated Italian ladies who played with the tray tables and exclaimed, "Bella bambina!"

These trips weren't the only time the Ma's came in handy, however. When I was about seven years old, we started moving around with increasing frequency and not just from house to house—these moves were from continent to continent. London was a starting point, at least for Maya and me, but my mother had come there via South Africa and my father via Brooklyn, New York. We did substantial global hopscotching as they searched for the right place to settle. We moved so often, in fact, that today, my parents are hard-pressed to reconstruct the moves between 1969 and 1971. During that short period, we lived in two different London homes and three in New York. The Mariannas set up in each one of these.

As we grew older and the game became more sophisticated, Maya and I invented more complex surroundings and emotional states for our Ma's. Sometimes the Ma's would be destitute, reduced to wearing rags and eating scraps of bread (we always had tea, though—we'd rather die of hunger than do without tea). We sighed and talked about how difficult it was to exist under these conditions:

"You know, Ma', Harry still hasn't gotten a job and now we don't have any lights! I had to use a candle to read my book last night."

"Really? That's terrible, Ma'. It's even worse for me. I have holes in my shoes and there's no money to buy new ones. And the floor is so cold to walk on with no shoes."

"But your Harry has a job!"

"No, he doesn't."

"Yes, he does."

"Well, he doesn't anymore. We are very poor."

Sometimes the Mariannas were fabulously wealthy and put on airs in our mother's mirrored velvet minidresses and platform shoes. This worked out splendidly until our mother discovered that we were popping the tiny mirrors out of her dresses so that they could serve as "jewels" and put a stop to our dress-up. When the Mariannas were rich, tea had to be served by a butler. Maya learned to make tea in short order because in these situations, she was forced to pull double duty as Marianna *and* the butler. Since I never took a turn as the help, it was a bit of a lopsided arrangement, but I considered this one of the perks of my position as older sister.

Occasionally, our Mariannas were famous. Even then, my Marianna sometimes envisioned her fame as a "book writer," but more often we donned our pink tutus and assumed the more practical career of prima ballerinas.

As time went on, the escape function of our game became more important. The Ma's didn't have parents, for example, who dictated and doled out cruel and unusual edicts. The Ma's were perfectly independent and adult and would never be told what to do. And if we were frightened (raging thunderstorms, parental arguments, or the first day in a new school), the Ma's were extremely useful. The Ma's could blow off emotional scenes as no big deal ("Where *is* that shouting coming from, Ma'? We're going to have to move out of this neighborhood") and fierce weather as just another minor discomfort ("It's a good thing that my house was built so that it can never be struck by lightning, isn't it, Ma'?"). Sometimes, the only way out of an unpleasant situation was through our Mariannas. There was the time, for example, when Maya and I decided to run away from home during one of our short stays in Brooklyn.

Running away was probably my idea. I'd recently given Maya the kind of swell haircut that can only be fashioned by an eight-year-old and my mother was furious with me. I hated my new school. I hated that I was even *in* a new school. And I never liked the apartment, it was dark and claustrophobic. But even though I might have made the suggestion to run away, Maya had to have been amenable to it. I would never have gone anywhere without her.

It was wintertime and very cold outside, so we put on our fake camel-hair coats with impossible-to-fasten toggle buttons and our giant furry hats that tied with pom-poms. We packed a few items in our matching plastic purses and we were ready to go.

"We're running away," Maya told our father, who was in the living room watching *Star Trek*. He looked at our serious expressions and winter gear.

"Okay," he said. "Why are you going?"

"We don't like it here," I said.

"What about you, Maya?" he asked her.

"What Debra said," Maya answered. I hoped he wouldn't try to convince her to stay, because Maya always folded long before I did and I wouldn't be able to leave without her.

"Are you sure?" he asked both of us and we nodded solemnly.

"Okay," he said. "You'll probably need some money." He dug into his pocket and gave us two quarters each. I was surprised, but also a little suspicious. I had expected resistance, some kind of protestation, or at least a plea to reconsider. I thought he was making it all a bit too easy. Nevertheless, my mind went to the vending machines in the lobby. There were potato chips and chocolate milk. Fifty cents would come in handy. Maya and I tucked the money into our purses and stood by the front door.

"Okay, bye-bye," our father said, and turned back to his show. I noticed that Maya had started watching as well and was becoming distracted from our mission. She's always been a big *Star Trek* fan.

"Let's *go*," I told her.

Once we were outside in the hallway, we hesitated for a moment, anticipating that our father would stop pretending he didn't care and come out after us as soon as we closed the door, but no. There was nothing coming through that door except the tinny TV sound of a transporter beaming someone up from a hostile planet. And so we were off, marching down the hall to the elevator. That was where we ran into real trouble. Neither Maya nor I could reach the elevator call button. Both of us tried reaching, stretching, and jumping, all to no avail. It never occurred to either one of us to look for a stairwell. We'd never used or seen stairs in this building. We lived on the tenth floor and assumed the elevator to be the only means of escape.

"What are we going to do now?" Maya asked me.

"Let's go ask for help," I said.

Back we went to the apartment.

"Did you change your mind?" our father asked.

"We can't reach the elevator," Maya said. "Can you come and help us?"

Our father had already been so willing and helpful, I was sure that he'd call the elevator for us at the next commercial, so what he said next came as a shock.

"No," he said. "If you want to run away, you're going to have to do it yourselves. And if you can't even reach the elevator, maybe you're not big enough to be running away."

We went back outside, back to the elevator, and still could find no way to get to the button. Sweating in our coats and hats, we were forced to admit we were beaten and go back to the apartment with our pom-poms between our legs. I was miserable, stewing in humiliation. I threw myself on my bed, coat still on, as if some miracle might happen and I'd be spirited away. Maya was no more than five years old at the time and her interest in running away had already waned, but she hated to see me upset or unable to handle any situation. It rattled her and she couldn't get comfortable until she knew I was all right. She looked over at me, a pleading expression on her face.

"Let's play Ma's," she said.

"Okay," I told her. "Let's."

Over time, the Mariannas became a channel for what Maya and I heard, saw, and didn't understand in the adult world. Thus, we had games where one or both of our marriages broke up and we consoled each other over the heartbreak. It was always difficult to get Maya to play the "my Harry left me" version of the game, though, because she was consistently uncomfortable in the role of miserable wife. Eventually I was forced to start *drawing* these scenes with my colored pens, creating whole picture books of marital tragedy. This suited Maya much better.

The Mariannas were tireless characters. They had a much greater willingness to sort through the mysteries and contradictions in the world around them than either Maya or I possessed. Together, there was no explanation that eluded them and no situation that they couldn't mold themselves to fit. More than anything else, when they were together, the Mariannas were safe. When we first began, the game would start by one of us saying, "Let's play Ma's," but that suggestion very quickly changed to "Let's *be* Ma's." In either case, the response was always "Yes, let's."

The Ma's were such an integral part of our relationship that I can't remember now what they talked about at their last get-together, whether they were rich or poor, or what country they were visiting. But I do remember, with striking clarity, the day they were sent away forever.

Maya was ten years old and I had just turned thirteen. We were living in New York again (upstate this time) and shared a downstairs bedroom below ground level that didn't get very much light. Grandma had knitted us matching quilts made up of squares in varying shades of blue and we displayed them on our identical beds. We each had a lamp and a stack of books beside our beds and a poster of the ill-fated racehorse Ruffian on the wall.

At night we lay in our beds and giggled in the dark.

"I don't get the joke," I told Maya. "Why *does* the mailman drive a blue truck?"

"To deliver the mail," she said wearily.

"Yes, but why blue?" I asked her. "Why is it a *blue* truck?"

"That's the joke," Maya said. "You know, like why did the chicken cross the road? To get to the other side. It doesn't matter that the truck is blue. He delivers the mail in it. Get it?"

"No," I said. "I don't get it. It's a stupid joke."

Maya sighed and rolled over in her bed. I could hear her breathing slow and deep. She still fell asleep before I did and once she was out there was no rousing her. Two years before, when our parents were out for the evening, I saw a mouse dart under her bed and started shrieking, "Maya, WAKE UP!! There's a MOUSE under your bed!! Aaauugghhh!" loud enough to make myself go hoarse. But even though I was less than three feet away from her, she never so much as fluttered an eyelash. I was happy that she got the mailman joke and I didn't. It always made me glad when Maya got things I couldn't figure out. I didn't want to go first and fall asleep last all the time, but that was usually the role I found myself in—the part I almost always had to play.

At thirteen, that part seemed to be mine permanently. I had just gotten my period. I'd been wearing a bra for a year. I'd started writing long, involved journal entries on whatever bits of paper I could find in the house, scratching out re-creations of daily events until late at night. My favorite book was Edith Hamilton's *Mythology*, but I was also reading my mother's collection of Carlos Castaneda and Gurdjieff. I was fascinated by anything having to do with the occult and took the whole concept of magic very seriously. I believed, in fact, that I had magical powers I hadn't yet learned to use.

But the strongest sea change that summer didn't come from my solitary treks around the inside of my head but from outside, in the form of other girls my age. They were a collection of Tracys, Sharis, and Jodys; clear-skinned lovelies with smooth legs and shoulder-length hair cut into feathers. There were plenty of them living in Patio Homes, the uncreatively named, patio-sporting town-house community we lived in, and even more came up from New York City in the summer when their parents vacationed. Many of them had known each other since kindergarten. I wanted to belong to this group more than I could ever remember wanting anything. But it was a doomed proposition from the start.

My hair was never right, for one thing. It was very long and very straight and neither one of my parents would even consider taking me to get it chopped into some trendy cut. My legs were a problem, too. My father insisted that I was too young to shave my legs so I had to sneak around with my mother's always-dull razor with results that were less than spectacular. The other girls rotated through each others' houses, making a weekend event out of sneaking into their parents' well-stocked liquor cabinets and getting drunk when nobody was looking. I was consistently left out of this party because my parents didn't have a liquor cabinet. I'd never so much as seen a bottle of booze in our house. Instead, my parents had a bottomless stash of fine Colombian and rolling papers and I wasn't about to divulge *that* information and appear totally strange. Therefore, I was consistently unable to participate in the circular conversations about how wasted Shari or Denise or Jody or I got last weekend ("Did you see how many times she threw up?"). Nor could I chat about my new haircut, the benefits of depilatory creams over shaving or how much things had changed since second grade. What I had to bring to the party was my knowledge of astrology, my ability to read Tarot cards, and the fact that I'd lived in a few different countries. I learned that these were not popular attributes.

Most of the time, I tagged along on the outskirts, struggling to insinuate myself into the inner circle. I invited the girls over, offering tea and cookies instead of alcohol. I allowed them to call me Debbie, although I despised the nickname. For their acceptance, I would probably even have signed it with a big heart over the *i* had anyone asked me to. I gladly participated in the ever-popular fainting game, which was to make yourself hyperventilate and then have another girl grab you around the waist, cutting off your air supply and making you pass out. The girl who blacked out longest was the winner. I banished my disapproving sister Maya to our bedroom for these get-togethers. I simply couldn't stand the why-are-you-selling-yourself-out-to-these-idiots look I saw on her face. She was too young and too immature, I told myself. What did she know of these sophisticated goings-on?

For a while, the girls tolerated me, although they tended to ignore me when we were all together. I often found myself sitting in somebody's crowded living room, outside a circle of matching jeans and sneakers, listening to and observing the conversation rather than participating in it. Occasionally someone would look over at me in surprise as if to say, "Oh, right, *Debbie's* here," but there wasn't much attempt to include me and when the girls paired off and went to each other's houses, I just went home. Eventually my best efforts to fit in with the girls failed and they phased me out altogether:

"Oh, Debbie, I'd come over but I'm sleeping over at Shari's tonight and, you know . . ."

"You don't need to come by, Debbie, because I'm baby-sitting and she only allows me to have, like, five friends in the house at one time. . . ."

I didn't take this well, especially considering that I never really got much of an explanation for why I couldn't be one of the girls. In an ill-conceived attempt to avenge my hurt feelings, I made the mistake of mentioning to one of them that I had the power to cook up a spell or two. Well! Seemed my witchy ways had freaked them out from the start and, in a 1970s version of *The Crucible*, Goody Shari and Goody Tracy banished me from the village for good. I was a pariah. None of the girls from Patio Homes ever spoke to me again. Not even when we were all clustered outside in subzero weather, teeth chattering, nostrils freezing together, waiting for the school bus that would take us to our last year of middle school.

I was crushed.

And Maya?

Maya was in fifth grade, reading Agatha Christie and learning how to dance the hustle in her gym class. She'd started taking violin lessons the year before and really loved her new instrument. She did the crossword puzzles in the *TV Guide* and was partial to jokes of the "Why does the mailman drive a blue truck?" variety. She was not an adoring little sister who wanted to be just like me and my friends. She never could stand those girls and made no effort to hide her disgust.

"Why do you like them so much?" she asked me once. "They aren't very nice."

"You wouldn't understand," I told her. But in my confused adolescent heart, I suspected she understood very well indeed.

One cool Sunday, shortly after my disastrous summer with the girls, when I was still trying to work out what went wrong, Maya turned to me, and said, "Let's be Ma's."

It had been less than a year since the Mariannas had gotten together to discuss their adventures but, at that moment, I couldn't imagine a way to call them back. Had Maya not noticed that everything was now different? I was so dumbfounded that I couldn't even answer.

"Let's be *rich* Ma's," Maya added, trying to be helpful. There was nothing for it, I had to tell her.

"I don't want to," I said.

"Why not?" she asked me.

I looked into my sister's face and saw the expectation there and all the years of her following my lead. I'd created the game, but she'd followed me into it and made it ours. Now I was going to have to toss it aside like a dress I'd grown out of. The two years and nine months between us stretched out like an ocean. I'd crossed a line and she was still on the other side wanting to play. And it wasn't really fair, I thought, because there could never be just one Marianna. Once I was gone, it was over. I wished there was a way I could have dragged her over with me. I would have liked nothing more than to have Marianna with me, helping to navigate the rough new landscape where I found myself. If there were anyone who could make sense of the senseless, it was Marianna. But unlike me, Maya was never in a hurry to exit her childhood. She showed absolutely no interest in coming over to my side. I couldn't take her with me and I couldn't go back to the place that I'd just vacated. I wanted to be able to play with her and I wanted her to understand why I couldn't. And neither option was a possibility because I was simply not sophisticated enough to explain it to her. Why not, her sea blue eyes were saying, why can't we play?

"I can't play Ma's anymore," I told her. "I'm too old."

If she'd protested, even scoffed, it would have made that moment easier, but Maya didn't say anything, she just stared at me with a look that pieced hurt, incomprehension, and acceptance into an impossible mosaic in her face.

"So don't ask me again," I said, sounding like the curt and officious big sister I was pretending to be. But my own Marianna was heartbroken. I felt I'd let myself and Maya down at the same time. I felt like I'd cut off an arm. I never gave Maya an explanation for why I stopped playing the game and she never tried to get one out of me. We wouldn't mention the game again for over twenty years. The issue of the Mariannas themselves, it turned out, was the only thing the Mariannas couldn't talk about.

A few days later, before we went to sleep one night, I asked Maya to teach me the hustle. There has never been a simpler dance invented, but I couldn't get the sequence of steps right.

"It's so easy," Maya said. "I don't know why you're not getting this."

"I don't know," I said. "Why does the mailman drive a blue truck?"

Maya made a disgusted noise and got into bed. She turned her light off and rolled over so that her back was to me. Soon after, I clicked off my light as well and lay motionless in the darkness. As always, Maya was sleeping long before I fell into unconsciousness in the bed next to hers.

When I was eighteen, I moved out of the house and went away to college. When I was twenty-five with a newborn son, Maya moved in with me. We are still living together. We have lived together, in fact, all but seven years of our lives—long enough to run out the bad luck of a broken mirror. In the last fourteen years, we've shared a checking account, a couple of jobs, and, quite often, my son's care. Maya, in fact, was the very first person on earth to see my son's face as he left the shelter of my body. Ours is truly a domestic partnership. Until he was about seven or eight, my son referred to the two of us as "my parents."

We've done things together as adults that the Mariannas couldn't have conceived of. There were the hospitals, for example. The two of us sitting in emergency rooms at three, four, and five o'clock in the morning with my sick child. These were times when Maya never slept, but stayed awake with me, making jokes about the seizure and suicide-attempt patients next to us in order to keep my mind off the fact that my son was blue and gasping for breath.

We've also done things that the Mariannas would have loved, like sharing a suite at Beverly Wilshire Hotel the night before I had a TV interview for my first book, noticing that room service popcorn cost ten dollars (*before* delivery charges and tip), and wondering if we should order some just so that we could get a sense of what ten-dollar popcorn tasted like.

Fairly often, Maya will start a sentence and I will finish it for her before she gets to the main point.

"I was going to say that," she tells me. "Why don't you get out of my head and get your own thoughts?"

"I was born first," I answer her. "I had those thoughts before you."

When Maya gets stuck in conversation and can't remember the word or phrase she's looking for (and, as we all get older, this kind of thing tends to happen more frequently), her standard response is, "I'm sorry, I can't get the words right now. Debra's using them all."

Maya and I don't share clothes. We don't wear each other's shoes or read the same books. Our views on men, relationships, and affairs of the heart are different enough to be diametrically opposed. We have different eyes, hair, and bone structure. But we have the same voice. When we sing together, it sounds like the same person on two vocal tracks. Sometimes our own mother can't tell us apart on the phone.

We have a house full of kitchen gadgets, books, and furnishings from Ikea. I work at home and she is out most of the time.

There are no Harrys. At least not in the way we envisioned them.

Maya is still my first reader, just as she was when she was Marianna. Then, Maya would listen to my stories whether they were about the Ma's or some other world we were creating together and give me her opinion on how well they worked. Maya saw everything first whether it was a short story, a drawing, or a play the two of us would perform together. Today, it is the same. Everything I write goes through Maya first. Maya knows if it's not working because Maya, more than anyone, knows what I mean to say.

When I published my first book, *Waiting*, Maya went on the road with me to every interview, book signing, and radio show up and down California. One glance at her expression during these events told me how well I was doing. If I faltered, I looked for her face, a fixed star, and found my way back to center. If I'd needed any reassurance that the fabric of my life was inextricably connected with Maya's, I found it during one of those radio interviews in Los Angeles.

The show's host greeted us warmly when we got to the studio and told us, "We'll be live today. And we'll open up the lines for callers. Are you up for that?"

"Oh yes," I told him. "Sounds great."

"Okay," he said, "get yourself comfortable with the microphone. Your sister can sit in there," he gestured to a small glassed off area, "and she can hear the whole show."

Maya situated herself with a pair of headphones. She was behind glass but directly in my line of vision. The host warmed up and introduced the show. The on-air lights went on and within minutes the plastic squares representing callers started blinking madly. We were off and running. I could see Maya smiling, enjoying a call from a disgruntled waiter who claimed that customers were always asking for items off the menu and expecting servers to provide them. The host asked me if I thought customers generally had unrealistic expectations of their servers or if servers just complained too much. I told him it might be a bit of both, but yes, there were certainly times when customers made demands that couldn't possibly be filled. The host asked if I could give him an example.

It was then that I started to drift a little, my train of thought unraveling slightly and I felt I was on the verge of missing what I was looking for. For a split second I thought I was going to have to switch gears and move to a different topic. I looked up at Maya who was gesturing to me in her booth. She was mouthing a word but I couldn't quite figure out what it was. I shrugged slightly and she scribbled something down on a piece of paper. I just kept talking, although I wasn't exactly sure what I was saying any longer. Maya held the paper up against the glass and I saw that it said wasabi in giant letters.

And suddenly it was all clear.

"Well, here's one example," I told the host. "I was working in an Italian trattoria at one time, waiting on a large party of Japanese businessmen and the host asked me for wasabi. I told him I was very sorry, but we didn't carry wasabi, it being an Italian restaurant and all, but he got angrier and angrier, *demanding* that I find him some and absolutely fuming that we didn't carry it. 'You should always have wasabi!' he screamed at me. 'People want wasabi. It's outrageous that a place like this doesn't have it.' And then he asked me if there was somewhere nearby I could go and purchase some. And obviously I couldn't. So that would probably constitute a good example of when a customer has unrealistic expectations of his server."

The host loved this and the entire board lit up. Maya smiled and nodded, pointing in approval at all the flashing lines.

"Please be patient," the host announced, "the lines are full, but we're going to try our best to get to all your calls."

The rest of the show seemed to run by at hyper speed and we ran out of time before we could get to all the callers. Afterward, the host asked me if I'd come back and do it again and I told him I'd love to.

As we walked back to the car Maya said, "I can't believe you forgot that story."

"But you remembered," I told her.

Maya was working beside me in that Italian restaurant on the night of the wasabi fiasco, although that day was the first time either one of us had mentioned it since. I couldn't have said how many years had passed since then, because most of them had blended together. I knew only that she had always been there. That experience, like so many others in our lives, had been a shared one.

"I could do these shows, you know," she said.

"You could," I said. "Like the first runner-up. You know, if I'm unable to fulfill my duties. Something like that."

"Huh," she said. "Funny."

Back in the car, driving through a relentlessly bright August morning, I asked Maya to take a detour, to the corner of Sunset and San Vicente Boulevard in West Hollywood where we'd lived for a short time twenty-seven years before. We were sunburned girls then, dressing up for Halloween costume contests and putting on plays in the living room. We went to Disneyland in matching crocheted ponchos. For fun, my father drove us around Bel Air in our ancient pink station wagon and we pretended to be eccentric millionaires.

Our childhood exists like this; a kaleidoscope of different places layered into the past. It struck me then that we lived only one hundred miles from this particular piece of our history yet this was the first time we'd even come close to seeing it in a quarter century.

But Maya did not share my desire to plunge into the past.

"We don't have time for a trip down memory lane," she told me. "Let's go home."

Maya is less sentimental than I am. She is also more practical. The subtext of her words was very clear to me. There was hardly a need to rediscover our past when we were always carrying it, and carrying each other, with us. Our past is woven seamlessly into our present, and within that present the Mariannas are often there with us.

At night we still drink big mugs of tea, an addiction we've never kicked. Although we would travel miles for it, we are lucky enough to live close to an oxymoronic "British foods" store that carries imported English tea and we go through an eighty-bag box every couple of weeks. Our particular tea ritual consists of arguing over who will make it:

"I made it last night."

"Yes, but I made it all last week."

"It's your turn."

"No, it's your turn."

"I'll give you five dollars if you make tea."

"Not enough."

"How about that book you want? I'll buy you that book you want if you make tea. How's that? It's a *hardcover*."

"Okay, done."

Unlike the old days, we now have television with our tea.

Maya has at least a dozen shows she likes to follow. On any given prime-time evening, there is one show on the TV and two VCRs recording a couple of others. Sometimes I read while she watches and sometimes I watch with her. Sometimes I can do neither.

Like tonight, for example. It's after 11:00 P.M. and I'm on the couch, suddenly awake and disoriented. The living room is quiet except for the whir of the VCR rewinding a tape. Maya is holding the remote and flipping through the Living section of the newspaper.

"What happened?" I ask her. "I missed the last ten minutes."

"You didn't miss the last ten minutes," she says. "You were out for almost the whole show. I can't tell you what happened, it's too complicated and you missed too much."

"I saw some of it," I say feebly. "I wasn't paying attention."

"You were sleeping," Maya says.

"No, I wasn't."

"Yes, you were."

"I was?"

"Yes," Maya says. "I saw you. You should go to bed. I'm off. Good night."

I hear her door close and drag myself off the couch, turn off the lights, and head for my bedroom.

It took a long time, but these days Maya often goes first and sometimes I fall asleep before her.

Our parents, circa 1968.

3

Departures and Arrivals

may

It's Mother's Day, a big deal for our family, regardless of the old saw that "every day is Mother's Day, not just this one." Despite its significance, we never take our mother to a restaurant on this day. Every one of us has worked a Mother's Day brunch in a restaurant at one point or other and, after witnessing countless displays of bad familial behavior from the other side of the table, a restaurant is the last place any of us wants to be. Therefore, as it has been for countless Mother's Days past, brunch is held at my house.

My mother and I are the two mothers in this group, but, rightly enough, my mother is the one who gets the homage. I do get a little lift at the beginning of the day because Maya always makes sure that Blaze takes care of me in some fashion. Every year, she takes him shopping for a gift ("That kid's really going to owe me once he gets a job," she says with a laugh) and helps him make me breakfast, or at least coffee, in bed. Over the last couple of years, too, Lavander and Déja have started giving me small bouquets of flowers and cards that state emphatically what a great mother I am. These are the cards I always keep and the sentiments I hold dearest to my heart. That my sisters consider me a good mother is more important to me than their opinions on any other aspect of my being—as their sister or as a woman.

Those lovely bouquets are scattered throughout my house now and, since my mother hasn't taken hers home yet, the living room is an explosion of red, pink, and gold. We are sitting in the middle of it, having eaten our fill of bagels, fruit, and pancakes. I've made a second pot of coffee, but it will probably go to waste since everyone seems sated. Lavander and Bo have already left, citing obligations (work-related in Lavander's case, unnamed in Bo's). Déja is sprawled out on one of the couches and my father wanders through the kitchen, picking at the leavings. My mother sits on the second couch amid a bounty of colorful boxes and wrapping paper.

Gift-wise, my mother made out like a bandit this year and, I have to say, I am partially responsible for setting the bar so high. A few days ago, I took her shopping and bought her an extravagant moonstone ring for her birthday. It didn't take long for news of the Gift to spread and for me to get quite a bit of ribbing, albeit good-natured.

"That's just great," Lavander said. "And how are the rest of us supposed to compete with *that* gift?"

"Guess you're the favorite now," Maya said. "Got yourself in pretty good, didn't you?"

Déja said, "That was such a sweet thing you did for Mommy. Of course, now *I'm* going to look bad when I show up with my pathetic little gift."

Well, *whatever*, I told them all. She loved it, she wanted it, and I was able to get it for her. It made her happy. She's also very happy about the box of Godiva chocolates I got her for Mother's Day. So happy, in fact, that she's even *sharing* them with my father.

"Anything else for me?" she asks, and laughs to herself. "Or is this it?"

"Ha!" Maya says by way of response.

My father comes out of the kitchen, having found nothing there that satisfies him for the moment.

"How about another one of those chocolates?" he asks my mother.

"No way," she says, grabbing the box and shoving them under her arm.

"Come on," he says, hand out.

"And I said no. Get your grubby mitts away from my chocolates."

"You'll be sorry later when they're all gone and you can't have any of mine," he says.

"I don't want your sorry-ass domestic chocolate," my mother says.

"We'll see," he says. He turns to his daughters. "Don't worry, she'll be looking in my couch soon enough."

"You've got separate stashes?" Déja says.

"Oh yes," my father answers. "We hide from each other all the time." He turns back to my mother. "Time to go," he says.

"Right," my mother says. "Thank you, girls. It was lovely."

After they leave, Déja says, "You know, I think the two of them are getting a bit weird." Maya and I just laugh.

"Seriously," Déja says. "Do you think Mommy and Daddy are going to get old? Is that really going to happen?"

Déja seems wistful about this. She's not yet twenty-five and still wants to believe that everything goes on forever. She still has that sense of immortal youth. I can't figure out if I miss that feeling or not. In some ways, it's comforting to know that, at almost forty, my life is into its second half. And, of course, the older I get, the closer in age I am to my own parents and therefore, the closer our experiences, the more similar our life weariness. But Déja hasn't approached that place yet, nor should she. Nor has Lavander, really. But Lavander has the unique distinction among my sisters and me of being born when my parents fell into the average category. What I mean by this is that my parents were very young when they had Maya and me—barely out of their teens, in fact. Lavander and Bo (who are eighteen months apart) arrived when my parents were into their twenties, the time when most people their age were just starting their families. They were in their thirties when Déja was born at the end of 1977, an age then considered a little late to still be adding children to the family. As a result, Lavander's peers have parents the same age as she does. Maya's and my peers have parents who are much older, Déja's have parents who are younger.

Lavander is not philosophical about my parents aging, but she's damn funny. The issue of what one does when one's parents die came up recently when we were discussing the case of a Las Vegas woman who wanted to bury her mother in her backyard so that she could always be close to her. There were some municipal issues involved with the burial and that's why the case made it into the papers. Lavander stated emphatically that she would never consider burying our parents in the backyard, but she wanted always to be as close to my parents as she is now. When they die, she said, she planned to stuff them and seat them on her couch, "so they will always be with me." It says something about our family that all of us, especially my parents, found this tremendously amusing and that the only comment offered was that she was going to have to find a really good taxidermist.

"Debra, really, what do you think?" Déja repeats. "Do you think they're going to get old?"

"What do you mean by old?" I ask her. "They're already a lot older than they were when *we* knew them."

Now Déja's really confused. "What do you mean?" she says. Maya is laughing. My comment was for her anyway.

"I know exactly what she means," Maya says. "We knew them a long time ago. When it was just the four of us. Before all of *you* lot."

"Oh sure," Déja says.

"She's right," I tell Déja. "You missed quite a bit."

And it's true, our parents never had a nest egg, a set of silver, or a dinner service for six. With all their moves, they never even accumulated furniture. For many years, we sat on giant foam-filled pillows that my mother had created with reusable Indian-print bedspreads or swaths of wide-wale corduroy. We had tapestries and plenty of hanging beads to separate areas of space. There was a time when our living rooms looked like the inside of Barbara Eden's bottle in *I Dream of Jeannie*. Throughout my childhood, I was sure that only the elderly owned couches. Headboards were a foreign concept altogether and forget about curio cabinets. Those are still a mystery to me (what if you have to go somewhere—what are you going to do with all that stuff?). Our parents were perpetual renters. They never had what is now referred to as a starter home. They never bought any kind of home at all, in fact.

But my parents did have a set of starter children, me and Maya. They had the two of us, and we got the two of them, at their youngest, hippest, and most experimental. We got them in the days when their friends (few of whom had kids of their own) would come over, hang out, pass hash pipes or joints, and wax profound over the latest Doors, Rolling Stones, or Beatles album. We got them very early, when they were still figuring each other out and formulating what would become their personal ethos. When they wore long hair, shades, and floppy felt hats. In other words, we got them in the '60s.

Those were the days when my mother still wore makeup. She was the essence of mod. She had purses full of Mary Quant eyeliners and shadows in shades of gray and black. During one season, she painted a single tear below her left eye in silver liner every day. She had an eye for style, my mother did. She smelled of Shalimar and patchouli and wore little paisley and velvet dresses, snakeskin shoes, and knee-high leather boots. Her clothes were a child's paradise of tassels, embroidery, and mirrors. During her silver tear phase, she also wore the ankle-length black woolen cloak she got married in, which later became a central prop in the plays about witches and lost princesses that Maya and I would put on in the living room. I would spend years trying to emulate the way my mother looked during that time, but I could never quite pull it off. I may have inherited her good taste but I didn't get her long, lovely legs and I could never duplicate her sense of style.

My father was as hip as my mother was mod. His hair was long, but never too long and *never* in a ponytail. He wore boots, aviator sunglasses, and a turquoise leather jacket. He was rarely without cigarettes. Every shirt pocket he owned seemed to come with its own pack of Lucky Strikes. But he could also always be counted on to be carrying either a box of Crackerjacks or a handful of Bazooka Joe bubble gum because, while my mother was in charge of the passports, plane tickets, and rolling papers, he was the one who always had the treats. He was philosophical about most things and was big on hidden meanings (Maya and I pondered the lyrics to "For the Benefit of Mr. Kite" for years because he'd told us that when we could figure out what they meant, we'd really be onto something), but he expressed himself in a way that was straight out of Brooklyn.

"Would you die if you jumped off the fire escape onto the sidewalk?" I asked him once. I was staring out the high window of the Brooklyn apartment where Maya and I attempted our ill-fated running away.

"Yes, you would die," he answered.

"But what if you landed on your feet?" I asked him. "If you just landed on your feet, you'd be all right, wouldn't you?"

"No," he said.

"Why not?" I asked. He didn't say anything then about the force of gravity or the effect of impact or bodies falling through space. He said, "Because your *feet* would go right through your *head*, that's why."

End of discussion.

My parents would never have considered themselves hippies. They rejected mass movements of any kind, for one thing, and, to this day, they harbor an intense dislike for anything communal. They didn't go to Woodstock even though we were living close by because they couldn't stand the thought of sitting in traffic. They same year we went to San Francisco for about a week with the thought that we might move there, but my father claimed the Haight Ashbury scene made him "itchy," and we ended up watching the Mets on TV from the comfort of a motel room.

My parents also disagreed with the "loose" way some of their peers were raising their own kids and they were fairly vocal about it. They held no truck with any of the pop psychology coming in and out of vogue. There was something of a "children should be free to set their own boundaries and explore their own space and shouldn't be told negative words like 'no' " movement happening in those days that my parents shared with Maya and me and then laughed at outright. My parents had an extremely firm belief in the word "no" and the only space that was going to be explored was the one they provided and controlled. Unlike many of the parents they knew then, my parents did not think that children should be setting their own boundaries or making their own decisions. I would say they even leaned generously to the seen-and-not-heard school of thought. My father once pointed to the passage in *Alice in Wonderland* (my favorite book at the time) where one of the characters tells Alice that she's thinking again and that makes her forget to talk, and said, "See this? This is important because, in reality, the exact opposite is true. When one is talking, one forgets to think. The words come out of your mouth, but you don't know what you're saying. Always remember to think first. And don't talk unless you've really got something to say."

Whatever the reasons, there were rarely other children around in those days. Because we so often switched schools, Maya and I didn't have time to develop friendships there either. In effect, we were the sum total of our own peer group. I never perceived any of this as a lack. Aside from Maya, I thought most children were much less interesting than adults, at least the adults I knew, because my parents' friends were nothing if not interesting.

Altogether, these friends made a Venn diagram of two circles that intersected in the middle. We switched back and forth between London and New York several times between 1969 and 1971. There was a circle of friends in each city and then a few who drifted back and forth between them as we did. There was Sara, for example, a New Yorker who lived for many years in London. She was already married and divorced by the time she was in her early twenties. I thought she was one of the most exciting women I'd ever meet. Sara dressed like the characters that populated my mother's deck of Tarot cards. In velvets, robes, and scarves, she was alternately the Fool, the Empress, and the Magician. When she lived with us in London, all the sheets, pillows, and blankets in her room were printed with Tom and Jerry cartoon characters. Sara shaved her head bald and wore a giant ankh around her neck. She always spoke to me as if I were a small adult instead of a seven- or eight-year-old. She told me that she'd had a baby at the age of thirteen and had to give it up for adoption. Her eyes were big and sad when she told me this, but she didn't cry. I wanted to know more but couldn't figure out what questions to ask.

And then there were David and Wanda, Londoners who didn't travel outside their city. David was beautiful to look at (everybody knew he was beautiful to look at and commented on it regularly), very talkative, and full of quips. He was one of very few people who could consistently make my mother laugh. David was an aspiring actor and always had a story about an audition or a film set. He was terribly glamorous and I always loved it when he was around. When he told the story about breaking his arm during an audition for a Shakespeare play, my heart wanted to break.

Wanda was David's girlfriend and perpetual fiancée. She was even more beautiful than David, but it was the ethereal, milky-skinned, limpid-eyed kind of beauty, as if she was some sort of landed ocean sprite. I always felt comfortable trading a joke or two with David, but Wanda was just too beautiful. I couldn't talk to her at all. Although everyone had more than a working knowledge of astrology in those days, Wanda was the expert. Every chart passed through her hands first. She told my mother that, although I seemed more gregarious than Maya, our charts dictated that as we grew older, Maya would become a much more social person than I. Maya would be externally motivated, she said, whereas I would spend a lot of time examining my own head. I never forgot any of this. These are the kinds of things one tends to remember. Especially when they turn out to be true.

Harold, a South African expatriate who ended up in London, was another fascinating character who appeared on the landscape fairly frequently. Like David, he could be counted on for a colorful story, but his stories usually involved being arrested and jailed somewhere for smuggling drugs. Harold was the one who usually brought the hashish to the party. By the time I was eight, I knew that there was blond hash and black hash and that everybody usually preferred the black, although I couldn't explain why. Wanda said that Harold had a glitch in his chart. By all indicators, he should have been a handsome man, she said, but he was small, dark, and gnomelike. He had an intercepted twelfth house, she said, and that's why prison would always play a role in his life.

The two others I remember clearly, George and Sondra, were among the few who never met each other and this was a good thing for me because I found them both inaccessible and daunting. Sondra was my mother's friend. She was tall, imposing, and made up of sharp lines; a blond-haired, black-robed sepulchral image. Sondra was a self-confessed child hater. She saw absolutely no use for children whatsoever, called them "nasty things," and made no bones about her distaste. It was hell visiting her house; a cold hell because she was too cheap to turn her heat on. Maya and I had a tiny cubic area of space we could occupy while we were there and we were not to touch anything, talk to anyone, or breathe too strongly in anyone's direction. Sondra was the stuff of childish nightmares, something of a Roald Dahl character come to full-bodied life.

George didn't hate children, but he wasn't sure what to make of them either. In a field of people who had given themselves a 1960s license to be bent, George stood out as weird. When we lived in New York, he'd ride the subway over to our apartment, often bringing his own bottle of Jack Daniels with him. He lived with his parents, which I thought was strange, and he never had any kind of girlfriend. He would speak in riddles and quote TV commercials when talking to me and then laugh at my frustration when I didn't understand him. Nothing he said made any kind of sense at all and that made him somewhat frightening to me. All I could decipher from him was only an intellectual and intense dissatisfaction with everything. Sort of like an extremely sarcastic Eeyore. George was fonder of Maya than he was of me, which was fine with me since I found him both dark and indecipherable and therefore scary. When Maya turned seven, George gave her Candy Land as a gift and made her a giant poster-sized card on which he modified the words of an Alka-Seltzer commercial into a birthday greeting. And he didn't just buy her the game, he played it with her, too.

In both London and New York, it seemed as though there were always people wandering in and out of our apartments and flats, especially at night. There were constant "happenings" in those days and I didn't want to miss any of it. If I was very quiet, my mother would let me stay up and join the party for a while. Maya was never interested in any of this, not when there was sleep to be had, so it was just me, sitting on the outer perimeter of the circle, trying to appear as small as possible so as not to be noticed. Most of the time, I brought a drawing pad and some colored pens with me because it made me look busy and I didn't want my mother to notice that I was paying too much attention to what was going on. Generally, when she caught me watching or listening too closely, she would order me off to bed, so I learned very quickly how to observe without being observed. For the same reason, I never asked my mother any direct questions about what I saw or heard. Afterward, in the quiet of my bed, I would try to make sense of it all. Ultimately, my conclusion was that adult behavior wasn't a huge mystery. Mostly, they were just stoned. And when they were stoned, staring into candle flames or pontificating about being and nothingness, they were interesting but intellectually unreliable.

In addition to all the metaphysical talk I overheard during

these nighttime sessions, there was also quite a bit of conversation about money. Nobody had any and everybody was always scrambling for it. A few of my parents' friends had rich parents who supported them and a few had actual jobs (George worked in a record store, for example), but most of them seemed to exist, as my mother would say, "on the sniff of an oil rag." My parents traded off which one of them would work at any given time. My mother worked as a secretary for a while and my father worked in restaurants. Their jobs came and went with the same regularity as their moves, but they always seemed to manage. They—we—were untethered and free, tied to nothing but each other. And then, at the beginning of the new decade, when I was eight years old and Maya was six, my mother announced that she was having a baby and our family began a slow but permanent shift in its shape.

Maya and I had no experience with babies, having been exposed almost exclusively to adults to that point, and had no idea what to expect. I wasn't yet three years old when Maya was born and she'd never seemed like a baby to me anyway. Both of us were excited and looked forward to meeting whoever the new person might be, but in an abstracted way. The event seemed unreal and very far off when it was first announced. We were living in London at the time and my parents decided that it was time to leave once more. We were going to move back to New York, permanently this time, they said, and settle down for the new baby.

In June of 1971, then, we left London for good. This time, we made a crossing of the Atlantic. And it *was* a crossing. There's just no other word for it.

We'd always flown prior to this trip. In fact, Maya and I were already veteran air travelers and knew enough to charm the flight attendants (we called them air hostesses back then) into taking us to the cockpit where we could meet the pilots and look at all the lighted controls. And we were familiar enough with that transatlantic flight to know where the extra blankets were stashed on the plane and what to expect for meals. I loved flying. Airports, however, were a different story altogether.

For a woman who did as much traveling around as she did, my mother was never comfortable in transit. And she was downright anxious in airports. There was always a minor panic with passports or tickets or getting the luggage tagged. Often, there was too much luggage and always a concern that we would go over our allotted weight. My mother was also terrified of being late and missing flights. She had a singular airport gait, a jerky half run, as she dragged me in one tightly gripped hand and Maya in the other. Going through customs was never a pleasant experience either. My mother's tension level always ratcheted up then. I could feel it like a small electric shock sent through my hand as she squeezed it. My father wasn't nearly as uneasy in airports as my mother, but her anxiety was pervasive and I absorbed it. I still get irrationally nervous in airports and, to this day, I hate checking luggage and fly with carry-on only.

For our last London departure, there would be no plane. My parents decided to go large, in keeping with the gravity of this particular move, and booked the four of us a passage on the giant and very fancy S.S. *France*. We would sail across the ocean for four days until we reached our final destination, an easy and pleasant way to make the transition between our past and our future. There were swimming pools on board, we were told, and an excellent restaurant. It was all seriously upscale. For the occasion, my mother bought Maya and me matching pairs of black corduroy hotpants with small blue stars stitched into the bibs. The two of us were in a state of high excitement and the Mariannas were in ecstasy.

As it turned out, our passage wasn't particularly easy or pleasant. My mother was seven months pregnant at the time and spent almost the entire trip puking violently in our tiny cabin. The ship's doctor made more than one visit. My father kept us busy, running up and down the grand staircase and along the deck, as much for our sake as for hers. Seeing her curled up in the dark, groaning and spitting into a damp cloth threatened to send everyone into a panic.

At first, Maya did well on the high seas. The photos we have of that trip show my father by the ship's swimming pool, wearing denim cutoffs, his thick hair curling around his shoulders. Maya and I are smiling next to him, wearing yellow "floaties" on our arms and brand-new bikinis boasting peace signs and flowers. But by the end of day two, the fun was over and Maya succumbed to seasickness, joining my mother in the cabin of pain. This put an end to all our games and cavorting. As for the hotpants, they hadn't yet gotten out of the suitcase. I was, ungenerously, very annoyed by this turn of events. As far as I was concerned, there was absolutely no reason for Maya to be sick when *I* was feeling perfectly well.

Only my father and I were strong enough to venture outside the cabin on day three, but even he admitted to feeling "a little nauseous." The seas were wild that third day and it was impossible not to notice the thrill-ride rocking of the ship. My father attempted to take me out onto the deck for some air but was forced to hold on to me and drag me back inside for fear I would get blown right over the railing in the gale-force winds.

"They must do this on purpose," he said. "They shake the boat up for one day so that the ship's doctor gets some work. There's no way a boat this size should rock like this."

Running up and down the ship's grand staircase wasn't at all fun without Maya. Nor was playing with the butter curls in the ship's restaurant, although the waiter (perhaps alarmed by the dwindling number at our table) lavished me with attention and spent a lot of time teaching me how to say, *"Je suis fatigué."* And without Maya, the ship (and the move) was no longer an adventure. Despite walks around the deck and all the butter curls I could smash, the trip began to seem endless and I started to feel some trepidation about what waited for us on the other side. I was looking forward to the arrival of the new baby, but I was also starting to understand that our family dynamic was about to change forever, that we would never again be a two-set unit of four, and I had no idea what that would mean.

By the time the Statue of Liberty came into view on the fourth day, the excitement I'd felt at the beginning of the trip was gone. It was the first time I'd seen her, despite our previous time in New York. She was shrouded in fog, looking cold and solemn, a perfect reflection of how I felt inside. The last snapshot of our S.S. *France* adventure shows much the same feeling. Taken by my father, it's a blurry tableau of my mother with one arm around Maya and the other resting several packages against her rounded belly. The ship looms large in the background. I can be seen off to the side, already walking away.

My father's mother was waiting for us when we disembarked, having driven from Brooklyn in one of the series of Impalas she owned. Grandma was still an unknown factor at that point. Our shifting geography had prevented any close connections. As we straggled off the ship, considerably more subdued than when we'd gotten on, I looked for her, hoping that the sight of her would provide some kind of stability to counterbalance the shakiness I felt. It didn't take long to spot her.

She was wearing a nautically themed outfit in navy and red, set off by white patent leather sandals and a large pocketbook to match (with Grandma, it was always a pocketbook, never a purse or a handbag) and she smelled of Jean Naté Body Splash. I didn't know what to say to her or how to be. I'd lost my tongue the minute we'd left the ship. But Grandma required very little. She put her hand under my chin and turned my face up toward her. "Hello, Princess," she said.

For several days, we packed ourselves like sardines into Grandma's tiny Ocean Avenue apartment. By day, we piled into her Impala and went apartment hunting. At night, we sat on her plastic-covered red couch under the air conditioner, watching TV until we passed out in its blue glow. The search seemed to take forever. It was devilishly hot in the city that summer and even hotter in the car as we traversed Brooklyn from one end to the other. The apartment buildings we looked at were dark and all of them, improbably, had Tropicana orange juice vending machines in their lobbies. We always asked to see the "super." When the super arrived, he was often disgruntled and always holding a massive ring of keys.

After viewing each apartment, my parents would debate its merits and drawbacks as we drove to the next. And then they would turn to me and ask, "What do you think? Do you like it? Should we live here?" I became something of an apartment medium, a high-rise canary in a coal mine. My parents were very sensitive to vibes, good and bad, and saw me as a conduit of both. If I was neutral on an apartment, my parents would attempt to size it up against the next one we saw. But if I really hated the place (and there were quite a few of those; some I found too depressing to even walk through), my parents wouldn't even consider it.

The one I liked the most had a dinette, two bedrooms, and a living room window that looked out on the fire escape. It felt bigger than anything else we'd looked at. More importantly, there was light, although the name of the neighborhood, Gravesend, seemed to imply the exact opposite. We moved in. Characteristically, we had almost no furniture. The living room was decorated exclusively with a wall tapestry, a turntable, a stack of record albums, and a television set that Maya and I moved from my parents' bedroom every time we wanted to watch cartoons.

Almost immediately, my father went to work driving a taxi in Manhattan. His shifts were long and his hours were erratic. Sometimes he left for work at four in the morning, sometimes at four in the afternoon. My mother was in a constant state of panic over this job, always worrying that he'd be in an accident or pick up a dangerous fare. Grandma, who started coming over more frequently as my mother neared the end of her pregnancy, was most often on the receiving end of these fears.

I lost almost all of my baby teeth that summer and continued to put them under my pillow, even though the Tooth Fairy no longer came to visit. Maya and I slept in bunk beds and, because she had a tendency to roll, I got the top bunk. Perhaps the Tooth Fairy had trouble finding me there, I fantasized, all high up and tucked away. It was important for me to hang on to concepts like the Tooth Fairy, even though in my heart I knew she didn't really exist. My parents had encouraged this kind of fantasy in their way. For my parents, but especially for their friends, Maya and I were little cosmic miracles. We were often referred to as the fairy girls, a couple of tabulae rasa who, in our innocence, somehow held the secrets of the universe. How else to explain the fascination they showed when we stood outside in our huge furry hats eating snowflakes as they fell from the sky? Or their delight when we donned our matching pink tutus and twirled around the house? How else to figure why, every time I made up a story about princesses and witches and dictated it to my mother, it was viewed as a work of great significance and deeper meaning?

During the summer of 1971, though, that fairy-child status was changing. I was still a little girl, my parents often reminded me, but now, with a new baby coming, I was about to become the *eldest* and, therefore, someone who would always be old enough to know better. My mother encouraged me to play with dolls, but she often spoke to me as if I were an adult. She gave me the minute details of menstruation, pregnancy, and birth to the point that I could easily have sketched the female reproductive system by the age of nine, but she never spoke to me about sex. I had no clue how a baby got started, but I could tell you exactly what stage of development it was in at any given trimester.

So when my mother came into our bedroom very early one late August morning and said, "Girls, you have to get up, my water broke," I knew exactly what she was talking about.

"That means the baby's coming," I told Maya, who was blinking uncomprehendingly. This was another essential part of my role, explaining things to Maya. Luckily, she never questioned my authority and pretty much accepted anything I told her.

We waited for news of the birth with a stack of comic books on Grandma's plastic-covered couch. Maya read *Wendy Witch* and *Casper the Friendly Ghost*. I read *Archie* and *True Romance*. We never read each other's comics. When we were finished, Maya and I speculated on the baby's gender.

"I think it's a girl," Maya said.

"It's definitely a boy," I told her. "Grandma said she could tell."

"She's carrying like a boy," Grandma interjected. She was sitting by the phone, smoking double-time and playing solitaire. "But it should only be healthy, God willing. Boy, girl doesn't matter."

"I hope it's a girl," Maya whispered. I didn't disagree. Boys were cute, but girls were a known quantity.

The phone rang sometime before noon. Grandma jumped out of her chair and grabbed the receiver as if it were a fire she needed to put out. Maya and I watched while she conducted her end of the conversation, punctuated by sniffing, reaching for tissues (Grandma always had a box handy), some mild chest clutching, and "Thank God" and "Oy Gottenyu" thrown in several times for good measure. I never, ever saw Grandma get hysterical or even seriously worked up. But she could get *verklempt* with the best of them.

"It's a girl," she said hoarsely when she hung up. "Ten fingers and ten toes. Thank God."

That night, our father took Maya and me out to dinner to celebrate and filled in some of the details.

"She's very tiny," he said. "And she has very long fingers. Her name is Lavander."

" 'Lavender's blue, dilly dilly,' " Maya sang. I pictured a plump cherub sitting in a purple flower. Another fairy girl come to stay.

"Can we go see her?" I asked.

"Children aren't allowed in the hospital," my father said. "She'll come home in a couple of days. It's very exciting, don't you think?"

"Oh yes," we said. What a question. Who wouldn't be excited to meet Thumbelina in person?

The baby my mother brought home two days later was not Thumbelina. She wasn't, in fact, at all who I had expected. She was small and alien, and looked way too fragile. I was alarmed when my mother insisted I hold her for a photograph. I wanted to refuse, to say that I'd hold her later, maybe, but my fear of how bad this would sound won out and I allowed my mother to position Lavander on my lap. I put my arms around her awkwardly, afraid to move, afraid I would break her. She had that exhausted and somewhat startled look on her face that newborns all seem to share, as if they can't believe that this is their final destination after the odyssey they've just made. She was little and red and covered with a downy fuzz. Like a lively peach, I thought. She lay there on my lap, a light but completely unfamiliar weight. I was terrified she would twitch, slide off, and crack into pieces. She seemed so helpless, I thought, and so dependent. And I just didn't know what to do with her. Only when my father snapped the photograph and my mother finally took Lavander off my lap did I let out the breath I'd been holding. My arms were stiff with the effort of trying to keep them around her.

When I look at that photograph now, it appears to be simply a picture of big sister holding new little sister. I see myself looking intently down at Lavander, my face obscured by a long fall of hair. Lavander's eyes are closed and her mouth is set. It's the same expression she gets now when her mind is made up, which it usually is. It all looks very sweet and natural. Nobody looking at the photo would be able to make out my fear and confusion—not knowing how to hold her, terrified that I would hurt her.

A couple of weeks after Lavander was born, Maya and I started school; first grade for her, fourth for me. It wasn't easy to fit in at my new school. To my classmates, and to myself, I was foreign in every sense of the word. There was my British accent, for one thing. And the fact that, for the first time and for reasons unknown to me, my schoolwork, especially math, was very difficult. I was too shy and scared to ask for help at school and tried to just blend into the woodwork. And there was the clothing issue. Let's just say that nobody else wore hotpants at that time. My parents were a half generation younger than those of my peers and so I was, unwillingly, ahead of my time. I had no desire to stand out or set trends. I wanted to be like everybody else. That year gave me my first inkling that I wasn't.

At home, the parameters had begun to bend into a pattern that would eventually become permanent. Though never wildly social people at the best of times, my parents were becoming steadily more insular. They stopped going out at night altogether. My father spent many of his waking hours working. My mother spent a lot more time cooking than she ever had before. And, ever so slowly, people stopped coming over. The gatherings (too laid-back to really be called parties) that had been a frequent occurrence in our house became smaller and smaller until they vanished into the smoke of their own incense.

My father cut his hair.

My mother stopped wearing makeup.

Maya and I lost our identity as the "fairy girls." We were now, all three of us, "the kids."

Lavander became the living room centerpiece, lying on a yellow receiving blanket with toys scattered in a circle around her. It hadn't taken long for her to grow out of the delicacy that terrified me the first time I saw her. Maya and I played our games in a slightly wider radius, dragging Lavander back to center when she started to crawl. We incorporated her into our games whenever possible ("Look at this baby I just found in the woods!") because she made a splendid, if somewhat unpredictable, prop. Most of the time Lavander tolerated us, gazing at our machinations with a look of puzzlement, but there were often times when she just opened her little mouth and wailed like the damned. One of us would have to take her then and rock her on our knees or hold her high in the air and spin her around. As an infant, Lavander hated to be left alone or even left out, and, before she started walking she wanted very much to be transported to where the action was. More than anything, though, she wanted *out*, disliking confinement of any kind.

Lavander's bassinette was in the bedroom I shared with Maya, but she spent most of her sleeping time with my parents. When awake and stuck in her crib, she'd pull herself up, grab hold of the bars, and swing until the crib started banging rhythmically, and loudly, against the wall. If that didn't work, she'd grab her bottle by the nipple and hurl it across the room. She was an absolute champion at making herself heard. If my mother had been cautious at first to allow Maya or me to lift Lavander out of her crib or balance her on the bassinet, we never knew it. Typical scenarios went something like this:

Lavander sits in her high chair, a small plate of mashed bananas in front of her. She's had enough of the food, of the chair, of everything. Bananas hit the floor with a wet thunk. Lavander looks up with an expression that says clearly, "Yeah, I did it, so what—get me out of here."

"Somebody take her out," says my mother.

Lavander is behind a closed door, "napping." Bang. Bang. Bangbangbang. A brief respite and then, thwack, as her bottle hits the wall. She gives us a two-minute grace period before she starts shouting indignantly.

"Somebody go get the baby," my mother orders.

Lavander is on the floor, kicking her legs and trying to get off the blanketed spot she's grown weary of. Maya and I watch *Petticoat Junction* a few feet away, lying on our stomachs, elbows propped, chins in hands. Lavander looks at the pillows surrounding her, blocking her from sliding out of her spot, and her mouth turns down at the corners. There's a brief moment of silence followed by an angry howl.

"Somebody pick her up," my mother calls from the kitchen.

It was never clear to me where Lavander wanted to go once she got out, only that she couldn't—absolutely couldn't—stay where she was for very long.

By the spring of 1972, I'd lost my British accent. I no longer referred to swimsuits as bathing costumes and both Maya and I had switched from calling our mother Mummy to the much more American Mommy. After several grueling sessions with my father, I'd finally learned my times tables. Maya watched, giving us a wide berth, while my father drilled me on both the multiplication and telling time. As a result, she learned how to multiply and read a clock long before she was required to for school. Maya, in turn, taught Lavander when Lavander was still a tiny thing. I'm quite certain that they both benefited immensely from my suffering.

By that spring, too, I'd managed to win a Citizen of the Month award presented during a school assembly. I had no idea what I'd done to deserve such an honor, other than stay silent for the entire school year (perhaps that was enough), but I was very proud of it nevertheless. I still hadn't found a social group of my own to replace the adults who used to wander through our home, however. And although Maya had managed to collect a large enough group of children to fill up our dining room table for her previous birthday party, she wasn't going out on play dates either. We remained each other's primary peer group.

It's impossible now to tell whether or not that would have changed, had we stayed in Brooklyn, or even in the United States, for another school year. Because while my parents' taste for people who weren't produced by or directly related to them had diminished substantially, their desire to leave had not. We had been in New York for less than one calendar year when it was time to pack up and move again.

We had added another person this time and, once again, we were changing continents. For reasons that were never clear to me and lost to them over the ensuing years, my parents decided to move to South Africa, where my mother's family still lived. It was as big a move as we'd ever made. I shared our destination with as few of my classmates as possible because invariably their response was, "You're going to *Africa*? Are you going to live with lions? And elephants?" At that time and place, there probably wasn't another place on earth that would have seemed as exotic or primitive.

The preparations went on for weeks as my parents obtained visas, renewed passports, and decided what would stay and what would go. For reasons that were part financial and part not wanting to be bothered, my parents did not believe in the magic of shipping. Essentials (mostly clothes) went in the same suitcases that we'd dragged off the S.S. *France* less than twelve months before. Nonessentials (toys, books, record albums, and my mother's small but very classy pottery collection) were packed into four large, green army duffel bags. Those duffel bags were deep and dark. Maya and I could both fit into one empty one and could pull the top up almost to our heads. I watched my mother take a giant black marker and write our last name and our destination ("Rep. South Africa" underlined four times) on each one. They weren't exactly easy to maneuver once they were full and getting them all out of the house on moving day was quite a feat.

Our plane was due to leave in the evening, by which time my mother had worked herself into a larger, more comprehensive version of her usual airport anxiety. Just as she'd been the one to see us in when we'd arrived, Grandma was the one elected to drive us all to JFK International. She was not happy that we were leaving, never mind going to the Dark Continent. On the drive to the airport, her lips were tight and her face was drawn from her reluctance to let us go. Once we got to the airport, however, everything got much worse and there was no time for the kind of orderly, weepy departure that Grandma was no doubt expecting.

We were over our weight limit. Way over, it turned out. About three duffel bags over, in fact. My father was cursing. My mother was crying. Lavander was wailing. Grandma smoked, her lips getting thinner and paler. My father explained to her that she'd have to take three of the duffel bags home with her. There was some verbal scuffling between the two of them as he insisted that she take them and Grandma told him that there was no way she'd be able to store them in her tiny apartment and what was she supposed to do with them and how could she even get them out of her car when she got there? Maya and I stood quietly, watching. I had the hideous panicky feeling in my stomach that would accompany me to every airport from then on. I wanted it to be over and I wanted us to all be sitting on a plane, flying to somewhere else.

I'm not sure how we selected the one duffel bag that did make it onto the plane. The bags had all been packed haphazardly and there was no real order to the contents. In the end, frustrated to the edge of his limits, my father just grabbed one and threw it after the suitcases. Although the details of what happened to the other three remain hazy in everyone's memory now, the generally agreed-upon story goes that Grandma stored the duffel bags at the airport until she found someone to help her haul them out. After that, assuming that we were never coming back or that we didn't care too much what happened to them, Grandma pieced out the contents and gave everything away. Where it all finally ended up will be forever lost to the mists of time.

The bag that made it across the ocean with us was the one that contained Lavander's baby toys, Maya's and my B list dolls, my father's astrology books, and most of the family photos. What was missing represented what had been the individual elements in our collective family identity prior to that point. All of my father's record albums were gone. He wouldn't listen to the Doors, Hendrix, or Cream again until his children became teenagers and brought it around one more time. My mother lost her pottery and the will to try to replace it. She also lost all of her mirrored dresses, the only clothes that weren't in a suitcase.

Maya and I had put all of our favorite dolls (we never had toys, only dolls) in the same missing duffel bag. Also gone were our ballerina tutus and all of our books, an impressive collection of fairy tales from around the world. For a long time, it wasn't even possible to know exactly what was missing. We discovered the absence of most of these things when we went looking for them. For years after in our house, there were conversations that began and ended this way:

"Hey, where's my—?"

"It was in the duffel bags."

"Oh."

They were only things, of course, and things can be replaced by other things. Over time, we collected different books, different dolls, and different music. What my parents never sought to replace, however, was what all these missing things signified. They left a way of life behind along with all the people who were part of it. Our family was coalescing and becoming an entirely new entity. I was the only one who ever wondered what became of my parents' friends, the people who wandered through our houses on their way to somewhere else.

"Don't you want to know where they are? Who they are now?" I asked my parents decades later.

"They were all your mother's friends," my father said to me. "And I never liked your mother's friends."

"They weren't my friends," my mother said. "Some of them were just people I knew. The rest were Daddy's friends. And Daddy's friends were always weird."

There were some other items that never got replaced. Maya and I didn't get new ballerina outfits, for example. Nor did we stock up on fairy tales again. Our roles as the fairy girls had come to an end and new roles had taken their place. I wouldn't get a real fix on the exact nature of my own role for many years, but on the day I hit double digits, I began to have some sort of inchoate understanding. My mother had given me a book for my birthday. On the inside cover, she wrote, "To my eldest lovely daughter, turning ten today. Your loving Mummy."

The title of the book was *Lavender's Tree*.

I still have the book my mother gave me for that birthday. Next month, it will be thirty years old, half a decade older than Déja is now. I look at her now, this sister of mine, and realize that it will never be possible for me to explain to her who our parents were all those years ago and how we were formed and changed together. She wasn't even a spark in the ether when we moved to South Africa. Even Lavander, the line of demarcation between how we were and what we became, is too young to remember that we stayed there for only a few months and that when we left for California, my mother was pregnant again, this time with our brother, Bo, who was born a mere year after we ditched those duffel bags at JFK.

For all Déja knows, our parents never had friends or a social life that didn't involve their children. She'll never remember them as longhaired groovers, traversing the globe with their fairy girls in tow. She's known them only once. Maya and I have known them twice and for a long, long time.

"You know what?" I tell her now. "I don't think they ever will get old. They'll always be exactly who they are."

Debra and Déja.

4

Already Seen

june

Tonight, I am finally off to see Déja's play. I am the last one to go. Lavander has already been twice, each time bringing a posse of her friends and making sure to pay full price at the door. "It's brilliant," Lavander says. "And Déja is so great. I've never laughed so hard at one of her plays. It's hysterical."

"I could hear her laughing in the audience," Déja says. "You know that laugh Lavander has. You can always tell it's her. I had to keep from laughing myself when I heard her."

Maya has been three or four times. I've lost count. She offered up clothes for costumes and went to the dress rehearsal. And she's watched the whole performance with a number of her friends.

"It's different every time I see it," Maya says. "I can really see how it's come together over the course of a few shows."

Déja calls Maya every morning after a performance, whether it's one Maya has seen or not, to discuss the specifics of her and her cast mates' performances and to gossip about the production. Maya knows all the players by now and jumps right in.

"I don't think she should wear the apron up so high on her waist," Maya says one morning. "And I love that thing where you pop out from behind the couch—and that whole Cuba scene."

"Hey," I yell, "do you mind? I haven't seen it yet. You're going to ruin it for me."

"Sorry," Maya says. "I keep forgetting that you're the only one who hasn't gone. What are you waiting for?" From the other end of the receiver, I can hear Déja faintly but quite clearly saying, "When *is* she coming? Ask her, will you?"

My parents have seen the play, too. My father remarked with conviction, "Funniest play I've ever seen. Period," signaling that everyone else should find it the funniest play that *they'd* ever seen, too, or else there was something very wrong. "And Déja," he added, "is just . . . She just lights up on stage. And she's just so good." He doesn't get any arguments there.

Even my brother has beat me to this play and he's usually the last to go to any event, if he makes it at all. Unlike almost everyone else, he's only gone once, but he, too, professes it "hilarious."

And Danny . . . Well, Danny has been to every show. He goes every single night without fail. He doesn't pay and is now in training to take over the lighting to fill in for the production designer who is going on vacation. After the first performance, word has it, Danny stood up, clapping wildly and turned to my mother saying, "You are a very lucky woman. And I . . . I am very lucky, too."

"It's so cute," Maya said. "He's in love."

And now it's my turn.

I have to laugh a little to myself on the way to the tiny theater, remembering the last time I went to see Déja perform two years ago. This play has the same director, but Déja assures me that the two plays are nothing alike. Which is a good thing. I can't even remember the title of that play—it was something like *The Scavenging* or *The Degrading* or *The Violating*. Some kind of gerund indicating the destruction of any kind mental peacefulness. I call it *The Torturing* when I refer to it now because that's more or less what the whole production ended up being. I'd gone with Maya, my brother, and his brand-new girlfriend, who was meeting us for the first time.

There was my little sister in the black box, costumed to look like a Dumpster-diving teen runaway, smeared with running mascara and white makeup. Her character wailed and sobbed and cried. *Loudly.* When she wasn't crying (with real tears) and screaming, she was cursing and spitting out lines such as, "Shut up, goddamn it, you fucking jerk-off!" And all of this under the glare of a single, blazingly harsh spotlight so we could see the full extent of her character's agony.

Her pain very quickly became ours. If there had been any chance of escape, I would have left, but I was trapped, along with everybody else, in the black, sweaty confines of the small room. As the scenes escalated in anguish and I heard Déja become hoarse from shouting, I turned to Maya, and whispered, "How long is this going to go on? I can't take it." Maya, who always rushes to defend from criticism anything Déja does, could only shake her head in agreement.

"This is not art," I hissed. "This is horrible."

"Sshhh," Maya whispered, but she was grimacing. I looked down the aisle to my brother, who looked as if he might be redefining the word *uncomfortable*. I couldn't see his new girlfriend's face from where I was sitting and couldn't even imagine what she was making of all this.

It went on and on. In reality, the play was an hour-long one act, but it had obviously been written in dog minutes because it seemed at least seven times as long. It wasn't so much that I was offended by the material, although I started to feel that the writer desperately needed psychiatric help, or that Déja's character was one-dimensionally nightmarish. I just couldn't stand to watch Déja *emote* at such a shrieking pitch for such an extended period of time. I didn't feel that I was watching a play. I felt as though I was watching my sister have an onstage nervous breakdown.

When the lights finally came up, I could swear I heard the entire audience exhale at once. We stood numbly waiting for Déja to come out and say hello as people filed out of the small side door onto the street.

"I thought it was never going to end," I said finally. "Made *The Crucible* look like a comedy."

"That was really an awful experience," my brother said.

"What did you think?" I asked his new girlfriend.

"She was really good," the girlfriend said diplomatically.

"Wait," Maya said, to the girlfriend, "have you met Déja before?"

"No," said the girlfriend.

"So this is the first time you've seen her?" Maya started laughing. "She's not really like that, you know."

"Did you think you really had to make that clear?" my brother said.

Déja came out of the wings, black streaked tear lines still on her cheeks. She looked exactly as she always did after she'd been upset and crying. I couldn't stand it. "Hi, everyone," she said. "What did you think?"

"Why didn't you warn us?" I said.

"I told you it was a heavy play," Déja said.

"*Hamlet* is a heavy play," I said. "This was something else entirely."

Our brother took that moment to introduce his new girlfriend to Déja.

"Oh, hi," Déja said, smiling through her mask of misery. "It's great to meet you."

That play, and our reactions to it, became something of a joke around the house. My imitation of Déja wailing her way through the endless scenes was always good for a laugh, although I was careful not to do it very often. *The Torturing* settled one thing, though. I told Déja that I couldn't watch her in another performance like that. It had nothing to do with lack of support. She would always be my baby sister and I just couldn't watch her in that kind of pain, real or imagined.

When I get to the theater now, I choose a seat in the front row. This is an unusual choice for me. I'm almost always a few rows back and as inconspicuous as possible. But tonight I can't deal with the thought of somebody sitting in front of me (and lately, wherever I go, the biggest person in the crowd has to be sitting *right there*), blocking my view. I don't want to have to lean this way or that and miss something in the process. I don't want to have to notice the breathing, fidgeting, or cologne of the person in front of me instead of the visual subtleties on stage. So here I am, parked and ready. There will be no torturing this time, I've been told. This time it's a sexual farce. And that's all right with me. I can deal with Déja sexualized. It's only agonized I have trouble with.

The lights go down on the audience and up on the stage. There are several scenes before Déja makes her appearance so I have time to form an impression of the play itself before I see her. The energy level is high onstage and I find myself laughing at the clever dialogue, full of double entendres and clever one-liners. When one of the scenes moves off the main set and to the edge of the audience, I am slightly alarmed to find out that my front row seat has actually put me inches away from the action. I can actually see the pores in the actor's skin. I think that maybe I am just a tiny bit too close.

After twenty minutes or so, I am so involved in the play that Déja's entrance gives me a start. She's wearing a beehive wig, mod jewelry, and false eyelashes. And she is so lovely. It could all be my imagination, of course, but I'm sure I can hear a sigh of appreciation coming from the audience as she launches into the dialogue. I watch Déja vamp across the stage and find myself slipping out of the objectivity I've so carefully constructed. It's always been difficult for me to be objective about Déja, whether the objectivity is in regard to her performance on the stage or in life. In a sense, I almost feel as if I am able to be more objective about my own child. After all, I have always been his mother. Our roles in relation to each other have always been very clear. It's not as clear with Déja. There was a time when I was more of an intermediate mother to Déja than a sister. And for a while, we had the best of both of those worlds.

My position as sub-mom for Déja is one that neither Maya nor Lavander shared. When Déja was born, Maya was twelve years old and Lavander was in first grade. Our sweet little brother, Bo, was four years old. I was six months from turning sixteen and she could easily have been mine. And until I moved out of the house three years later, Déja *was* my baby. In a way, we've been trying to redefine ourselves as sisters ever since. I look at her now and I can't help but see the outline of those baby features in the curve of her woman's face—can't help but notice the passage of time as it reflects through her. And I can't help remembering, again, the person I was when she was born and the person she helped me avoid becoming.

In 1977, we were living near Monticello, in the Catskill Mountains, where we'd been for four years, an epic stretch in one place for my family. Of course, we *had* changed addresses several times over that period, moving from a house bordering a cornfield to a condo on the edge of a lake, and then to a spare, concrete apartment complex. The fourth house was everyone's favorite: an L-shaped ranch-style house on a long leafy street. There was a rolling lawn in the front and a forest of aspen and fir trees in the back. We were never really sure how far back the trees went because after seeing a black bear, a few deer, and a wild turkey stroll by within spitting distance of the breakfast table the first winter we spent there, nobody was brave enough to chart a course through them.

The house suited my parents more than any other I could remember. In the winter, it was possible to look out the window and be convinced that you were completely alone on the planet, an illusion my parents had been striving to create for some time. Our driveway was a shining slope of ice then and the lawn was covered with drifts of snow. Our street wasn't a major enough thoroughfare for the snow plow to make its way there after the constant winter storms, so when the snowfall was measured in feet rather than inches, everybody simply stayed put. On those days the sky was low, the same off-white as the ground, and there was a quiet stillness, punctuated only by the occasional crack of frozen branches.

"Snow day" school closings were announced every morning at 5:00 A.M. on the local radio station. When the school bus could make it through, it arrived with orange-haired, scarlet-lipped, tough-talking Val driving, heavy chains on its tires, scraping through salt, ice, and gravel. It took almost an hour to get to school. Maya dozed next to me on the bus while I read. When we got into town, we'd pass a light board that displayed the air temperature, often in the single digits. That was my cue to wake Maya up. Her drop-off at the middle school was first, then Val careered over to the high school where the rest of us stumbled off in our clogs and Frye boots to negotiate the skating rink of a parking lot.

We had neighbors on either side of our house, but we never saw or heard them in winter. Both my parents, especially my mother, loved this arrangement. Hunkering down around the wood-burning stove in the dead of winter surrounded by their own children was an idyllic experience for them. My feelings were exactly opposite. For me, this rural, tucked-in existence was a form of involuntary confinement. In October, I started feeling claustrophobic and by the time the first snows started falling, I was suffocating. School was really the only time I got to go out at all and, for that reason alone, I was fanatic about not missing it. My school attendance record would have been near perfect, in fact, were it not for my parents. They believed that we went to school entirely too much and needed more frequent breaks than we got.

"Why don't you and Maya stay home tomorrow?" my mother would say. "It's below zero and Daddy thinks you could use a day off."

"I'll miss my homework," I'd say, or, "I have a test," but neither parent bought these as excuses. I was always ahead of my schoolwork and never brought home anything lower than a B on my report card. This they knew. When I refused to capitulate, though, my mother sometimes got sneaky, turning off my alarm so that I'd simply oversleep and have to stay home. When I woke up anyway and went to school, she actually got angry.

I started to feel trapped at home and said so on more than one occasion. This was definitely a term that didn't go over very well with my parents. Both my mother and father told me regularly that I had a selfish attitude, that I was unwilling to be a giving part of the family, that they were working their asses off for me and that all I did was complain.

They weren't entirely off the mark. In the period preceding Déja's birth, both of them had jobs at the same time, an uncommon arrangement for our family. Prior to this, they had traded off working and staying home with the kids, so that one of them was always with the children. Quite often, my mother worked and my father was home. When she was pregnant and when my siblings were infants, my mother was home and my father worked. When I was about thirteen, though, my parents felt comfortable leaving me in charge and, when they could, they went to work together. Since Maya and I were in school during the day and the other two had not yet started at that point, my parents worked night jobs in hotels because they never believed in child care—never believed that the care or raising of their children should be left in any way to strangers. Had they really been motivated to make money, I suppose that my parents could have alternated shifts so that they could always have had jobs at the same time, but that was never an appealing prospect for either one of them. Although they had plenty of arguments, often at high volume and with great drama, the fact was that my parents didn't like to be apart for very long. They have always been each other's favorite people. The kind of working arrangement that would have them greeting and parting at the door on their way to their different shifts wasn't a possibility for them. Besides, they viewed jobs only as a financial means to an end rather than as careers. As far as I could see, for most of my life, their children were my parents' career and family bonds were of paramount importance to them.

Although time, the disparate personalities of all their children, and a changing attitude toward money have gone a long way to pummeling and reshaping this philosophy, the essence of it remains true for both my parents. When, after many years of struggling to get into print, I published my first book, my father pointed out to me that, "At the end of your life, it won't matter that you've written a book. What matters is that there are people who love you and that you love the people who love you. That is the real accomplishment." And by "people," of course, he meant family.

This was a difficult ethos for me to swallow at the age of fifteen, when all I could dream of was the day when I'd have my own identity apart from the family unit. My parents rejected any such notion and seemed concerned, even worried, that I'd be having such thoughts at all. My mother, particularly, became incredibly rattled if I mentioned going away to college after high school, getting a job, and, especially, wanting to date (although we never called it that—it was always referred to as "having a boyfriend"). And so, for the first time in my life, I found myself unable to talk to my mother about my feelings. This was doubly distressing for me because I'd always felt that one of my mother's best virtues was her ability to listen to her children, as well as a genuine interest in what they were saying.

My father was definitely out as an advisor, being the primary enforcer and arbiter of all moral standards. He didn't allow earrings, leg shaving, or cheerleading, so it was more or less pointless to even broach the subject of, say, dating, with him. It's worth noting here that my father always considered himself very liberal and considered his house very free and unconstrained. And it was true, there was a constant exchange of ideas happening in our house, but my father was very clear that mine were as yet unformed. I was his first teenager, after all, and when I was going through my teens, he was still fond of saying things like, "You're not old enough to know who you are right now."

I didn't have much luck cultivating the kind of best-girlfriend relationships I saw among my schoolmates at this point, either, although it wasn't for lack of trying. For one thing, I could never find enough common ground with these girls to gain secure purchase there. When it came down to it, my family really didn't fit into any of the social categories in our area, which meant that I didn't either. Which is not to say that we were so strange that we really stood out, because we didn't. But there was a collection of little things that made me feel as though I was always a half step off the beaten path.

For example, our town bordered a ski resort and ski weekends were major winter social events. We didn't ski. This was an alien culture to us. My parents would sooner have parachuted out of an airplane than strapped on a pair of skis and they simply couldn't understand why anybody else would want to either. The only person in our family to even attempt it was Maya. After she spent an afternoon dragging up and down the slope in her pink ankle-length sheepskin coat, she gave up the idea forever.

We had also just become vegetarians in a place that was known for its deer hunting. In fact, the seasonal parade of cars with freshly killed, still-bleeding deer strapped to their roofs was a major contributing factor to our decision to stop eating meat. Our revulsion over what was considered to be not only a fine sport but also a natural way of keeping the deer population in check wasn't an attitude that went over particularly well with anyone else.

Aside from all of this, we just didn't have the kind of collective identity that could have shoehorned us into any particular category. We'd come from everywhere generally and nowhere specifically and never stayed anywhere for long. Social distinctions were important to the girls I knew. More important, even, than what one had to bring to the party in terms of personality. I could never figure out where those social lines were drawn, which ones I could cross, and which ones defined me. I suppose this might have been basic garden-variety teenage alienation, but, even though I occasionally accused myself of being "typical," I'd had no experience with it and didn't know what to do with it. I was the leader of the pack in my family, the one who always had to go first, and there were no footsteps to follow. In one of the many ledgers that would serve as my journals, I described it for myself this way:

> *I have this incredible feeling of being left out of something*
> *I want very much. Everyone has their own station in life.*
> *Everyone has their niche. Except me. Everyone I meet seems*
> *to belong to the world or at least to themselves. I'm alone. I*
> *just don't fit. If I were a genius, or a raving beauty, or even*
> *extremely ugly, I would be someone. But I'm just someone*
> *else and I don't know who that person is.*

If there was one person who might have been able to understand all this, who might have been able to say, "Yes, it's just like that for me too," it would have been Maya. She had always been my confidante as well as my foil. But in the dark winter days when I was caught between fourteen and fifteen, Maya was too far away from her own adolescence to understand my sense of suffocation and yearning to breathe air that was different from that in our own house. At least, this is what I assumed and it was an assumption she never tried to dispute.

During the previous summer, when we'd been living in a sterile but overpopulated apartment complex, I'd had my first flirtation with one of the neighbor boys, something I'd made her swear on pain worse than death to keep from our parents. It was an innocent bit of fiction as those things go, existing mostly in my head, but the spark itself was enough to warrant parental hysteria. Maya hated carrying that secret around, almost as much as she hated the boy himself and the very idea that I would be interested in flirting with him at all (let alone *kissing* him or anything as revolting as that). Maya could never understand how coquetting it up with some gangly teenager would be more appealing to me than playing jacks with her on our big redwood dining room table while Marvin Gaye's greatest hits cheered us along. I would have explained it to her if I'd had any idea myself, but my behavior, along with the motivations that spawned it, was as much a mystery to me as it was to her.

At any rate, her disgust over the whole thing put her squarely in the too-young-to-understand category for me, as well as establishing a sort of off-limits zone for all future conversations relating to romantic involvements. But my natural inclination, almost from the day she was born, was to tell Maya everything. Despite my sense that she didn't understand what I was feeling and was vaguely disapproving besides, I didn't want to stop our constant conversation. So the two of us developed a sort of communicative silence that would play an important role in our relationship from then on.

I'd pull out my journal and write furiously while Maya lay on her bed opposite mine, reading one of her mysteries. When I couldn't write anymore and sat staring into the blue space of our bedroom, Maya would come and sit next to me, both of us resting our chins on our knees, saying nothing. Sometimes she put her arm around me. Sometimes she just sat close enough so that our shoulders were touching. If our silence went uninterrupted for long enough, she would suggest a cup of tea or putting my hair into a French braid and we always ended up doing one or the other. I put my journal away, shoving it between my mattress and box spring. It was a hiding place in plain sight, really. Maya always knew it was there. But she never once read it.

My journals became the only place where I could dump all the feelings I couldn't express to anyone else. I filled two of them that year, each entry more angst-driven and frustrated than the last. Sometimes, the journals themselves became part of the frustration. "Just sitting here in gray depression," I wrote.

I must keep writing, because I don't want to go to bed. I'm sick of dreaming because, even in my dreams, I'm an idiot. I can't stay up and be depressed by my miserable family anymore, so I must write. When I write, I am suspended between love, hate, anger, fear and apathy. But I am still depressed and there's nobody I can talk to or tell about it except this paper I'm writing on and it can't answer me.

For a while after this, the entries got much shorter. "I wish I was dead," I wrote one day. The next day's entry read, "I really wish I was dead. I think death has to be better." The third in this series consisted of an entire page filled with the words "I wish" over and over again until the last line, which said, "I was dead." I worried a bit about writing this down because, although I knew that Maya would never read my journal, I wasn't as convinced about my mother—with good reason. When I turned eleven, my parents gave me a diary for my birthday, complete with a lock and tiny key. I loved that diary more than any other present I'd ever received and wrote in it religiously every day of the year, leaving it out, near my bed, foolishly believing that its lock would protect my secret thoughts from prying eyes. But no. My mother read it, "cover to cover," as she hastened to tell me. It was phenomenal to me that she felt she had every right to read my diary and made no secret of it, but what was even more stunning was that she *took issue* with its contents, berating me for saying terrible things about her and my father in its pages. I don't remember now what those terrible things were, because, after our argument over the diary (during which my mother insisted, "And I'd do it again!"), I burned it, page by page, in the fireplace. It was a violated and ruined thing after that and I couldn't stand to have it near me.

Because I was compelled to keep writing, I started hiding subsequent journals in various spots around my bedroom, sometimes leaving decoy journals in plain sight that charted events like the weather and what hits were on the Top 40. Even with all these precautions, though, I didn't feel entirely safe about writing down my innermost thoughts in plain language anymore. I started writing in code, using metaphor and allegorical short stories to describe what was going on. Despite this, though, I assumed that everything I wrote from then on was going to be read by someone else and so, from that point on, I wrote with an audience in mind and tailored even my most boring journal entries so that they would be interesting to that audience. It was in this way that my mother became, indirectly, my first and best writing teacher.

It was in anticipation of this audience that I stopped writing that I wished I were dead. In those terms. The thought of my mother discovering these feelings and then sharing them with my father was worse than the thoughts themselves. So I started writing stories full of suicidal ideation, becoming progressively more detailed as I really started to explore the concept itself. Suicide fantasies started becoming a form of escape. I couldn't have said then where I was heading with all of this. I knew only that I was miserable, guilty about being miserable, and blind as to how to make it any better.

Right around this time, close on the tail of the first spring thaw, my mother announced that she was pregnant again. What I found peculiar about this was not that she was pregnant (I'd certainly seen *that* movie before), but that she was so delighted about it. This was a *planned* pregnancy. At my age, when one out of every four girls I knew was either sneaking off to Planned Parenthood to get birth control or dealing with the consequences of not using it (there were plenty of girls calling the help line that year), it was a bit strange to think that my mother and father were intentionally adding to their family.

My parents are among the very few people I've ever known who actually planned their children. It's still difficult for me to imagine what that decision-making process must have been like, even though both my mother and father have, jokingly, described it as going something like this:

"Shall we have another baby?"

"Yes, okay, let's have another baby."

Maybe there was more to it than that and maybe not. My parents have always loved the very idea of babies, as well as the notion that, together, they could make new people. By 1977, they already had four children, broken by our ages into two sets. Maya and I, in our teens, formed the original set. Lavander and Bo, who were only eighteen months apart and inseparable from infancy, formed the second set. They were still little, but no longer babies when my mother conceived again. Lavander had already started school and Bo was right behind her. In other words, there was no baby in the house and so my parents decided to make one more.

When she's in the right mood, though, my mother will sometimes claim that she had Déja for me. It was a way to keep me out of trouble, she says, meaning that, if there was a baby available to satisfy my burgeoning maternal instincts, I wouldn't feel compelled to rush out and have one of my own. "You were at *that* age," she says. "Who knows what you could have done?"

Naturally, she never discussed any such thing at the time. Nor did Cindy McGill's mother, who was due the same week as mine. Although Cindy and I had been in several classes together at school, we'd had nothing in common until both of our mothers became pregnant at the same time. The uniqueness of this situation drew us together and we formed a tentative friendship. Cindy had only one brother who was four years younger than she was. Things had been pretty quiet in her house for some time. Unlike mine, Cindy's new sibling was not planned. And unlike mine, Cindy's mother continued working at her job in the local department store where, in those pre-mall days, everybody had to shop at some point. Cindy's mother worked in the housewares section and my mother made a point of visiting her there when she was on shift to say hello and compare notes. Although they were around the same age, Cindy's mother seemed worn, tired, and older than mine. I got the sense that Cindy's mother wasn't exactly overjoyed about her new baby. Cindy merely seemed nonplused by the whole thing and, in this, we were somewhat united. It was a little strange to be anticipating new babies from our mothers at our age and neither of us could quite figure out how these new people would affect the structure of our families or, more importantly, how they would affect *us*. Speculating on whether we'd be changing diapers or wakened in the middle of the night gave us enough conversational fodder for many study halls.

"What do you want?" I asked Cindy. "A boy or a girl?"

"My mom doesn't care," Cindy said, shrugging. "She just wants it to be healthy."

"Of course, healthy," I said. "But we all want a boy. It's definitely a boy."

"I guess a girl would be nice," Cindy said. "But it doesn't really matter."

She spoke like a girl who had no sisters.

The weather report predicted a blizzard on the day Déja was born. The air smelled like snow and the sky was the color of gunmetal. We went to school anyway. Up in the mountains it was always business as usual until there were several inches of white on the ground. It was lunchtime and I was working in t vice principal's office, filing papers and trying to catch the e a senior boy on whom I'd developed an annoying crush my father came to get me. I looked up and he was just there, calmly waiting for me to notice him.

"Is it time?" I asked him, suddenly more excited ' for months.

"It's time," he said. "Let's go."

My new sister arrived less than six hou

never showed up. My father called as I was washing the dinner dishes. I was almost disappointed, having prepared myself for a long night of waiting, wondering, and drama.

"It's another girl," he said.

"Really?" I asked.

What I'd told Cindy was true. Before she was born, we were all convinced that the new baby was a boy. It seemed like a logical assumption at the time that we'd end up with three girls and two boys. My parents were so sure, in fact, that they didn't even bother debating girls' names and had come up with Dustin as the only choice.

"Yes, another little girl," my father says. "She's perfect. Ten pretty fingers and ten toes."

"How much does she weigh?" I asked.

"Seven, eleven," my father said. "It's a lucky number."

"What's her name?"

"Well, we're going to have to think about that," he said.

That decision came the next night. My father sat with me at the kitchen table, coffee in hand, debating the choices. Obviously Dustin was out, but he was still working with the letter D.

"I was thinking about Desiree," he said. "I really like the sound of it. What do you think?"

"Very pretty," I said.

"But it means 'desire,'" he said. "I don't like that. We don't want her to have to start her life with desire. Too heavy."

"Hmm," I said. "That's true."

He went over a few more, sounding out Daisy, Della, Dahlia, and Delilah. Together, we rejected all of them.

"Desiree sounds so nice," I said. "Maybe we should go back to Desiree. Or, what about Dusty?"

"Dusty . . ." my father said. "Definitely not. She's definitely Dusty." He ruminated a little longer and then, on the back of an envelope, wrote Desiree next to a few of the rejected names. "Looks nice on paper," he said. "But what about this?" On the bottom of the list he wrote "Deja."

"Like déjà vu?" I asked him. "But then you have to put an accent on the *e* and the *a*." I added the appropriate diacritical marks and we looked at the result.

"I like it," my father said.

"But it means 'already,'" I squeaked, using my limited knowledge of French.

"Well, we *already* have three girls," my father said. "But still . . ." He erased the accent on the *a*. "There," he said. "That's it."

"Yes, that's it," I said.

"Good," he said. "Let's call Mommy and see if she likes it. She'll have the last word."

My mother agreed with us. Already or not.

When Déja came home, nothing changed, but everything was different. Almost immediately, as if there had been some sort of tacit agreement between the two of us, my mother handed her over to me. This wasn't out of a desire on my mother's part to be less involved, because she was very much attached to Déja, as she was to all her children. But this time it was as if I had become a satellite and Déja was the shared link between the mother ship and me. There was never any discussion between the two of us as to how to care for her, what her sleeping and eating schedule was, or how to soothe her. My mother just assumed that I knew all these things and she was right.

Every day, when I came home from the school, the first thing I did was bundle Déja up and take her into the unused family room where we kept the stereo and rock her to sleep under the speakers. Because she squirmed if I sat down, I always stood with her in my arms, watching her eyelashes flutter as we moved back and forth. I recorded songs off the radio for this express purpose. We'd start with James Taylor and Stevie Wonder, and move into Billy Joel and through Boz Scaggs. She was almost always asleep by the time we got to "New York State of Mind," but she was so warm and sweet, I didn't want to put her down. I'd hold her like that for hours sometimes, afraid to disturb her peace, afraid to disturb mine.

On the weekends, I had her all the time. I walked around the house with her attached to my hip. I bathed her, changed her, and fed her. She lay on my bed when I did my homework. She sat in her high chair next to me when I did the dishes. When there was a family outing in the offing, I always opted to stay at home with her because it was too cold for her to go outside for long. It was during these times, when we were alone together, that I started talking to her. I spun out my thoughts for her in a way I couldn't tell anyone else. I stopped writing suicide fantasies in my journal or anywhere else. In Déja, a captive but happy audience, I'd found a place where I could share my secrets. It didn't matter that she didn't comprehend what I was saying (although I believed that somewhere in her preverbal innocence, she had a fundamental understanding), because I didn't need answers from her. Her small need for me, her contentment in being with me, was all the response I needed.

Cindy's mother delivered a boy three weeks after Déja was born. For a couple of months, we continued to trade baby news when we saw each other at school. But it was soon clear to me (and probably to Cindy, too) that she didn't have the same kind of relationship with her new brother that I had with Déja. "I guess he's kind of cute," she said, "but he cries all the time and I don't know what to do with him when he's screaming. My mom takes care of that." Our conversations became briefer as the weeks went on and soon they were limited to:

"Hi, Cindy. How's your little brother?"

"He's good. How's your little sister?"

"She's great."

Finally, as if by mutual agreement, there wasn't even that

much. We passed each other in the halls and smiled at each other, slightly puzzled, as if we weren't sure why we even knew each other in the first place. Unlike Cindy, or even my other siblings, Déja and I had developed a bond, the parameters of which fell somewhere short of mother but beyond that of sister. And in my relationship with her, I found some sense of the identity I'd been searching for. Maya claims that all three of our younger siblings spoke her name as one of their first words (after "mama," "dada," and, in Lavander's case, "no"), but I know that Déja was different. She was just a little blond thing when she first looked at me, raised her arms, and said, "Deb-deb. Up." For the first two years of her life, I was always the first one Déja looked to when she wanted to be picked up and carried. And every time I lifted her, she brought me up with her.

I watch Déja stride across the stage now, all glitter and mascara, a cigarette smoking between her fingers. My family is absolutely correct in their assessment of her performance. She's very good in this role, beautiful and funny, with an adopted maturity that belies her actual age. Despite the humor in the script, though, my eyes are blurry with tears. It's always this way with Déja, and I suspect that it always will be, no matter how many years are stretched between that New York winter and now. After a while, I'll be able to pull myself out of this sentimental slide and focus my attention on Déja's art and may even be able to tease my notion of her away from the role she's playing. But for this moment, the moment when I first see her spotlighted up there, all I can think about is what I selfishly consider her first role, that of *my* baby sister.

In a sense, my mother is right. Having Déja did keep me out of trouble, but it's not the kind of trouble she had in mind. Déja didn't save me from becoming a wayward daughter or teen mother, she saved me from myself. I like to think I gave her something back that was worth as much, but I doubt it. She was not quite three years old when I started college and left home to live on campus. My school was only a half hour away and my parents didn't want me to move out, but I went anyway. At that point, I welcomed the separation from everyone in my family except Déja. I felt irrationally guilty about leaving her behind and wasn't sure what we'd be to each other when and if I came back to the fold. My parents could sense what I was feeling. When I moved in with my boyfriend after my first year of school instead of back with my family, my parents were both furious and distraught. We barely spoke to each other for almost a year afterward. Maintaining this fraught silence didn't stop them from putting Déja on the phone, however.

"I miss you, Deb-deb," she said. "When are you going to see me? When are you coming home?"

I burst into tears after every one of these conversations. And every time he witnessed it, my boyfriend felt compelled to comment.

"Why do you let them manipulate you like that?" he said.

"It's not them," I told him. "It's Déja."

"What about Déja?" he said testily. "She's just a little girl and not perfect either, you know."

"Yes, she is," I said. "You don't know . . . you don't understand."

I never tried to explain it to him—never attempted to make clear how much "just a little girl" (which is how my father often referred to me the year before Déja was born) could mean or how much heart she could possess.

I never tried to explain this to Déja either, I think as I watch her steal another scene. I wonder how much of those early years is buried in her. I wonder not what she remembers but how much she knows. In the last year, I have started talking to her the way I did when she was an infant, which is to say that, once again, I am sharing secrets with her that nobody else knows. And now she is answering.

The play gets wackier and more farcical as it goes along and I'm soon laughing as loudly as anyone else in the audience. Déja's character gets progressively more sexual and provocative and I'm proud of her for being able to pull it off so well. Before the cast takes its final bow, I've managed to get in a good laugh *and* a quick weep. Can't really ask for more than that.

The audience files out and I'm left sitting in the empty theater for several minutes while I wait for Déja to emerge from backstage. I watch as other cast members come out, chat with each other, inspect the night's ticket take, and drift backstage again. I've almost given up, thinking that maybe Déja doesn't know I'm here, maybe she thinks I left, maybe she left through some back door I can't see, when she comes bursting out. The beehive wig is off, as are the false eyelashes, but her lips are still a particularly hot shade of scarlet and her eyelids a particularly electric shade of blue.

"Where's my sister?" I hear her calling and then, when she sees me, "Debsie!" (a mutation of Deb-deb which seems to have stuck over the last twenty years or so). "What did you think?" she says as she hugs me tight. "How was it? Did you think it was funny? It was funny, wasn't it? Did you think it was good?"

"You were great," I answer. "It was very funny. I really enjoyed it."

"Really?" she says.

"Of course, really," I say.

"Because, you know, I was really nervous that you were coming tonight."

"But why?" I ask her, genuinely puzzled.

"*You know,*" she says. "You're my big sister. What you think really matters to me. Not that nobody else matters, but you're always so . . . *critical* isn't really the right word, but . . ."

"When have I ever been critical?" I ask, critically.

"Not critical, okay? I mean, you're not just going to automatically think it's great just because I'm in it. You're harder to please. You have higher standards."

"Thanks. I think."

"I told everyone you were coming tonight," Déja says, "and that I was nervous. And then I look out and you're sitting in the *front row*. Why did you sit in the front row? Nobody else sat in the front row—not Maya or Lavander or anybody."

"I know," I tell her. "I'm sorry about that. I just didn't want anybody else to get in the way."

"I saw your little face from backstage," she says. "I was checking to make sure you were laughing. I saw you laughing."

The director walks out as she says this and smiles in Déja's direction.

"Mike, Mike, come here," she says, waving him over. "This is my big sister, the one I told you about. You know, the one who hated the *other* play."

"*The Torturing*," I offer. "Or whatever it was called. That's what we named it."

"Yes, Déja told me about that," Mike says.

"But this one was great," I say hastily. "Loved it."

"My big sister," Déja says again, putting her arm around me and resting her head on mine. "Look how tiny she is. Tiny cute little person."

"Funny, Déja," I say.

"She used to rock me to sleep when I was a baby," Déja tells Mike, who nods as if he's heard this story before. "She took care of me," Déja says.

Mike says, "Nice to see you," and takes his leave.

I tell Déja I'm going to leave and let her take off the rest of her makeup and do whatever she does with her fellow thespians after a performance.

"Did you really like it?" she asks me.

"You were wonderful," I tell her. "Really."

"I'll call you in the morning," she says. "And then you can give me details. I want to know what you thought of everything, down to the last detail."

"Okay," I tell her. "But you were still great."

"Next time maybe don't sit in the front row, okay?"

"*Okay*," I say. "So kill me because I wanted an unobstructed view."

She hugs me for a third time and kisses me hard, leaving the perfect imprint of her red lips on my cheek. "Love you," she says.

"Love you more," I tell her.

"No, I love you more!"

"More!" I laugh and walk away.

"More!" I hear at my back.

When I get to the theater door and turn around to give her a last wave good-bye, I can see her standing there, still mouthing the word "more" until I am out of sight.

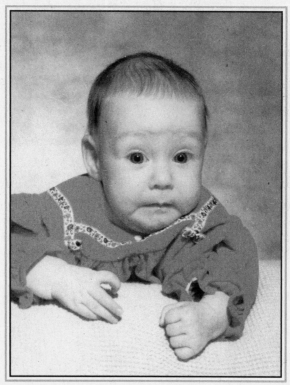

Lavander, 1971.

5

Mirror to Mirror

july

Lavander is in crisis.

I am the first of my siblings to hear about this. I'm on the phone with my mother and the weight in her voice is like that of a teetering seawall.

"I don't know what to do with her," my mother says. "She rejects everything I have to say. She's accusatory. I don't know why she's so angry at me."

"What's the problem?" I ask my mother, but we both know that it's about Tony. Bad Boyfriend, as he is becoming, is behind it all. And Lavander herself stands behind Bad Boyfriend, alternately defending him and vilifying him. The story is the same as it has been for the last few months, none of us would care who or what Tony is if Lavander was *happy* in the relationship, but she clearly isn't. Now, my mother tells me, she's broken up with him, or maybe he's broken up with her, she isn't clear on the details. Whatever it is, she's distraught and my mother is to blame. At least, this is what Lavander is currently projecting.

I was in New Mexico over the weekend and I bought my mother and each one of my sisters a turquoise bracelet. I thought about the choices carefully, even though I bought them all from the same vendor in Santa Fe, a wizened Native American woman with a hearing aid that squealed every time I asked the price of her jewelry. I got my mother a bracelet with big green-tinted stones. Maya got one made up of silver beads with designs of suns and arrows etched into their surfaces. For Déja, I picked one with small, perfectly round, deep blue stones. Lavander's bracelet looks very much like my mother's, the only difference being that the stones are slightly smaller. This morning, I went to deliver the bracelets with Maya. I figured that since Lavander lives in a condo nineteen steps from the one where my parents live (we counted them one night and there are exactly nineteen steps), I could give both of them their bracelets at the same time.

"Where's Lavander?" I asked my mother after I'd taken the bracelet off my wrist and fastened it on hers. I was keeping Lavander's bracelet warm on my own wrist as well until I could give it to her.

"I don't know," my mother said. "Maybe she's home. Why don't you go check?"

We were standing between the two condos when Lavander clicked her way up the concrete stairs from the street below and walked toward her door without so much as a greeting.

"Hi!" Maya called over to her.

Lavander turned and looked at us. Her expression was one that I could only classify as dangerous: a mixture of misery, disgust, hostility, and desperation.

"I'm taking the rest of the day off," she said in slow, measured tones. "I don't want to be disturbed, so please don't call me." She went into her condo and closed the door behind her.

"Well, I guess that's that," I said, touching the turquoise stones on my wrist. I could feel the hard silver clasp pressing into my skin.

"What's the matter with her?" Maya asked my mother, and my mother shrugged as if she didn't know, as if she wasn't privy to Lavander's every dot and dash.

Now it's close to five in the afternoon and I'm on the phone with my mother and it's clear that nothing has improved.

"She's screaming at me," my mother says. "She threw me out."

"Maybe you should try to detach yourself a little," I tell her. "Just leave it alone for a while."

"Can you detach yourself from your children?" my mother asks. "*You* know. You're a *mother*."

"I know," I sigh, "but you are so involved. And the two of you react to each other in the same way every time. It's a pattern."

My mother is too miserable to listen to this. She talks about Lavander's choices and her own inability to influence them. "She doesn't listen," my mother says. "She never listens." It goes on like this for several more minutes and then she hangs up, citing emotional exhaustion. I feel depressed and angry at the same time. Lavander doesn't retreat into her sadness, she uses it as a weapon.

The phone rings a half hour later. This time it's my father.

"Where's Maya?" he wants to know.

"She's out working," I tell him.

"All right, I'll call her on her cell phone," he says.

"What is it?" I ask him, knowing already, but wanting him to say it anyway.

"It's Lavander," he says. "I think Maya should go over there and talk to her. She needs a sister right now."

"And what about me?" I ask. "I'm not a sister?"

"You can't go over there," he says. "You've got Blaze."

"I could go if I was needed," I tell him. "But I'm not. Lavander doesn't want to talk to me. She's barely spoken to me in the last six months anyway." I say it without bitterness and more as a statement of fact.

"What do you mean?" he asks.

"She doesn't want to hear what I have to say about anything, Dad. I don't know why." There is a pause and I think he's going to give me an answer I've heard many times before: that one has to keep trying, that you never give up with family, that if one approach doesn't work, another one has to be tried. But there's none of that this time.

"Why don't you just consider yourself lucky that you're not in this one," he says and it's not a question, it's more like a directive. "I'm going to call Maya now. I'll speak to you later."

Maya comes home an hour after this conversation. She's obviously gotten the message.

"It's Lavander," she says by way of greeting. "I'm going to eat something and then I'm going over there. I might spend the night—I'll call you and let you know. Déja's meeting me there as soon as she finishes work."

"So Déja's in this now, too?"

"Déja's coming as *my* support," Maya says.

Now, I have to admit, I feel a little put out. I want to know why my advice and sage counsel aren't deemed necessary. Why nobody seems to think that I am capable of helping. Of course, that's not entirely true. My mother will be the one who ends up needing me. I will be the one she calls, again and again, to talk about Lavander until both of us are so tired the only thing we can do is sit in front of our respective televisions and watch something mindless. I know this is coming, because it's always been this way with my mother. I am the only one of her daughters who is a mother and that has added a layer of understanding to our communication. When it comes to my siblings, especially my sisters, she talks to my father first and then to me. When she and my father disagree on any given issue, she speaks to me first. Sometimes my mother and I are able to discuss my sisters so objectively that they become other people for us, detached from their roles as sisters and daughters. I have no doubt that my mother also discusses *me* with my sisters, but I know that, for them, I come up more as a passing topic, not as the center of the discussion. It would never happen, for example, that my mother would spend an afternoon with Lavander, Maya, or Déja and talk about nothing but me. But she and I have spent many mornings and afternoons together with one, two, or all three of my sisters as our sole focus. I suspect that we'll be talking about Lavander for quite a while. Lavander has been stressed, unhappy, and not particularly pleasant about it for some time. My mother always gets the cutting edge of Lavander's moods, whether these are angry, conciliatory, or distressed. I suspect this is because they are more alike than either one of them even knows.

"I'll call you," Maya says now. "I'll let you know what's going on."

"Right," I say.

But the hours pass and she doesn't call. Nobody answers the phone at Lavander's house. My mother doesn't want to talk anymore, either. I try Maya's cell phone, finally, and she answers only after several rings.

"I can't talk now," she says. Her voice is low and stressed and I think I detect a note of officiousness as well.

"What is going on?" I ask.

"I said *I can't talk,*" Maya replies. "I'm hanging up now. Don't call me again. I will call you when I can."

"Oh, come on, what is this?" I snap. "What could be so—"

She disconnects me midsentence. I am furious for a second or two and debate calling her again just so that I can hang up on her, but I stop myself and settle for yelling "COW!" into the quiet phone in my hand.

I decide I'm going to ignore the whole scene with all its entanglements and implications and settle in with a book or a sitcom rerun, anything so that I won't have to think. Not surprisingly, this doesn't work. I am irritated with Maya, but I know that will pass soon enough. More knotted and difficult is the combination of anger and worry I have about Lavander. The anger operates on a couple of different levels. On one hand, I am angry because her anguish is creating plenty of anguish for everyone else. On the other, I am angry that, despite the fact that she knows the miserable trajectory of my own past love life, that I've been there and back and there again, that she never comes to me. I am the only one of her sisters who has had experiences similar to the ones she's having and yet that's not enough for her to confide in me. I wonder, sometimes, if she likes me. And she is the only person in my family who makes me question this. I wonder, too, if she sees me as inaccessible. I have the reputation in my family for being emotionally bulletproof. Maybe that makes me seem aloof to her. Maybe she thinks I judge her, even though, having integrated so many personal fuck-ups, I am probably the least judgmental person in my family at this point. And maybe we are too similar on a level deeper than either of us wants to look at. I know that Lavander can push my buttons more effectively than anyone else I know. She alone is able to send me into an ugly rage and rage is not a state I enter into easily, with my sisters or anyone else.

As a group, my sisters and I have never been fighters, hitters, or hair pullers. Our arguments manifest verbally and conflicts are usually resolved the same way. Although certain items have occasionally gone flying through the air, there have always been better ways to strike strategic blows with correctly aimed verbal darts or the ever-popular silent treatment. In fact, among the four of us, there has been only one all-out physical brawl. And that one was between me and Lavander.

Lavander was sixteen and I was twenty-five. I'd given birth to Blaze less than two months before. I was single and living in a tiny studio apartment in downtown Portland, Oregon, where I'd moved two years prior, after graduating from college. My family was living in a suburb about a half hour south of me in a comfortable house with a big backyard, surrounded by Portland's ubiquitous greenery. Maya had taken a leave of absence from her university the year before and was living at home and working full-time in Peppy's, our family's pizza place. I'd spent most of the previous year sitting right there beside her, but after Blaze was born, I confined myself to my apartment for several weeks as I adjusted to a major shift in my priorities, most of which fit into the narrow space occupied with midnight feedings, disposable diapers, and an elusive quest for sleep. I was fine during the daylight hours—confident, happy, even optimistic. But the nights were difficult. When it got black and quiet outside and it seemed as if everyone in the world was sleeping except for me and my squalling infant, that was when I began to have doubts about my ability to navigate the course my life had taken.

Occasionally Déja, nine years old at the time and on summer vacation from school, came to spend the night with me. There wasn't much she could do to help me with Blaze, of course, but she was wild about him, thought he was "sooooo cute," and loved to walk around the tight confines of my room with him balanced in her arms. We ate Peppy's pizza together and watched TV. She made herself a bed on the floor and was passed out cold by ten o'clock—the time when my night was just beginning as Blaze started wailing, ready for another all-night party. Amazingly, Déja rarely woke up during these sessions. I'd pace around her, jiggling Blaze and attempting to will him to sleep, while the blue light of the TV danced across Déja's sleeping form on the floor. Sometimes, if Blaze was crying particularly loud or long, she'd raise her head and ask if I needed something. I always said no, because there was nothing more she could do for me. The quiet solidity of her presence was, in itself, very comforting.

Déja's field trips to my apartment were necessarily limited, though, so on the weekends, I put Blaze in his wicker basket and went to stay with my family. The nights were so much easier when I was surrounded by the sleeping bodies of my parents, my sisters, and my brother. There were people around me who I trusted and who would know what to do in the face of infant disaster. There was a safety net I could fall into if I needed to. Those weekend nights were the only times I could truly relax in the first few weeks after Blaze's birth. I didn't get a free pass, you understand. Nobody got up in the middle of the night to walk Blaze or change him. In fact, one particularly sleep-deprived Saturday, I woke to my mother shaking me by the shoulder.

"Excuse me," she said, "your baby's crying. Get up."

During the day, Blaze was cuddled and passed around the daisy chain of his relatives. I ate and even slept sometimes. This halcyon period was the first time I could remember allowing myself to openly need—to lean on someone else's shoulders emotionally. In the half-submerged part of me that wasn't busy fretting over my baby, I felt somewhat disappointed in this need, but I let it go. I allowed myself to cry in front of my mother, even allowed myself, occasionally, to break down completely.

In a sense, I'd been on something like an emotional hiatus from my family for about six years. I'd moved out at eighteen, gone to college, and attempted to forge some sort of identity for myself over that time. Although we were in close physical proximity, I didn't see my family very often and took mostly a surface interest in what was going on in their lives, since I was fairly one-pointed about what was going on in my own.

Over those years, Maya finished high school and started university. She found her own niche and developed some close friendships. She went to Grateful Dead concerts. She fell in love, but wouldn't discuss it—at least, not with me. Very rarely, she came to visit me. I always sensed an underlying wash of disapproval from her, although I was never sure whether this disapproval was over my friends, my lifestyle, or my personality. It was almost as if she was waiting for me to get on with it and get to whomever I was supposed to be. Not that I knew who that person was. And I never asked her. Like so much of the emotional undercurrent between Maya and me, this stayed in the realm of the undiscussed, never quite reaching the surface. On a barely conscious level, though, I knew that she had a better understanding of who I was than I did. And she knew that eventually our circles would intersect again. For this reason, I never really felt Maya's absence. Nor, it seemed, did she feel mine. It was somewhat different for the rest of my siblings.

While I wasn't paying attention, Déja had left her babyhood and started school. At nine years old, she'd become an individual with preferences and dislikes I knew nothing about. She had a schedule, activities, and playmates. She had opinions. She had, too, a distinct position in our family. No matter who moved out, went away, or came back, Déja would always be the youngest. She would always be the baby.

And my brother would always be the only boy. Since I'd moved out, he'd really become my father's only son. Bo was a jock, no longer a little boy at fourteen years old, and no longer content to hang out at home or ever be the center of familial attention. I had to admit I didn't have much of an idea who my brother was. For his part, he seemed to view me with a kind of wariness, something like trepidation, especially after I gave birth to Blaze. It was if the role of uncle was undefined for him and too much to integrate.

But, for me, it was Lavander who had undergone the most startling transformation during the time I'd been absent. She'd morphed from a saucy little girl to a wild sixteen-year-old and I had no recollection of what had come in between. Lavander was the first of the Ginsberg offspring to drive. I'd never gotten my license and Maya wouldn't get hers until she was almost twenty-three. For Lavander, getting a driver's license was almost an afterthought. She'd already been driving for years—whenever anyone would let her take control of the wheel. Once it was official, she was *out*. For the first time ever in my family, my parents bought a second car and Lavander was given free reign over their old Mazda. When she was home, which wasn't very often, she was on the phone—her own personal line, because in those days before call waiting, there was a constant busy signal when Lavander was in the house. She was extremely popular, constantly in the middle of one drama or another and was always in transit, either on her way out or just stopping at home briefly on her way to somewhere else.

Lavander was also the first (and only) one of us to have secret parties in the house while the parents were away. My parents never took vacations, so "away" meant when they were out of the house for any reasonable length of time. When Peppy's first opened, my parents (especially my father), Maya, Déja, and I were there until closing every night. Lavander was then, as she is now, the consummate party planner. She made excellent use of the hours between five and eleven.

When my parents pulled into the garage after a night at Peppy's with Maya and Déja in tow, they often sensed a vibration in the air, a displacement of ions, like the sudden stillness after a tornado or the wake of a speeding train. They could never quite put their finger on what it was that was different, because nothing had been moved or broken inside the house and everything was clean. Had they lingered in the garage for any length of time, they might have noticed the faintest odor of beer and cigarettes, but their senses were somewhat dulled by the constant onslaught of garlic and tomato sauce from Peppy's and the only thing anyone wanted to investigate after a full day of work was a package of cookies and the inside of a bed. Lavander, of course, was gone by the time everyone came home.

Bo was the only witness to what went on during these hours and would have sooner sacrificed his limbs than divulge to my parents what he'd seen. Even so, his grateful astonishment over the level of partying in which he was included caused him to slip somewhat over time, but only to his sisters. ("Dude," he once revealed with the reverence of someone recounting a mythic tale, "you don't even *know* what she pulled off. She had *kegs* in the garage. She had *whole bands* playing music in there. *Whole bands.* With instruments and amps. And it was all gone by ten. Gone, without a trace. No cars, no beer, nothing. It was *amazing.*") It must have taken a Cat-in-the-Hat type of cleanup effort for Lavander to get the house back in shape after these shindigs, a supreme display of organizational ability. My brother still looks back on it as some kind of miracle.

This all came to an end after I had Blaze. From then on, my mother, Déja, and I spent much less time at Peppy's. On top of that, my father had started closing the restaurant earlier on weeknights and altogether on Sundays. Lavander reacted to this shift by going out even more often. I barely saw her, but when I came home on the weekends, I began to get a sense of the storm her adolescence had become. Since there was no spare room for me when I came home with Blaze, I slept wherever there was a free bed. Sometimes I took my brother's room and sometimes Déja bunked with Maya and gave me her bed. Most often, though, Lavander was absent and I slept in her room, surrounded by her scattered notebooks, hair spray, flame-blackened candles, and the jittery scent of rebellion.

When I was in Lavander's bedroom, I tried to keep myself and Blaze in as small a space as possible. Diapers and receiving blankets had absolutely no place among her Aerosmith and Motley Crüe cassettes, glittery lipstick, and acid-wash jeans and I felt like a rude intruder. The disordered order of her room rejected anything maternal or soothing. When I sat up to feed Blaze in the wee hours, I let my eyes follow the trail of hair ties, folded notes, and matchbooks on the floor, looking for clues as to what might be going on in Lavander's head. There were tiny worry dolls in a box next to her bed. She had a corkboard tacked full of photographs of her friends and one framed photograph of our parents on her nightstand. Random keys were carelessly scattered on the floor, as if she'd decided to jettison her responsibilities to whatever they opened. There were small books with decorated covers that looked as though they might have been diaries, but they were sitting out in plain sight and I couldn't fathom how anyone would leave her innermost musings in a place where they could be read and judged. I didn't touch them. I touched nothing, in fact, despite my vexed curiosity. The air around my sister vibrated with the tension of a stretched rubber band and I didn't want to touch or disturb anything in her room, didn't want to investigate the icons of her existence, for fear of breaking it and getting stung in its snap.

These best-laid plans came to ruin one Sunday morning. I was on one of my weekend visits and Lavander was temporarily without a place to go or people to see. She sat on the couch disheveled and smudged with last night's makeup, wearing a look of utter disdain as I planned an outing to the mall with my mother and Maya to buy Blaze a new stroller.

"You're always *shopping*," she barked at my mother. "Doesn't it get boring? Doesn't that baby have enough *things*?"

"You can come with," I told her.

"Yeah, *right*." She sneered.

As the tension in the room ratcheted up by several notches, Maya and my mother dissolved into other parts of the house. The unmistakable odor of confrontation was in the air. I stayed where I was, preparing Blaze for an outing, which involved maneuvering his infant limbs into a one-piece, getting socks on his feet, and a blanket wrapped tightly around his body. Lavander watched my machinations with disgust. I could feel waves of hostility splashing over me. She muttered something unintelligible but distinctly unfriendly.

"Have you got something to say?" I asked her, matching her tone.

"Yeah, I do," she said. "You think you're so special, but you're not. You can't get anything together by yourself. You and your baby. Debra's *baby*, Debra's *baby*, that's all I fucking hear about anymore. Why don't you learn to DRIVE already? Get yourself a nice car and drive off to your own apartment with your baby and get yourself a life!"

"What are you talking about?" I asked her, stunned almost to the point of laughing.

"I said, why don't you get yourself a *life* and stop leeching off Mommy and Daddy!" She was actually snarling.

Angry thoughts exploded in my head like firecrackers. How dare she accuse me of being financially dependent, I seethed. I'd been fully self-supporting and financially independent for seven years and had never asked for or received any monetary help from my family in all that time, nor was I now. Until Blaze was born, I had worked an average of three jobs at a time. That she knew none of this, had never even bothered to know any of this, threw me into a blind fury and I reacted without compassion or a trace of rationality.

"Why don't *you* just go to fucking HELL!" I screamed at her.

"What did you say?" She was up off the couch.

"I said fuck OFF!"

That was it—we were at each other, fists and feet, kicking, snarling, pulling, and punching. In the small part of my brain that wasn't consumed with rage, I had two useless thoughts. One was disbelief that I was actually engaged in a physical battle with my sister in front of my infant son and the other was that the tight white leather skirt I had squashed my postpartum body into was seriously inadequate fight wear. The rest of me merely wanted to rip her face off.

Before any real damage could be done, Maya and my mother came running from their hiding places to break up. Maya started yelling at the two of us for acting like babies and my mother burst into loud tears, threatening to tell my father and exact punishment. Lavander retreated to her room, all the while spewing vitriol about what an unbelievable bitch I was and how she had been grievously wronged. *As usual*.

When we finally reassembled and headed out to the mall (because fight or no fight, shopping would not be denied), I was still trembling. My mother continued to sob in the car and Maya clicked her tongue in dismay. I could feel the anger pulsing off me in steamy waves and it nauseated me. But worse than that, I was deeply embarrassed—and not because of my own loss of control. I was embarrassed because Lavander's words had an underlying ring of truth. If I had taken even a second to think about the subtext of what she was saying before I leaped at her, I would have understood Lavander's frustration. I would have seen how my reappearance after such a long absence (with a baby in tow, no less) constituted a major intrusion for her. It was undeniable, when I was there the family revolved around me and my new baby. Lavander, in a precarious battle with her own entry in womanhood, was relegated, again, to middle-child status. And she was right about the fact that I depended heavily on my family, just not in the way she thought. I could understand Lavander's irritation with my prodigal daughter reappearance at the family table, but I still couldn't figure why she seemed so repulsed by my life and why she was so intent on shutting me out of hers. Of my three sisters, only Lavander seemed to find my new motherhood repellent.

When I told Maya I was pregnant, she'd just finished playing the *Messiah* at a Christmas concert in Eugene, Oregon. We'd driven down from Portland, en famille, to see her. It should have been her moment, but I'd taken the opportunity of the long drive to break the news to my parents and they insisted I tell her on the spot. Her face lit up much brighter than mine and she actually jumped up and down. "So exciting," she said. "So, so exciting."

Maya sat beside me for almost my entire pregnancy, experimenting with different menus for my confused palate, talking to my belly, and organizing a baby shower for me at Peppy's. We went to childbirth classes together and secretly made fun of the instructor. She managed to find a Mother's Day card for me before I delivered that was printed with "For the mother-to-be with love from her sister." Maya was my labor coach. She was an oasis of sanity when I thought I was losing my mind during the delivery. Her connectedness and part in this experience was never in question. I couldn't have imagined going through it without her.

Déja was as excited as Maya about becoming an aunt. She was also curious about the pregnancy. What did it feel like inside when the baby kicked, she wanted to know. How did I know it was a boy? How would I be able to tell when he was ready to be born? She put her hands on my belly and giggled when she felt the skin rolling. She promised me hours and days of free baby-sitting. She was the only one who was less patient than I for the baby to be born. On the day Blaze was born, Déja waited in the hospital for thirteen hours, refusing to sleep and refusing to go home until she could give me a kiss and tell me how much she loved me.

From the day I announced that I was having a baby, Lavander's reaction was markedly different. It was if she couldn't find a way to connect with the whole situation and it pushed her away. I was aware of this on a mostly subconscious level in the months leading up to Blaze's birth and couldn't have defined it if I'd been pressed. And, of course, I was very focused on my own experience and not looking to explore anyone else's. As Lavander pointed out, it was pretty much all about me at that point. There was one moment, however, when Lavander's feelings became very clear to me. I was in the end stages of labor and had passed into that phase of teeth-gnashing pain where even the strongest of women start cursing their lot. I'd kicked everyone but Maya out of the delivery room because I couldn't stand the thought of anyone, especially the people closest to me, seeing me in that state. That's when Lavander made her entrance. She'd come to the hospital late and walked into the room, a girlfriend in tow, just as the labor nurse bent both of my shaking knees back and reached into me up to her elbow. Neither the nurse nor Maya noticed the two of them standing by the door, but, over the IV, fetal monitor, and the giant rise of my belly, I saw an expression of naked horror on Lavander's face. The girlfriend backed out of the room as quickly as she'd come in, but

Lavander stood there for a few moments, undecided about what to say or do. Maya and the labor nurse turned toward her then, aware of her for the first time.

"I'm sorry, Deb," she said. "I'll come back later." She turned and left. I didn't see her again for several days.

It was that look of dismay I kept seeing over the twenty minutes it took us to drive to the mall after my fight with Lavander and I felt both my anger and embarrassment dissipate, giving way to a heavy disappointment. I didn't know how to reach my sister. I didn't even know if she wanted to be reached. Even if she did, I thought, I wouldn't be high on the list of people she'd want there.

A few days after our altercation, Lavander drove herself to my apartment to apologize. I made her a cup of tea and we sat in the only two chairs I owned. She started crying. Great big teardrops splashed down her cheeks and fell unchecked onto the table.

"I'm really sorry," she said.

"It's okay," I said. "I'm sorry too." I put my arm around her and she buried her head in my shoulder, sobbing hard for a minute and wetting my shirt with her tears.

"I didn't mean it," she said, pulling back at last. "You know I didn't mean what I said."

"You weren't altogether wrong," I told her. "I *do* spend a lot of time at home lately. I should try to get my life more together, figure out what I'm doing. It's just . . . the baby . . . Blaze . . ." I trailed off, unsure of what I wanted to say or how to present it. I didn't want to shut her out again by talking about my motherhood or my baby.

"I think you have a great life," she said. "I *love* your life."

"You do?"

"Yes, I do. I think you're *cool*, you know. I do. And you're a wonderful mother. You're doing this all on your own and everything. I know it's not easy. I totally look up to you. I always have."

"It's not . . ." I started again. "I mean, I'm not perfect. I'm just trying to work it out like everyone else." I stopped for a second and looked at her. She was waiting for some sort of explanation, some sort of insight. I wanted so badly to give it to her.

"There's just one thing," I told her. "I don't take money from anyone. I never have. I've always supported myself. It's really important to me that you know that. It's the one thing, you know, that I've always done. I've always taken care of myself that way."

"I know," she said quickly.

"No, you didn't," I said. "But you do now."

"I don't know why I said those things," Lavander said. "It was just a bad day, you know? Sometimes it's hard. . . ."

"What's hard?" I asked her, but she shook her head no. "It's just hard sometimes," she said. "That's all. It's not you."

There was a small silence between us. Lavander sighed and wiped her eyes. I noticed, for the first time, that there was a bandage around her hand.

"I'm really, really sorry," she repeated.

"What happened to your hand?"

"Nothing. I kind of hurt it the other night. I was at a party . . . I fell on a glass and cut it. It feels okay but I think there might still be some glass in it."

"Let me look at it."

Lavander unwrapped the gauze and I took her hand. Jagged red lines bisected her palm. I searched for glass fragments in the wound.

"How did you do this?" I asked. "You fell on a glass? How is that possible?"

"It's okay," she said, and gave me a look that begged me to stop questioning. Her hand was trembling a little and she smelled faintly of cigarettes. It occurred to me then that I wouldn't know how to begin to ask her what she was getting into. The problem wasn't that she couldn't relate to my experiences, I realized, but that I couldn't relate to hers.

I had a flash of the two of us when *I* was sixteen and she was seven. I was always the first one up in the mornings and so it was my job to make sure that Maya and Lavander got out of bed and ready for school. Every morning, Lavander sat spaced out in front of her cereal, staring into nowhere. "Eat, Lavander, eat, eat," I would tell her. Sometimes she would lift the spoon and sometimes not. Either way, she never broke that long-distance stare. I'd hustle her off to the bathroom after that to brush her long, fine hair and put it up in barrettes. Then I'd tell her to go finish her breakfast. When I left for school with Maya (our bus arrived before Lavander's), she'd be back at the table, still zombielike, but resigned and ready to go. I could still see that gaze of hers. Somewhere in there, she was watching.

At sixteen, I went to school and came home. I read one book after another. Much of my social life existed within my own head. I didn't have dates and I never went to a single party, let alone threw one of my own. I was ridiculously naive about most things. I thought the kids who listened to Led Zeppelin were dangerous and that the best way to start a conversation with a boy was to ask him about rack-and-pinion steering (as if I had a clue what that was). I didn't start many of these conversations anyway, though, because I was so terrified of rejection. I preferred to stay inside my own brain where I knew I'd be secure. I wouldn't have had the moxie to go storming through sixteen as Lavander was. I wouldn't have had the courage to confront someone like me about the choices I had made. I didn't even think I had it now. In a way, Lavander was the sixteen-year-old I'd always wanted to be. She drove. She went out. She took chances. She wasn't afraid to bust me or anyone else.

I thought she was brave. And I thought that when I was her age, I had chosen to play it safe.

"I don't see any glass," I told her and rewound the bandage.

"Yeah, it's okay," she said. "I'm okay. But I am sorry for those things I said."

"You weren't altogether wrong," I said again, and I gave her back her hand.

Lavander and I didn't get deeper into that discussion that evening and we didn't broach it again afterward. Nor did we ever come close to having another fistfight. Lavander remained the more combustible of the two of us, but I learned to steer clear of her when it looked as if she were headed for an explosion, especially if the blast was going to end up revealing my flaws. How much of this was self-protection and how much was lazy avoidance, I still don't know. I do know that I didn't venture further into an exploration of Lavander's inner life at that point. Nor did she come looking for me. I was in my midtwenties then and it was easy to believe that time was an unlimited quantity in which everything would naturally work itself out without too much effort on my part.

But here we are, almost fifteen years later, and I'm sitting in my living room, wondering, like an idiot, why Lavander doesn't come to me with her problems. I could laugh at my own blindness if it weren't so foolish.

Around eleven o'clock, Maya calls to tell me that she and Déja are going to spend the night at Lavander's place. Lavander has stopped speaking altogether and so Maya and Déja have cued up *The Matrix* on DVD and are planning to just sit next to her on the couch until she becomes more communicative. Or not. I don't ask her if anything's been worked out with Bad Boyfriend, or what, besides making microwave popcorn, anyone is doing to help Lavander get through this rough patch. I don't even ask whether or not it's the breakup that's the problem or if there's more to it than that. I'm assuming I'll get the information later in several different forms from several different people.

"I'll be home in the morning," Maya says.

"Whatever," I say. I know this is a childish response, but I don't care. I'm still irritated that she hung up on me and I'm holding on to my singed feelings. I put the phone in its cradle and get ready for bed. I turn off the lights, including the one Maya's left burning in her bedroom, and go into Blaze's bedroom to make sure he's sleeping soundly and give him a kiss on the cheek. I look to see if the front door is locked and that no appliances have been left running in the kitchen. But the very last thing I do before I get into my own bed is to take Lavander's bracelet off my wrist and put it back in the little bag it came in. I don't know when I'll be giving it to her now and I don't want to risk breaking it before I have the chance.

It's been three weeks since that night and I still haven't seen Lavander. I've spoken to her on the phone, but only after that conversation was negotiated by various other family members; meaning that my father, my mother, and Déja alternately told Lavander that I wanted to speak to her and then told me that she didn't actually *object* to talking to me. Maya's out of it now because the morning after she stayed over, Lavander told her that she was all right, everything was okay, and that Maya could just leave, please, and nothing needed to be discussed again. Maya was hurt, is still hurt, and doesn't want to leave herself open again.

"You try talking to her," Maya said. "Good luck."

So I called her.

"I'm not mad at you," was the first thing Lavander said to me after she returned the message I'd left on her cell phone. She was in her car and I could hear the usual sounds of traffic and rushing air that punctuated every one of her conversations.

"Are you sure?" I asked her.

"Yes, I'm sure," Lavander said. "You know, this has nothing to do with *you*. This is about me and what I'm going through."

"That's my point," I told her. "You can talk to me about what you're going through. I mean, why can't you? Unless you're angry at me for some reason."

"I can't be judged, Debra. I don't want to be judged and that's the problem. I mean, Maya . . . I feel so bad because Maya's always there for me. I mean, she always shows up, right? She's always there. But she *judges*. I always feel like I'm letting her down. I can't do that, I just can't do it."

"I can't speak for Maya," I said. "I'm not going to say anything about what she thinks or how she feels or whether or not she's judging you. But I am not Maya, okay? We are not the same person. We have different opinions. We have different things to offer."

"I know," she said, but she sounded unconvinced.

"Well, then, you should call me," I said, sounding terribly lame. "I'm here. Use me."

"I'm fine, I'm fine," she said. "I've got to go. I *will* call you. I don't feel like talking about it now, anyway. But I promise I'll call you."

That was two weeks ago and I haven't heard from her since. Of course, I haven't called *her*, either. But today, I'm having some romantic problems of my own. The man I've been seeing for almost a year has told me that he's still not sure whether or not he can really commit emotionally to our relationship. He'd like to, he says, he's just not sure if he *can*. The fact that we live in different cities has made committing on any other level unnecessary, so it's this one that's come up now. He says that it's clear that I want more of an allegiance than he does at this point. He can't predict how he will feel next month or next year, he says. He just can't tell. And that's where we've left it for the moment.

The rational part of me understands that this is an almost textbook relationship issue that will have to be discussed and worked through. But the rational part of me is very, very small at the moment and a raging tide of emotional response threatens to drown it altogether. Like Lavander, I'm not particularly stoic when it comes to the affairs of my own heart.

Generally, I'm able to do a pretty effective triage for most parts of my life. I can run work, motherhood, and family simultaneously even if there are aspects of each that are off track, stressful, or temporarily demanding most of my attention. It's rare that everything runs smoothly all the time, but I can manage. I can get things done. But when I'm in some kind of romantic twist, I come to a complete standstill, unable to switch gears or focus. I'm aware that this is a major failing. It's also the reason that this relationship is the first one I've had for several years.

I'm lying on my couch, staring out the window at the contrast of greens in my tiny backyard. This is my usual pose for these occasions. Ficus, bougainvillea, and palm. My eyes go over every leaf, overlaying the same circular thoughts on each one. Ficus: why can't he commit? Bougainvillea: why wouldn't he want to? Palm: will he ever? I visualize a full night of this paralysis and realize that I'm going to need some kind of help.

I call Lavander.

"What's up?" she wants to know.

"Do you want to go out tonight?" I ask her.

"Like, where?" she asks.

"I don't know, dinner?"

"You want to go out for dinner?"

"Or whatever," I say. "Just somewhere. Out. The two of us."

"Why?" she asks.

"Because I could use it," I tell her.

She doesn't hesitate. "Okay," she says. "I'll pick you up at six."

When she arrives, Lavander seems both hurried and somewhat perplexed by my sudden invitation. We get into her car and drive without a destination in mind. I'm not very hungry but she wants to eat something and, really, what else is there to do? I start feeling stupid for initiating this get-together in the first place. Now that we're together, I don't know what to say and am thinking that I'd have been better off silently sulking into the leaves. I glance around the inside of her car, which holds as much information about her daily life as a diary would. She's got water bottles, empty and full, scattered around the interior. She has two cell phones with battery chargers for each one. She has gift baskets and football tickets in the backseat for potential clients. She has assorted shirts and shoes, both casual and dressy, next to the baskets in case she has to go to dinner, a club, or an office. She has affirmations—positive mantras that she needs to repeat every day—tucked into the passenger-side visor. I eye these with interest.

"Don't laugh at my affirmations," she says.

"Why would I laugh?" I ask her. "Do they work?"

"I don't know. Maybe."

"Well, if they help, what's the difference?" I say.

We decide to go to a nearby restaurant I know well, having spent many years there as a waitress. It's right next to a restaurant where Lavander worked as a cocktail waitress, so it seems like a fitting choice.

"So, what is it?" she asks, once these plans have been made. "What's going on?"

I tell her, somewhat sketchily, the woes of my love life. I make it sound as if it's not really that big of a deal because now I'm wishing it wasn't. "I don't have the energy for these kinds of highs and lows anymore," I tell her. "It used to be easier."

"You know what you should do?" she says. "You should *date*. You should get out there and go on some dates. I mean, this guy, he's not so great. If he can't commit to you, what do you need him for? Kick him to the curb. Find somebody else."

I have to laugh. "I don't date," I tell her. "You know that. I've never been a dater. I can't do that sort of thing, I find it depressing. Besides, I don't *want* to find somebody else. I like this one. That's why I'm with him."

"But he's not treating you right!" she exclaims, indignation permeating her voice. "How can you go out with someone who treats you so badly?"

"He's not treating me badly," I tell her. "Who said he's treating me badly?"

"You know, you don't have to be physically abused to be treated badly," she counters. "By telling you that he doesn't know if he even wants to be with you, he's treating you disrespectfully. You don't need that."

"Well, I don't agree," I tell her. "That's not what this is about."

"I don't think you know what this is about," she says. "That's why you're not happy."

All right, she's got me there, but I don't know how to answer. This conversation isn't going at all the way I thought it would.

"I've asked you so many times to do one of those Internet dating things with me," Lavander continues. "I don't know why you won't do it. You should get yourself out there. With me."

"Because I don't want to," I tell her. "I don't want to date, Lavander. I don't want to go looking for men on the Internet or anywhere else. I want the one I've got to get it together."

"You're so stubborn," she says, and I have to laugh again.

"It's not such a big thing," I tell her. "Just another bump in the road. It'll work itself out."

"Hmm," Lavander says, unconvinced.

We get to the restaurant and decide to eat at the bar. The bartender on duty remembers me from the old days and we catch up on each other's lives.

"Have you ever met my sister?" I ask him.

"Oh yeah, I'm sure," he says, extending his hand to Lavander. "You're—wait, I know it—Violet, right?"

"Lavander," says Lavander. "But you're close."

"Didn't you work here too, for a while?" the bartender asks her.

"I don't know. Did I?" She looks over at me and I realize that she's serious. She can't remember. My sisters and I have worked in several of the same restaurants over the last ten years. Obviously, the chronology has gotten mixed up for Lavander.

"You worked next door," I say.

"Right, next door. But I'm thinking maybe I worked here for a minute, didn't I?"

"I think you applied, but it never happened. I think I'd remember."

The bartender tells us that his marriage is doing much better. There was a time when it looked pretty bad, he says, but now it's worked out and they're both very happy. They don't have any plans to have kids, he says, because, really, the two of them are enough. He takes our order, collects our menus, and turns away to help another customer.

"I really don't need to get married," I tell Lavander. "I don't need a husband. That's not what I want."

"You know," she says, "it's actually *okay* to want that. You don't have to pretend that you don't want it because you think you're not supposed to. It's okay to want a wedding and a house and a ring. That's *normal*. I don't know why you feel that you have to say you don't want it. You don't give anything up by wanting all that, you know. You're still an individual. You've still accomplished things on your own, supported yourself, have your own personality. You don't have to give that up by wanting a husband. It doesn't make you weak."

"I agree," I tell her, but I know we're no longer talking about me. "I don't feel like I'm being dishonest with myself when I say that I don't want to get married. I didn't say I wanted to be alone for the rest of my life, because I don't. I just don't need to have the trappings, it's just not necessary anymore. That doesn't mean it's the same for you. It's okay for *you* to want all that. Why not?"

"I love him," she says, and quickly adds, "I know you don't like him so I don't expect you to understand."

"It doesn't matter whether or not I like him," I tell her. "I'm not the one involved with him. Only you know what goes on between the two of you. Only you know what the nature of your relationship is and what you're getting out of it. The only people who can judge a relationship are the two people inside of it. I can't tell you anything about him. All I can say is that you have to be happy—at least, most of the time. If it makes you unhappy, what are you doing it for? The security? Because you think you won't find anyone else?"

"It's complicated," she says.

"It's always complicated. That's the nature of relationships." I don't know who I'm talking about anymore, myself or her. I feel as if I'm holding a reflection of myself in a mirror, watching the image repeat endlessly into infinity. There's a name for that phenomenon. I wish I knew what it was.

"I'm not going to freak out again," Lavander says. "I'm working it out. So nobody has to worry."

"You don't have to work it out alone."

"I know that," she sighs.

"It's not easy being a woman," I tell her. It sounds flip, as if I'm summarizing a self-help article in some women's magazine, but that's not how I mean it. I believe that it's true. And I believe that, in the nine years that separate me from my sister, the choices we've had to make as women have only gotten more difficult. I don't tell her any of this, though, and it seems I don't have to. She looks at me with tacit agreement and I can tell that, for a moment, we've transcended personality and history and reached some sort of common border. Our most vulnerable sides are touching.

The bartender delivers our dinners, along with some more tales of life behind the bar. We listen to him and we eat. Our conversation shifts. We talk about the merits of fresh mozzarella and the best way to prepare a pasta sauce. Her cell phone rings and, although she doesn't answer it this time, she'll have to the next. Our time together is reaching an end. She asks if I want to go somewhere else and I tell her that I don't, that I'm tired and am looking forward to an early night. We split the bill and head out.

"I've got something for you," I tell her as we get back into the car. "I almost forgot." I pull her turquoise bracelet out of my purse and fasten it on her wrist.

"I love it," she says. "And turquoise is very in right now."

"Well," I answer, "one has to be in, doesn't one? It really suits you. It's a great color for you, brings out your eyes."

We are mostly silent on the drive home, but when she turns the corner onto my street, Lavander says, "This was nice. We should do this more often. Why don't we?"

"There's no reason. We should."

"You know, all you have to do is ask," she says. "That's all you have to do. Just ask me and I'm there."

"And I'm always here for you," I tell her. "Please know that."

She gives me a hug and a kiss and we say good-bye. I watch her back out of my driveway and disappear around the corner. In my mind's eye, I can see her headed for the highway. Her phone is ringing and she's picking it up to answer the call.

Maya and Debra.

6

Misters and Sisters

august

It's August again and that means that Maya's orchestra is putting on its annual summer pops concert in the park at the Mission San Luis Rey. Despite the fact that I always go, we have the same conversation every year.

She says, "You should come. It's a nice program and you can bring a picnic."

And I ask, "What are you playing?"

This year, the program includes a tribute to Frank Sinatra and themes from *Star Wars*. Blaze will like the concert, he always does, although in years past, he's spent more time splashing water out of the fountain than sitting on the grass enjoying the music. Still, he's always eager to go, always asks Maya complex questions about the music and the composers, always remembers every tune, and always likes best what Maya and I both assume he will like the least. Maya has several concerts during the year, and Blaze actually attends more of them than I do, as he sometimes goes with Déja or with our parents. Maya rarely urges anyone in our family to attend her orchestra events unless she thinks the music will be particularly appealing, but the pops concert is always an exception.

My uninspired idea of a picnic consists of a few nectarines, some energy bars, and a couple of organic colas. I throw these items into a plastic bag, elicit promises from Blaze that he will remain quiet during the actual performance, and we're ready to go. As we have in years prior, we're going to make the half-hour drive to the mission with Gwen, Maya's stand partner.

Maya and Gwen have been friends and stand partners for almost a decade. They play in the first violin section, in the third and fourth chairs. On the face of it, they seem like unlikely pals. Gwen, a midwestern transplant, grew up during the Depression, married her childhood sweetheart, raised three boys, and never worked outside the home. Gwen steadfastly refuses to divulge her real age, but it doesn't matter, because she looks and acts more youthful than most fifty-year-olds I know and refers to women much younger than she as "old ladies." Still, she keeps referring to forty (the age I'm currently bemoaning) as "child-hood." Age difference notwithstanding, her background and Maya's are as dissimilar as any two could be. But the surfaces of age and background are notoriously deceptive. Gwen and Maya both possess the wacky eccentricity common to all the musicians I've ever met (especially those with classical training). They share the same offbeat sense of humor and both reject any kind of sentimental attachment to the past. And both Gwen and Maya are completely devoid of bias when it comes to class, age, or religion. Perhaps it is their shared love of music that allows them to transcend those barriers or perhaps they *are* musicians because this transcendence is innate. In either case, the bond is there, strengthened by real affection and mutual respect.

On their weekly rides to rehearsal in Gwen's Cadillac (which Maya drives, because Gwen, who didn't start driving until she was nearly forty, doesn't drive at night) Maya shares details about her life or feelings with Gwen that she doesn't think of telling me. And I know this because when Gwen calls during the week to chat with Maya, she often gets me on the phone instead and we have our own conversations.

"So, Maya's going to Las Vegas for the weekend?" Gwen will ask me.

"First I've heard of it," I'll answer.

Or Gwen will say, "Has Maya told you about that good-looking cellist we've had sitting in with us? I think the two of them could really hit it off."

"Well, no," I'll respond. "She hasn't."

But Gwen and I don't confer about Maya very often when we talk because Gwen's always very up on what's going on in *my* life as well and that provides plenty of fodder for discussion. Gwen knows all about my books, knows all about Blaze, knows all about my siblings, and knows all about my love life, which, until recently, she mourned.

"I don't know what's the matter with you girls," she said. "You're so lovely and talented. I just don't know why you aren't with anybody."

When I did start seeing someone seriously, she was one of the first to know.

"So Maya tells me you're seeing a real nice fella," she said. "I just think that's great. And, you know, Maya's so excited for you, says he's just a great guy."

"She does?"

"Oh yes, she's so happy for you, you know. Now if we could just find someone for her. . . ."

We're taking Gwen's Caddy again today, and along for the ride and the concert is Gwen's sister, Judy, whom I've met once before on a similar outing. Gwen and Judy live within ten minutes of each other. They see each other often and speak to each other every day. When they get into the car, I can feel the ease between them. The subtext of their relationship, at least what I pick up on an instinctual level, feels very familiar to me.

Maya drives and Gwen sits in the front. I sit between Judy and Blaze in the back. I give Judy a long look and decide she must be Gwen's younger sister. Like Gwen, she has a very youthful appearance. She's small boned, but doesn't appear frail in any way. She's dressed impeccably and I'm envious of her perfect makeup, which is understated but enhances all of her best features. After studying her for a while, the word *elegant* comes to mind and stays there.

Maya has told me that Judy is a retired librarian and that her daughter makes sculptures out of butter. I can't find a jumping-off point conversationally with either one of these topics. I also know that, unlike Gwen, she's been married more than once, which doesn't give me much to work with, either, so, for the time being, I remain silent. Judy is much quieter than Gwen, who is laughing with Maya over another viola joke (the violists being the constant butt of gibes by violinists).

"How can you tell when the violists are out of tune?" Maya says and doesn't wait for a response. "When their bows are moving. Wait, here's another one: why do violists put their violas on the dashboards of their cars?"

"Oh, I haven't heard this one," Gwen says.

"So that they can use the handicapped parking," Maya says and Gwen howls with laughter.

"Musician humor," I say to Judy, and she smiles. It occurs to me that she's probably been hearing these kinds of jokes for as long as I've been on this earth. "Why do you always pick on the violas?" I ask Maya.

"Oh, jeez, because it's so easy," Gwen answers, which makes Maya laugh but doesn't really answer my question.

"I'm not positive," I tell Judy, "but I'm starting to think that musicians are even weirder than writers. And that's saying something."

"Really?" Judy asks. "Why do you think writers are weird?"

"They spend too much time inside their own heads," I say. "They tend not to have the best social skills. But at least they don't pick on violists."

"You don't play an instrument?" Judy asks.

"No, Maya's the musician in the family. My parents always encouraged me to write. I don't remember being offered music lessons at any point." I raise my voice slightly at the end of this pronouncement so that Maya will hear.

"You could have played an instrument if you'd wanted to," Maya picks up. "You never asked."

"I would have asked if I thought it was an option," I say.

"You know, you're always complaining," Maya says, without any rancor. "Such a hard time you've had. So much neglect."

"Oh, you girls," Gwen says.

"Anyway, Debra sings," Maya says. "We sing together sometimes."

"Maya does great harmony," I add.

"Oh?" Gwen says. "Judy sings, too. She's got a lovely voice. Let's sing something together."

"Oh yes, yes," Maya says, excited, as always, for the opportunity to belt one out. This is a woman, after all, who bought her own karaoke machine.

"No show tunes!" I implore.

We debate the music choice for a while and I'm pleasantly

surprised by how willing Judy is to burst into song. I would have thought she'd be more reserved. We settle on "Amazing Grace" because it has unlimited possibilities for harmony and everybody loves it. We're all a bit tentative at first as we find our places in the music, but we are soon comfortable and the sound of our four voices together is actually pretty good. Blaze has a huge smile on his face. He just loves this kind of thing, especially when Maya and I sing together. "Amazing Grace" carries us almost the entire way to the mission. We only stop when we run out of verses.

Gwen's having problems with her knees these days, so we pull up as close to the stage as we can get and climb out of the car. Judy carries Gwen's violin for her as well as a folding chair she's brought for the occasion. I sense that this isn't the usual way with the two of them, that Judy doesn't normally carry anything for her sister and that Gwen dislikes that fact that Judy has to in the first place. I realize that my sister is loaded down as well with her violin, a box for tickets, and a bag full of music, so I offer to take something for her. Like Judy, this is not usually my way.

Maya and Gwen head over the stage and Judy, Blaze, and I spread a blanket on the grass and settle in. Because we are here with performers, we're early enough to take the best spot, right in front of the orchestra where we can see everything through the yellow glare of the slowly setting sun. Judy dons her sunglasses (as tasteful and current as the rest of her outfit, I notice) and studies the program.

"Good music," she says, and smiles at me. "Don't you love these concerts?"

I smile back at her in response.

When the music starts and we watch our sisters lift their bows and start playing, I can feel the shared thrill run silently between us. For a moment, I turn my attention from Maya to Judy and study the small, satisfied smile illuminating her face. I have a fleeting moment where I can clearly see myself in her spot, watching my sister years from now and in all the years in between. I'm thinking that Judy and Gwen are the sisters I assume—no, I *hope*—that Maya and I will be decades from now.

This vision is very different from the one I had about ten years ago, on the heels of a nasty breakup with a man I was planning to be with forever but who walked away after two years. Maya, Blaze, and I moved out of the house we'd been sharing with that man and into a smaller condo. I was sure I'd reached the end of my romantic world then, as it seemed to be in too many pieces to ever put back together again. Maya and I were both working in the same Italian restaurant, sharing a couple of shifts, but mostly passing each other between lunch, dinner, and the occasional split shift.

"*Sorelle* Ginsberg," our Italian manager would say when the two of us showed up at work together in our matching black-and-whites. It was easy for me to see the two of us like that forever then, going to work and coming home, the home we shared, until we were physically unable. I saw us slowly filling our house with knickknacks as one or both of us developed a need to collect something—frogs, maybe, or elephants, or demitasse cups and saucers. We'd get progressively more eccentric, start wearing black all the time instead of most of the time, read mysteries, and complain about the cold. In my mind, I saw us becoming two old Italian spinster aunties, sitting alone in our respective rooms until we died. And I say Italian, specifically, because in all the old Italian films I managed to find on video, there were always a couple of these women (hovering, dressed in black) who never married and who, whether or not they had each other (and some spectacular failed loves in their pasts), had missed an essential element of existence by living out the best parts of their lives without a man. Usually, in the films and in my own scenario, when one sister died, the other couldn't live without her and passed on shortly after. There wasn't much emotion attached to this mental picture I'd painted for myself. It was merely something I could see spinning out of the place we were in.

I was thirty years old and Maya was still in her twenties when I had this vision of our future. We'd only been living together for five years. I was beginning to doubt that I could have a successful domestic relationship outside of or in addition to the one I had with Maya. And she showed no signs of entering one herself that would disturb our arrangement in the least. And did we talk about this? Did I share my Italian-spinster-aunt vision with her? Had we ever talked about what would happen when or if one of us met the man of her dreams and wanted to move out, move away, move on?

No, no, and never.

Long before, when Maya and I were Mariannas, it was I who created the husbands Harry. My need to flesh out my make-believe mate with details as to his looks, preferences, and dragon-slaying abilities could possibly be explained by the fact that I was the older of the two of us. But, even when she grew older, Maya's Harry remained almost an afterthought, an add-on who existed mostly to react to my Harry. While I was creating marital storms and passions as part of our game, Maya's imaginary domestic life was always "fine." Beyond that, she had little to say and hated to be pressed. This never changed. There has always been an unwillingness on Maya's part to discuss affairs of the heart—hers or mine. Perhaps this was because, even when we were little girls and far away from actual romances, I was already creating relationship "issues" to go with the invented ones (it was rarely smooth sailing with my Harry) and she just didn't want to deal with it.

Because of this, the Harry component of the Marianna game

slowly faded out of prominence. Gradually, too, I stopped trying to press Maya into discussions about romance, boyfriends, or the desire for either. In fact, desire as a general concept was removed from our conversations. There was something she seemed to find distasteful about it all—at least in the way I presented it. So I didn't confide in her when, at twelve, I watched Donna and Frank (both fourteen) make out on the bus every day on the way home from school and wished that I was old enough to be in Donna's place. I didn't tell her about the boys I thought were cute (we always had such a divergence of opinions in this area anyway that to mention I thought someone was good-looking was to invite ridicule for my poor taste) or the boys I wished would ask me out.

When I had my first real boyfriend in the summer of 1978 when I was sixteen, I didn't talk to Maya about what we did, how I felt, or what he said to me. She indicated quite clearly that she didn't want to know. Nor did she have any desire to start up the romance I encouraged with my boyfriend's younger brother who was the same age as she. I thought that this would be a neat little package, the brothers and the sisters together, but Maya, thirteen years old at the time, was repulsed by the very idea. She wasn't crazy about my boyfriend to begin with and thought his little brother was an immature tool.

Maya's aversion to my romantic choices was an ongoing theme (I think it's possible that she didn't even like the Harry I'd created), although she always stopped short of outright con-demnation. She was more subtle about her dislike, exuding a whiff of disappointment, like an imperceptible head shake in the negative. It was her opinion, always, that I could do better and that I was selling myself short. In this respect, she adopted the role of older, wiser sister, a sort of Jiminy Cricket ever whisper-ing in my ear that I was making a mistake. There were two ways to deal with this as I saw it. I could try to corrupt her and draw her into my adventures as an accomplice (such as the attempt to get her to pair up with the boyfriend's younger brother), or I could completely separate that part of my life from my relationship with her. It didn't take too long to decide on the latter option.

Maya and I had always been dedicated and extremely loyal to each other. Neither one of us had ever ratted the other out, to our parents or anyone else. Never once had either of us attempted to blame the other for something she didn't do in order to escape punishment. In fact, both of us would feign ignorance of the other's wrongdoings if questioned. And, although Maya was rarely in the wrong, she would go to the mat to defend me. For many years when we were growing up, Maya had the reputation in our family as being the "sweet" one, whereas I was the "sullen" one. Rather than reveling in her elevated status as the more pliable daughter, Maya took great pains to convince our parents that I deserved that status as well. She didn't idolize me, but she would have followed me, literally and metaphorically, wherever I asked her to go. Rewarding that kind of devotion by taking advantage of it was something I was unable to do. I couldn't ask, pressure, or demand that she go along with something she felt was wrong or even unpleasant, and therefore I couldn't draw her in as a co-conspirator in my amorous escapades, real or imagined. What's more, I even felt the need to protect her from them, and so I stopped sharing my thoughts on the subject altogether.

There was a certain dissonance created in our relationship by this gap, but I wasn't fully aware of it until one August night in 1980, a few weeks before I was scheduled to start college. I had one girlfriend, Charlotte, in my last year of high school. Charlotte was very rich, very smart, very refined, very quiet, and had a wild streak a mile wide running through her personality. Just my type. Charlotte was dating a university frat boy (a sophomore, no less) and was on the pill. She said things like, "He's not really an intellectual, but the sex is very good," which I thought were just astonishingly sophisticated. Charlotte and I were slated to go to different colleges in the fall and she wanted to take advantage of our last few weeks together by inviting me to as many of her boyfriend's frat parties as possible. She was set on fixing me up with someone, anyone, so that we'd have more common experiences to share. I was heartily sick of being Miss Goody Pure Shoes and I can't say I was unwilling to go along with her plan.

Two parties were a bit of a wash. At the first party, Charlotte introduced me to several drunken Ricks (every male at these parties seemed to be named Rick) who were willing to chat for about ten minutes ("How old are you?" "What school are you going to?" "What's your major—uh—going to be?" "What's your name again?") before suggesting a trip to whatever bedroom was available. Because I couldn't stand the taste or smell of beer, I was not drunk and was, therefore, unable to convince myself (although I really tried) that Rick or Rick was interested in any aspect of my being other than what immediately met his eye. Charlotte suggested I take a trip to the keg, but I couldn't face the thought of meeting more Ricks in the kitchen where the Budweiser was flowing like ambrosia. Charlotte took me home early after that one, a little disappointed, I sensed, that I hadn't found a Rick to drive me.

At the second party (more beer, more Ricks, but this time there was dancing in the living room), Charlotte had an argument with her boyfriend and left, taking me with her, before we could really get settled in.

Charlotte took me to the third party to make up for the second where I hadn't "had a chance" to meet anyone. This last party was markedly different from the first two. For one thing, there was a bar with actual liquor available for anyone who wanted it. Charlotte, ever the aristocrat, got herself a gin and tonic and set me up with a vodka and orange juice, the first of four I would end up drinking that night. The music was different here, too. The previous two parties had blasted the Rolling Stones, the Police, and the Pretenders. This one had the decidedly more laid-back Eagles humming along at a low volume. People seemed to be talking to each other as opposed to shouting, and were actually sitting down on chairs and couches instead of endlessly milling around a keg. Charlotte had made up with her boyfriend by then and was eager to spend some quality time with him. She left me in the living room with my drink and a guy whose name was Joe, not Rick, and melted into another part of the house.

Joe wanted to talk to me. He asked me the obligatory questions about where I was going to go to school and what I wanted to study, but he didn't stop there. He started to talk about what *he* was studying (English lit) and he asked me what books I liked to read. He asked me what music I liked to listen to. He was drinking Jack Daniels, straight up, and smoking Camel cigarettes. After the first drink, I thought he was interesting. After the second, I thought he was *deep*. After the third, I was in love. After the fourth, I was so drunk I had to lean on his arm to keep from falling as he walked me up the stairs to an available bedroom. I saw Charlotte sitting with her boyfriend on the stairs as I climbed them. They were a amalgam of arms, legs, and lips. Charlotte's boyfriend had one hand on one of her breasts and the other sliding up her thigh. I couldn't see where her hands were. As I passed her, she broke her lip lock and looked up at me. That look was the clearest thing I'd seen all night. It was surprised, pleased, and vindicated. *Good luck*, it said. *You're on your own from here.*

It was Joe who took me home that night, not Charlotte.

"Maybe you should give me your phone number or something," he said as he dropped me off.

"Not necessary," I told him. "It's okay."

It was well after midnight, hours after I'd promised to be home, and I was terrified that my parents would still be awake when I crept into the house. I was deliriously relieved to find that all the lights were off and that nobody called my name when I locked the front door behind me. But when I slunk into my bedroom, the glare of Maya's reading lamp sliced into my eyes like a laser. She was wide awake, reading a romance novel, and eager to chat. She'd been waiting up for me.

"How was the party?" she said, bright as can be.

"It was okay," I said very slowly.

"Must have been better than okay, you're home really late."

"Uh-huh." I was a deer stuck in the headlights of her questions.

"Are you *drunk?*" she asked.

"No," I said. "Not drunk. Tired. I just have to go to the bathroom now. I'll be right back."

I sat on the bathroom floor, knees up, head down, for what seemed a spinning eternity. I fought, with every screaming-in-pain fiber of my body, to keep from retching into the toilet. It was essential that I not throw up, I told myself. Everybody would hear and the jig, all of it, would be up. To keep my mind off the nausea, I focused on the pain I was feeling in parts of my body I didn't even know existed. *Have to go back to my room,* I thought. *Have to pretend that everything's fine. Maya will know if I don't. Maya will know.* I tried to get up and get undressed, but the sight of my ruined underwear sent me back to the floor. Only then did I start to cry.

I never knew the real meaning of what it was to "collect" one-self until that night. Sitting in that bathroom, I had to make an effort to collect the sections I'd been split into and put them back into something that resembled the person I was before I'd gone to that party. I washed my face and brushed my teeth. I drank water from the faucet. I went back into my bedroom. Maya had turned the light off and had curled into a lump on her bed. I could tell she was angry, even in the dark, even in my altered state. I could tell because she was Maya and there were things I knew about her without having to see and without being told. The same was true, had always been true, for her. And that, I assumed, was why she was angry.

I slid into my own bed as carefully as possible. I wanted to tell her. I wanted to be able to say I *did a stupid thing. I made a mistake.* I wanted to describe that look on Charlotte's face when I passed her on the stairs. I wanted her to help me figure it out. But none of that came out.

I said, "Good night, Maya."

And she said, "Okay, good night."

I fell asleep that night as I had for as long as I could remember, in a bedroom with my sister, the person who was at once closer to and further away from me than anyone else would ever be.

My actions that night were only the beginning of a long series of similar mistakes I would make. For the next seven years, though, I didn't have Maya around to hide them from. I had little direct contact with Maya over most of those years, even though I continued to live close to home. The distance between us didn't strike me as peculiar. Like so much of our relationship, it seemed to be a thing that had been arrived at by mutual, unspoken understanding.

In my freshman year at college, I invited Maya to come visit me a couple of times, but she never found it in the least bit appealing. Maya didn't view these excursions as a chance to get away from home and live it up. In fact, the opposite was true. She viewed the whole college scene (at least, *my* college scene) with the vague distaste I'd come to know so well. Far from initi-

ating my sister or being in danger of leading her astray, I felt I
had to set a good example for her and was forever letting her
down in that respect. She didn't want to party, found my friends
pretentious, and my boyfriends unworthy even of comment,
although she never shared this with anyone else.

Just as she always had, Maya came to my defense when my
parents had a breakdown over my moving in with my boyfriend
at nineteen. They hated the whole situation, from top to bottom.
Taken alone, they didn't mind the boyfriend, who was well-
mannered and always pleasant around them. But the fact that I
was shacking up with him was too much for them and he went
on the hate list shortly thereafter. The fact that I was "living like
a lowlife" was a constant topic of conversation in the family
home for at least a year. I got to escape most of this, of course,
living as I was in the house of sin, but Maya got an earful on a
regular basis. She consistently refused to offer an opinion or a
judgment on my behavior to my parents, even though she disagreed with what I was doing as well and didn't think much of
the boyfriend, besides. I know this because, years later, when it
had all blown over and there were other daughters to worry
about, my mother told me how frustrating it was to get any kind
of commiseration from Maya, no matter how hard she was
pressed.

I think that Maya assumed I was more or less finished with my
run of bad relationships by the time we moved in together when
I was twenty-five. I'd pretty much hit the jackpot with the last
one, John, who had left me alone to parent the child he didn't
want me to have. Maya and I never discussed that relationship in
depth, either, although she'd sat next to me for the nine months
of my pregnancy, gone to childbirth classes with me, and stood
by my side when I gave birth. "What do you need him for if he
doesn't want to be there?" she said of John, but never offered

much more of an opinion as to what she thought of him or my inability to sustain our relationship. Instead, we attempted to write a romance novel together.

I was a writer in search of material at that point and Maya was a veteran romance reader. This was our way of talking about how we felt about love and men. Our effort turned out to be ineffective but quite enlightening. To begin with, we couldn't even agree with what our heroine would look like.

"You can't have a romance heroine with double D breasts," Maya told me. "That can't be a defining physical characteristic."

"Why not?" I questioned. "Maybe her big breasts have been a source of discomfort to her all her life. She got teased in high school. Everyone thought she was easy. Now she doesn't know whether or not men are attracted to her or her breasts. It's a problem."

"No, no, no," Maya said. "You've got it all wrong. She doesn't have any kind of past like that—not in this kind of book. And, anyway, it's not pornography, you can't talk about breasts."

"Breasts are pornographic? What about when they have sex? Can you write about them then? Wait a minute, they *are* going to have sex, aren't they?"

"It depends on what kind of romance you're writing. In some of the romances, the couple doesn't actually get physical," she said.

"*What?* What is the point, then?"

"Do you think sex is the necessary end point of everything?" she asked with severe disdain.

"Well, no, but I do think it's a necessary end point of a romance novel. Otherwise, how is her bodice going to get ripped?"

"A bodice ripper is a very specific kind of novel—and that's not what we're doing. Anyway, the point is *romance*, okay? They meet, they come together, they're forced apart, they suffer, they come back together, they live happily ever after. Get it?"

"I get it. But that doesn't mean they don't have sex."

"You know, perhaps if you didn't think the only conclusion was a sexual encounter, you'd . . ."

"I'd what?" I said.

"Nothing, never mind. This is a book, okay? It's a fantasy."

"You're telling me," I said. "Okay, fine." On the paper where we'd decided to put down the physical attributes of our characters, I wrote,

> *Heroine:*
> *Tiny little breasts (can't even be seen)*
> *Hair like a raven's wing*
> *Doesn't wear a bodice*

"You know, if you're not going to take this seriously, we should just stop," Maya said as she watched me write.

"Okay, okay," I said. "But it has to have some grounding in reality, otherwise I can't write anything."

"There's a formula," Maya said. "You know what to expect. It's just the details that are different and that's what makes it interesting. Besides, people like it when things work out in books. They don't want to read about reality. That's why they like to read romance novels."

"Maybe that's why *you* like to read them," I said. She folded her arms across her chest, an extremely annoyed expression taking over her face.

"Do you want to do this or not?" she said.

"Yes, I want to," I said. "Maybe you should just tell me what to write. That would be easier. Then I can just fill in the blanks, so to speak."

"I can't tell you that!" She flushed. "You're the writer. I can only tell you whether or not it's going to work."

"All right, let's talk about the hero, then," I said. "What's his name? Lance?"

"Again, if you're going to be facetious about the whole thing, it's not going to work. People will know if you're making fun of something while you're writing it."

"*Okay*. What does he look like?"

"Well, of course he's got to be good-looking. They all are."

"Can you give me more?"

"You can do that part."

"Right, high cheekbones. Maybe a Native American look. Maybe Italian. No, not Italian, forget that. Strapping and muscle bound. He can close his big, manly hand around her waist. And what's he like?"

"He can be brooding," she said. "Sometimes they're moody. You know, these guys, they just don't get it. That's usually why they don't get the girl right away."

"Hmm," I said. "Okay." On our character page, I wrote,

Hero:
Dark skin (Native American heritage?)
High cheekbones
Self-serving asshole

Maya took a look at the sheet and turned to me with a look of utter finality on her face.

"Forget it," she said. "We're done. We can't do this. It's obviously a bad idea."

"I'm sorry, I'm sorry. Come on, let's get back to it. I'll try not to be so—um—realistic. Come on, I'm sorry, really."

"No," she said. "You're too cynical to write a romance. You

have to like the concept, at least a little bit. You have to believe that things really could work out in the end."

She made a good point, but I felt compelled to argue it. I wasn't cynical, I claimed, merely practical. And I did believe that things could work out in the end. It was just that they often didn't. Maya shook her head in disagreement. If you don't think it will work out, then it won't, she said. One's orientation was everything. That, and the choices one made.

"What's better?" I asked her. "To take a chance and run the risk of making the wrong choice or play it safe and hope the right one just falls into your lap?"

"I guess it depends on how much you think you can take," she said.

Therein lay the specific difference between the two of us. I was the romantic risk taker. She was so unwilling to make the wrong choice that she didn't choose at all. And it seemed that as long as we didn't talk about this, everything would be fine. And everything was fine, more or less, until I met a man who I thought fit the very happy ending Maya claimed I couldn't conceive of.

Maya, Blaze, and I had moved to California from Oregon three years earlier and were living in a two-bedroom apartment that was walking distance from the beach. We were working as waitresses, alternating shifts so that one of us was always home with Blaze. We'd set up a joint checking account and pooled all our cash. We split all of the household bills and made all of our big purchases together, including furniture, televisions, and a car. There was never a moment of stress in this arrangement, never a question of who would get what if we were to split the house. Splitting the house was not a consideration. Nor did we ever have a single argument about money. We were more stable and more egalitarian about the sharing of funds and household duties than most married couples—so much so that Déja (who was fairly young when Maya and I first moved in together) told our mother that "if you and Daddy ever get a divorcement, I'm going to live with Debra and Maya."

Aside from our family, though, most of the people we met at work or socially (often the same thing in the restaurant business) assumed that our relationship couldn't be as well balanced as it seemed and that one of us had to be taking advantage of the other. Usually, I was the person assumed to be taking advantage because I was older, I had Blaze, and Maya often shared in his care. How could that be an equal arrangement, most people questioned? Why would a single woman in her midtwenties want to spend any time at home taking care of her nephew? Why would she give any of her money to her sister? Why would she feel she had any obligation at all to that sister?

Despite what I knew to be true—that beyond the fact that we were sisters, Maya and I actually *liked* each other, enjoyed spending time together, and had a very similar worldview—I often questioned whether or not Maya was the loser in our relationship and whether I was taking advantage of her. I could never bring myself to ask her directly, though, for fear she'd agree that I was. Instead, I tried to make sure that everything was as fair as possible. For a few years after we moved in together, I made more money than Maya and so I put more into the joint kitty. I kept Blaze's expenses separate and paid for those myself. I was the one with credit at that point, so it was always my name that those expenditures went under. And I rarely went out unless it was to work. Maya didn't stay home with Blaze while I was out gallivanting.

Still, I wondered if, somewhere, there was resentment building in Maya that she wasn't even aware of herself. Julian, the man she started dating around this time, didn't do anything to disabuse me of this notion. Julian, who was closer in age to our father than he was to Maya, wasn't particularly interested in becoming one of the family. His view was that Maya wasn't nearly autonomous enough and he found her attachment to her family puzzling. He preferred his own space to anyone else's and so didn't hang out at our house (he wasn't really the "hanging" type anyway). He didn't come to family dinners. His relationship with Maya didn't unfold under the scrutiny of the family eye. As was her usual way, Maya kept it close to the vest, steadfastly refusing to talk about it until the refusal itself became her primary source of communication where her love life was concerned. And, as was my usual way, I didn't press her for details and was left to come to my own conclusions.

I didn't have much inclination to discuss Maya's relationship, however, because around this time, I met Norman and all things domestic underwent a seismic shift. Actually, to say I met him is a bit misleading. I already knew Norman and even had a brief but intense romance with him ten years earlier when I was a college freshman. I took that romance very seriously, but Norman was in love with someone else, quickly dumped me, and disappeared. I was crushed and dealt with the heartbreak by drinking one too many homemade piña coladas and threatening to throw myself off my second-floor dorm-room balcony. It took my roommate telling me repeatedly, "You know, you'll probably just break an ankle or something," and at least three rotations of the Rolling Stones's "Can't You Hear Me Knockin'" on her turntable to finally get me to come back inside where more piña coladas were waiting. It wasn't one of my prettiest moments. It was, however, one I never forgot and so I never forgot Norman either. When he showed up one day (directed to me by a mutual friend), it seemed like kismet.

This was precisely where Maya was wrong about me. I wasn't cynical at all. I loved the idea that a man from my past had fallen into my present and that he was saying things like,

"Where have you been all this time?" Ten years later, the timing was finally right and he was in love with me. What's more, he considered the fact that I had a child, whom he seemed truly fond of, an asset. And he liked my family—every last one of them. It was heady and romantic in the extreme and I was completely caught up in the thrill of it all.

And what did Maya think of this? Although she tried mightily to hide it, she didn't particularly like or trust Norman. There was something about him that struck her as emotionally unreliable, but she swallowed her uneasiness. She was even more a sucker for a happy ending than I was and my delirious happiness was as beguiling to her as it was to me.

Norman was living in New York. We'd reconnected because he'd come to California on business. For the next year, we had a bicoastal courtship. Every couple of months, one of us would fly out to see the other. We had teary scenes at airports, walks through summer rainstorms, and afternoons at the beach—all the elements of a good romance novel, or perhaps a romantic film. By the end of that year, because we simply could not bear to be apart any longer, Norman decided to move to California. We pledged total commitment to each other. We wanted to spend the rest of our lives together. It was love, love, love.

I was convinced that this was forever.

Maya and I went looking for a house to rent for the four of us and when Norman arrived, we had already moved in. We never considered splitting up our household and moving anywhere separately. Forever, at least as I saw it, included Maya.

The philosophical, charitable term for what happened over the next twelve months would be *life lesson* or, perhaps, *learning experience*. I prefer the word *disaster*, which seems much more in keeping with what it actually felt like. The romantic in me died hard that year as all the elements of the dreamy happy ending I had envisioned collapsed and came apart like the house of cards that it was. I can't say that everything went wrong right away. More accurately, nothing was ever right.

Almost immediately, Norman started complaining about the house, the neighborhood, and the state of California in general. It was too suburban, too uptight, too fake, too *neat*. "This isn't who I am," he said over and over again. "I'm not the kind of guy who mows the lawn." This was a one-eighty from his position of the year before which was that he couldn't wait to leave the urban decay of New York City. Then the problem was everything was too spread out. There were no subways, nowhere to walk. Every excursion required a car. And I didn't drive, which had been kind of cute the year before, but was now a problem for him. He didn't like the fact that I waited on tables, thought it was low class, but it was the only steady income either of us was producing because, relegated as he was to the backwoods of southern California, there was no work to be had for him. And this wasn't all. The problems continued to pile up like bags of garbage that nobody wanted to take out. My vegetarianism became a problem, despite the fact that I'd made clear that it was the one, the *only*, issue that I would never compromise. I wouldn't eat meat, wouldn't cook it, and wouldn't have it in the house. Whatever he ate outside the house was fine with me. The year before this had been fine, even an admirable show of principle, but now it had turned into an indictment of him. Even worse, he claimed I was denying him proper nutrition by not allowing burgers, steaks, and ribs to be cooked in our kitchen. And how was he supposed to find a job or function as a human being when he was practically starving?

Inevitably, Blaze became an issue as well. Norman felt he was undisciplined and needed a firmer hand. His child-rearing strategies were in direct opposition to Maya's, who resented the fact that he even felt he had the right to an opinion on the matter. In my absence, Maya felt justifiably proprietary where Blaze was concerned. To say that she and Norman argued would be overstating. It was more like mutual, slowly seething antipathy. Of course, it was neither fair nor possible to expect me to take a side between Norman and Maya, each of whom complained to me about the other. Usually, I just ended up in tears, which drove Norman out of the house and Maya into her room.

And then there was Norman's cat, the most telling problem of all. That ugly, evil-tempered bastard of a cat became a metaphor for everything that was wrong with our relationship and an accurate predictor of how it would all end up. I am not an animal hater, although since I'd lost my hamster to Marlon's feline appetite, I hadn't been a real lover of cats. I'd also always been slightly suspicious of single men who owned cats. But Norman was attached to that cat, a purebred something-or-other gift from his mother, and didn't want to leave it behind in New York. Fine, I thought, love the man, love his cat.

This was not to be. First of all, it was an extremely unattractive cat. It was white, with short hair that always looked damp and unkempt, and it had a giant rear end that was completely out of proportion to the rest of its body. It didn't walk, it minced. It also hissed and hated every human being it came into contact with, except Norman. And the human it hated most was not me, as one might expect, but Blaze who was also the only human aside from Norman who liked it. While I was still in love-the-man-love-his-cat mode, Norman cajoled me into letting the damn thing sleep on our bed, which would have been acceptable, if not ideal, were it not for the fact that the cat didn't appreciate being relegated to the foot of the bed and consistently weaseled its way into the space between us. For many weeks, I woke up with my face full of dirty white cat butt. The cat's head, of course, was nestled next to Norman. It didn't take me long to believe that this was jealousy, plain and simple.

"Does this cat have to be in the bed?" I asked Norman.

"Come on, it's the only thing I've got that's really mine," he said. So I let the cat stay until it attacked Blaze, scarring his lip with a kick and scrape of its back claws when Blaze tried to "rescue" it from beneath the covers. I was nearly hysterical over this assault to my four-year-old.

Norman said, "Poor thing, it was probably terrified."

"It? You're calling Blaze *it*?" I said, incredulous.

"I was talking about the cat," Norman said. "Do you know how scared a cat has to be to attack with its back legs?"

"I want the cat out of the bed," I said.

After the scratching incident, I was no longer a friend to the cat. But my aversion was nothing compared to Maya's naked loathing.

"I hate that thing," she said. "It's the most horrible beast I've ever seen. And I am telling you, when it gets fleas, and it *will* get fleas, either it goes or I go. You know how I feel about fleas." Indeed, I did. Fleas were, and still are, Maya's bête noire. The sight of a single flea is enough to send her into hysterics.

"It won't get fleas," Norman said. "It's an indoor cat. It never goes out, so it can't possibly get fleas."

The cat got fleas, followed by flea baths, and bombings and flea collars. Maya stayed. The fleas came back. Norman grew more and more resentful, although he had started taking regular trips back to New York to "tie up loose ends" and I was often left to take care of this thing he cared about so deeply. Maya took every chance she got to insist that the cat be removed from the house.

"I'm telling you," she said, "that cat has to go. If it doesn't, it might accidentally get killed. You wouldn't want that on your head, would you?"

"How can I make him get rid of his cat?" I asked Maya. "He loves that cat."

"I found a flea on Blaze's arm today," Maya responded. "On your son's *arm*! Have you lost your mind? This is your child we're talking about."

"What can I do?" I told her. "I hate the thing, too."

Maya voiced her discontent to the other members of our family, who had become, by this time, completely disenchanted with Norman, his problems, and his cat. "The whole relationship," my father muttered, "isn't worth the hassle of dealing with a single flea."

What finally sealed the cat's fate was not the litter box, fleas, or even the scratch on Blaze's face. Rather, I had what I could only call a showdown with it one night when Norman was in New York and Maya was out. I was sitting on the couch and it stood in front of me, in total defiance of the no-cat-on-the-coffee-table rule, and gave me the coldest feline stare I have ever seen. I was convinced, at that moment, that I was not looking at a cat but at some sort of fur-wrapped spirit, perhaps a witch's familiar.

"Why don't you just leave?" I asked it out loud. "Make it easier on everyone, just take off. Nobody can stand you here. Don't you realize that by now?"

The cat leveled its green stare at me and hissed. Then it spoke to me. I know, I know, but I *heard* it speak, clear as the bell on its flea collar.

Fuck you, it said.

When Norman got back from New York, he was already planning his next trip. It was springtime, less than nine months after we'd all moved in together.

"The cat has to go," I told him.

Norman shook his head, looked at me in an *Et tu, Brutus?* kind of way, and said, "My cat. So now it's my cat, too?"

"What do you mean *too*," I said. "Like I'm out to get you. Like I'm not trying to help you."

"Please," he said. "You've made this as difficult as possible from the beginning. I'm the one doing all the compromising in this relationship."

"What?!"

"You know it's true. I'm the one who's uprooted his whole life and tried to fit into yours. I've got nothing, except my *cat*, which you're now forcing me to give up as well."

"What about me?" I sputtered. "You haven't got me? Wasn't that the point? Isn't that why you decided to come out here?"

"Again, your idea," he said.

I'd had enough. Echoing the cat, I shouted "Fuck you!" at him and stormed out of the bedroom onto the landing.

"What do you mean?" Norman said.

"Which word didn't you understand," I barked, "*fuck* or *you*?"

Norman slammed the door, fuming. I stood helplessly on the landing for a second, vibrating in my anger. I looked down to the living room and saw Maya looking up at me. She was laughing. "Good one," she said quietly. It seemed as if it had been so very long since either one of us had found mirth in anything. I couldn't help it, I had to laugh along with her.

A few weeks later, we found a home for the cat (and a good one at that) with a woman whom Maya and I worked with in the restaurant. She had several cats already and, for reasons that remained mysterious to us, really took a shine to this one. "I can understand how traumatic it is to give up a pet," she told us. "You can come visit it anytime if you want."

"I don't think so," Maya said. "Better to make a clean break, don't you think?"

Much as he professed to love it, Norman didn't miss the cat at all once it was gone. I was beginning to believe that this was how he approached everything he claimed to love, including me. This belief was confirmed three months later when Norman took another trip to New York and simply never came back.

Over time, I became thankful to Norman for taking off,

because it was something I never would have done. I'd made a commitment to him and I would have stuck it out, trying to honor the spirit of that commitment, until there was nothing left but gutted remains. In other words, much longer than would have been healthy for either one of us. As it was, we'd been at odds almost from the first day we moved in together. I can only imagine how ugly and destructive it might have gotten had we continued. At the time, though, I was anything but thankful. I was angry, confused, and deeply depressed by what I considered a spectacular failure.

Maya and I began a desperate search to find another place to live because our lease was up and we couldn't afford the rent on the one we were in. To add insult to injury, I had to pack up and move what Norman had left behind along with everything else (nothing vital, as it turned out, because Norman had either left in New York or subsequently taken back everything that was important to him). And, of course, there was the huge, gnawing question of what happened to the love. Had there ever been any at all or had I been gaslighted by my giant desire for a happy ending?

Maya and I found a little condo nearby and signed another lease together. She never once said anything even remotely along the lines of "I told you so." Nor did she offer me a shoulder to cry on. As far as she was concerned, we were all well rid of Norman and she couldn't understand why I'd even be sad that he was gone. On our last night in the house, we were on our hands and knees, giving it a thorough going-over with solvents and carpet cleaner so that we'd be able to retrieve our deposit. Maya wiped at a black mark on one of the walls, and said, "You know, I never liked this fucking house."

"I know," I told her.

"It was never right," she said.

"I know."

"I can't tell you how glad I am that we're out of here."

"I know that, too," I told her.

And at that moment, I also knew this:

Men leave.

My sister would always be there.

It's been ten years since that awful summer—long enough to reevaluate the conclusions I reached then. I am no longer sure that men always leave, not that I've given one a chance to do so in all that time. For something that lasted such a short while, the Norman episode left some long-term marks on my heart. I am, however, still certain that my sister will always be there for me, just as I will be for her, no matter what men come, go, leave, or stay. I don't know if this means we will live together for the rest of our lives (my Italian-spinster-aunt vision dissipated a long time ago, so I no longer see the two of us sitting in rocking chairs wrapped in black lace shawls and surrounded by Hummel figurines), but what would it matter if we did? The point is, I don't worry about it and neither does Maya. There is an ease in our relationship now that has been hammered out and refined by time. In the ebb and flow of days upon days, we are each other's most constant of constants.

This is why, despite the diversity of our backgrounds, I can see the two of us in Gwen and Judy and the two of them in us. They spent many years apart, when each was raising her own family and their physical proximity to each other has only been close for the last fifteen years or so. But they have been sisters for a long, long time. The effortlessness of their interaction, the unspoken communication between them, is testimony to the power of this kind of time in the indestructible bond between sisters. I can feel this time, the melted warmth of it, as I sit next to Judy on this beautiful summer evening watching our sisters play.

When the concert ends and Maya scrambles around delivering tickets, cash, and receipts to the treasurer (she's the orchestra president and in charge of these things), I take a bit of the load off Judy and carry Gwen's violin as well as Maya's. I order Blaze to carry Judy's chair.

"Why are you the only one with free hands?" I ask him. "Letting the women carry everything?" I don't care if this is sexist, it's time for him to pull some weight.

"Oh yes," Gwen says. "The fragile women."

Blaze snorts in disagreement. I can understand why. This boy has grown up around women who are anything but fragile or helpless. What can I expect?

"These damn knees," Gwen says. "I can't wait for the new ones."

On the way home, Maya and Gwen discuss Gwen's upcoming knee replacement surgery and then move on to the tastier topic of orchestra gossip. Judy and I remain silent in the back, listening. Nobody mentions singing again, which is just as well because it's hotter now than it was a few hours ago and we're all tired.

We say good-bye and switch cars back at Gwen's place. Blaze has taken my admonishment to heart and helps Gwen and Judy into the elevator with all their gear. When the three of us are back on the road home, I tell Maya, "Those two are so young looking and acting. I can only pray I look that good when I get to be their age."

"It just goes to show you," she says. "It's all about attitude."

"And good makeup," I say. "Genes don't hurt, either. Judy looks fabulous. She's younger than Gwen, isn't she?"

"Oh no," Maya says, "Judy's older than Gwen—the same difference as we have, I think, maybe even a little more."

"She looks really great," I say. "I can hardly believe it."

"Gwen says she never goes out unless her hair and makeup are perfect. She reminds me of you, actually. She puts on makeup every day and does her hair. She has a boyfriend, too. Can you imagine? At this point, a boyfriend."

"What do you mean?"

"Just, you know, to have a boyfriend at this stage of the game. . . . To still be working things out, building a relationship. I don't know, it just seems kind of . . . *tiresome*."

"Maybe that's what's keeping her young," I offer.

"Maybe," Maya says. She looks over at me and smiles.

"See?" she says. "I told you she reminded me of you."

Lavander and Bo.

7

About Our Brother

september

Lavander is turning thirty-one and our brother has inexplicably decided to host a brunch in her honor at the apartment he shares with Déja and Danny. Birthdays, and we have eight of them in our family (nine, if you count Danny), are a *big* deal with this group. Nonbirthday months are November, October, and April. Thanksgiving, which is arguably an even bigger deal than a birthday for us, falls in November, taking that month off the calendar as a free one. There is usually some sort of Halloween thing happening in October as well, so that month could be considered a draw. When you get right down to it, then, April is the only month when there isn't an obvious mandate for a party.

Over time, our birthdays have gotten bigger in scope, importance, and significance. People expect more, prepare lists of gifts they'd like (or must have), and request menus and specific kinds of cake for birthday dinners. Buying an off-list gift can be a dicey proposition because, like so much in our family, gift-giving is competitive. Gifts have to be store-bought, but also creative. Creative, because giving cash or gift certificates makes the statement that you don't care enough about the person to put any thought into a gift. Store-bought, because if the gift is homemade (paintings, soaps, poems, etc.), it implies you are too cheap to buy one.

Cards are also a very important requirement and are, perhaps, even more competitive than the gifts because they come with fewer restrictions. One is allowed (even encouraged) to make a card, although this is a rare occurrence. My brother has created a niche for himself in the card department by never buying a card that is appropriate to the occasion. For example, on your birthday, you might get a card from him that says "Bon Voyage," or "Congratulations on Your Bar Mitzvah," or, his favorite, a juvenile birthday card with all kinds of digits added to the single one on the outside. Lately, he's been particularly fond of giving cards in other languages. On our parents' last anniversary, he outdid himself and wrote his entire message (most of which didn't make any sense) in Spanish.

I'm not sure how the birthdays got to be such a tour de force with us, but I suspect that my mother was the primary catalyst. Many years ago, she and my father celebrated one of those milestone wedding anniversaries (I can't even remember which one now, which was part of the problem to begin with), and none of us (their children) acknowledged the event. Actually, that's not entirely true; my brother did present them with a giant bag of M&Ms, which, unbelievably to the rest of us, placed him on the only-child-who-cares list for quite some time. Determined not to be forgotten or overlooked again, my mother created a birthday and Mother's Day gift wish list for herself (no combination gifts allowed!) and now owns the month of May when both of those

It's Maya who has the reputation for being the master chef and caterer. That's why it's odd that my brother has suddenly decided to host an event (and prepare food) at his house. Generally, he's not too fond of having people (family members or no) in such close proximity to his personal space. Plus, if an event is in your own home, it's very difficult to flee if things start to get uncomfortable. I notice that nobody mentions any of these things, however. The novelty of a Bo-prepared fete is too enticing to ask for further details.

Brunch is scheduled for sometime between 11 o'clock and noon. Several hours earlier, I take my daily constitutional. These walks are my version of the gym. Gyms have never worked for me. This is not for lack of trying. We live in a gym-obsessed part of the world here and the pressure to join one is fairly intense. Maya is always dependable in this respect. She's joined a wide variety of gyms and followed a stunning array of programs— none of which seem to last very long. I joined a gym with her once and the two of us nearly killed ourselves jumping up and down on the aerobic step.

"I don't think it's such a good idea to turn purple," I told her as the two of us dripped sweat and gasped for breath.

"But it's good for you," she panted.

Maya dropped out of the gym shortly after that. Then it was Tae Bo. She bought all the tapes and was extolling its virtues for weeks. "Look how I'm sweating and I've only done the instructional video!" But when it came down to doing the actual regime on a daily basis, she dropped out of that too. I picked up the Tae Bo slack for a while, religiously working out to the tapes in our living room until I hurt my back doing some sort of weird scissor kick and had to give it up. Maya's next effort was to find a personal trainer. She was involved in a band that was playing odd gigs in coffeehouses and the drummer had a fireman friend who doubled as a trainer.

events take place. It didn't take long for everyone else to jump on the big birthday bandwagon.

Which brings me to the most important element of these birthdays, the party. There is always a meal involved, usually prepared by Maya, who is also the person who always bakes the birthday cake. Since nobody in my family eats eggs, store-bought cakes are usually out of the question. Maya demonstrated her skill with eggless confections a long time ago—nobody else can even come close—and so she is the designated cake-baker in the family. Unfortunately, this means that she also has to bake her own birthday cake, a situation she complains about every year. Occasionally, we'll collect en masse and go to a restaurant for a birthday lunch or dinner, but home-cooked meals are always the preferred ones and so the venue is most often Maya's and my house. Attendance at these affairs is strongly suggested. For example, "If you don't care enough about me to be around on my birthday, that's fine, but just remember that the next time yours rolls around."

I don't mean to imply that we don't have fun at these gatherings, because we do. Like any repeating event, though, some are better than others. Some are even inspired. When Blaze turned fourteen, he requested that the family join him for sunset and cake on the beach. This turned out to be one of the most enjoyable and relaxed afternoons we'd ever spent as a group. And one year, I decided to take everyone out for dinner on my own birthday, which ended up being one of the finest parties we'd ever had. But one of the best was my brother's last birthday which fell on the same day as the Academy Awards ceremony. We had a blow-out combination event, complete with an Oscar pool and hors d'oeuvres. My brother ended up winning the pool in addition to a series of side bets he'd made during the actual telecast and added a pile of cash to his collection of birthday gifts.

Mostly, though, it's Maya who prepares the food for the parties.

"Mmm, a fireman," I said. "Send him over."

"This is my personal trainer," she said. "Forget about your fireman fantasies."

The fireman came over exactly once and didn't accomplish very much.

Finally, Maya opted for yoga classes, joining several different programs and dropping them until she found one she liked with our mother. For the last few months, her attendance at this one has been pretty good.

Lavander has an interesting relationship with the gym as well. Usually, her method is to spend a lot of money joining whichever gym or system is most popular and then never go. I think the idea is that if you've paid for the thing, the rest will just come on its own. Déja's recently jumped on the fitness bandwagon as well and now she and Maya alternate swimming in the pool at Déja's apartment complex and yoga. They've tried to rope me in to these pursuits, but I'd rather walk. I've never been a driver, so walking has always been my default means of transportation, but now walking has become essential to my mental well-being, never mind a means of keeping in physical shape. It's a way of convincing myself that I am continuously moving forward. Sometimes, when I slip out the door and prepare to make my rounds, I fantasize that I could just keep going until I reach the end of whatever edge I'm walking at that moment.

This morning I'm following my usual route, which is to wind down the hill and to the supermarket. There's always something that needs buying, so the supermarket is ever a logical destination.

I reach the store and head over to the ATM inside. Before I get there, though, I see a good-looking guy chatting up one of the female checkers as he pays for his groceries. It takes only a fraction of a second for me to realize that the guy is my brother. I stand still, in the vicinity of the check stand without being close enough to get in anybody's way or attract attention. I am curious to see how long it will take my brother to notice that I am standing there and to recognize me. He continues to flirt with the checker and gathers his bags. I start to entertain the notion that he's going to walk right by me without so much as a glance. I spin a future scenario in my head:

"Hey, Bo, how'd your shopping go this morning?"

"How do you know I went shopping?"

"I saw you. I even know what you bought and what checker you were talking to. She's cute."

"How do you know that? Were you spying on me? Watching me? Where were you? What were you doing?"

My brother is fairly paranoid and while it's amusing to imagine playing on this paranoia, I start feeling a little annoyed that I've been standing here for a couple of minutes already and he hasn't even sensed my presence. For a paranoid person, he's not too well aware of somebody staring at him in a supermarket. I'm going to have to mention that to him as soon as he notices me.

Finally, as he is making his way to the door, he turns his head in my direction. A kaleidoscopic rush of expressions runs across his face in lightning succession. The first is a suspicious "Why is that person staring at me?" look. This is followed by a "There's a *girl* looking at me" expression, and then "It's my sister!" Finally, there is one more layer: "It's Debra!" As the eldest sister of the four he has, I am the original font of adoration. This is when he breaks into a huge grin, paranoia dissipated, and the transformation from slightly dark, enticingly mysterious player wannabe to baby brother is complete. "Debsies!" he says with genuine pleasure. "What are you doing here?"

"Took you long enough to notice me," I say. "I thought you were going to walk right by me. You don't look around much, do you?"

"You know how I feel about that," he says. I laugh, remembering the time a couple of years ago that Maya and I came to visit him at his summer job unloading cartons in the warehouse of the county fair. When we were still several yards away, I could see an admiring look on his face as we approached. By the time we got up close, that look had changed to one of mild disgust.

"What's up?" I asked him.

"I hate it when I'm checking out a couple of hot chicks and they turn out to be my *sisters*," he spat out.

"Maybe you should try directing your stare at their *faces*, then," Maya said. "That's never a bad idea."

"I would, if you weren't dressed like that," he said.

"I'm guessing that's a compliment," I told him.

I steer him away from the door now and into the floral department in the supermarket. "What are *you* doing here?" I ask him. "I don't usually see you around these parts." My brother has a long list of places he refuses to go, usually because he doesn't want to be recognized, although by whom and why it would bother him if they did, nobody has been able to figure out. It's not like he's graced the cover of *People* magazine anytime lately.

"Shopping for the big do," he says, holding up his grocery bags. "I've been to three stores this morning. Got bagels, a variety of juices, some fine coffee, and other tasty treats. Even bought pastries—two kinds, thank you very much. Raspberry and apple. And fruit. The fruit's for you, Debsie. Because I know how much you like fruit. Can you think of anything else I need?"

I smile at him. He's so cute, I can hardly stand it. "I think you've got it covered, brother," I say. "You're very well prepared, I must say. What's the deal, anyway? Why the sudden desire to have a party at your house?"

"Because I am the *man*," he says. "Maya's not the only one around here who can put together a shindig, you know. I'm going to show her up."

"Don't get too cocky," I tell him. "Soon all the parties will be at your house if you keep it up."

"Oh no," he says. "See, it's all part of my master plan. When

Maya sees how well I can put this together, she'll be determined to outdo herself in the future." He winks. "I'm no fool," he says.

"No, 'fool' isn't the word that immediately comes to mind," I tell him. "By the way, I think it's great you've decided to put together this party for Lavander, considering you didn't even bother to show up on my birthday."

"You know, you really need to get over that," he says.

"And I'm still waiting for my gift," I tell him.

"Yes, well, I've got to be off," he says. "Got to start preparing. Don't be late, okay?"

"Wouldn't think of it," I tell him, and he's gone.

He's such an odd duck, I think, as I watch him go. On the one hand, he's so intensely private, a hoarder of secrets that everybody already knows and an inventor of mysteries where there are none to be had. Even his simplest plans and activities (what he had for breakfast, what kind of shirt he wants to buy) are shrouded in cloak-and-dagger secrecy. It's impossible to get information out of him if you ask for it, and he gets downright surly if pressed. On the other hand, his outside persona is outgoing and absolutely charming. He is so personable and sincere that people like him instantly. He's always been popular with both sexes, but women, especially, find him captivating. And I know this is true because I've witnessed it firsthand. He is unfailingly polite and respectful, but never condescending or chauvinistic (in public, anyway). He has a fundamental understanding of the differences between men and women, but he's not one of those men who claim that women are an unsolvable mystery. He is genuinely warm and always seems interested. And he never appears to be faking it. Women love this. Just love it. Pleasant personality notwithstanding, I believe that my brother is able to consistently pull this off because of us, his sisters. That's right, I'm taking credit. And I pity, that is, feel genuinely sorry for men who have grown up without at least one sister. If you ask me, they (the men) get better life training from their sisters than we (the women) get from our brothers. Of course, my perspective on this issue is fairly skewed. Let's put it this way: I'm still not sure how my brother learned to walk because, for the first two years of his life, his feet never touched the ground.

Bo was the prince of our family before he was even born. The very location of his arrival seemed auspicious. We were living in Los Angeles then, in an apartment just beneath the Sunset Strip. It was warm all the time and the air had a permanent rose-gold glow. Disneyland was around the corner. We went out for ice cream at least once a week. And, unlike the other places we had lived, there was always a beach close by. I fell in love with the ocean and with California that year and wasn't entirely comfortable in any of the places I lived until I moved back here sixteen years later.

When my mother was still a few months away from delivery, she had a dream that she was sitting in front of a large, brightly colored bowl. In the bowl was a giant pea pod which she split open, revealing a plump, pink baby boy inside. She told me, in excited detail, all about the dream, and said, "It means that this baby is definitely a *boy*. I know it."

My mother said the word "boy" with a certain reverence. It wasn't that she believed that boys were somehow worthier than girls, because I've never for a moment believed that either of my parents had a preference as to the sex of their children. Rather, there was a certain awe that came from knowing that she could create a male within her female body. Even at ten years old, I had an unconscious understanding of this miracle and when I gave birth to a son fourteen years later, it struck me, all over again, how astonishing it was that a woman could produce a child who would become a man. I've since decided that it's entirely possible that some women never quite get over this sense of awe, which would explain quite a bit in terms of the sense of entitlement so many of their sons feel. My brother was born into a house that was full of awe-struck females just waiting to lavish him with adoration.

I was almost eleven years old when Bo was born and Maya was eight. I'd forgotten any awkwardness I might have felt handling a baby by the time he came along. Lavander seemed so fragile to me when she was born and, for a long time, I was afraid of breaking her. I never had this worry with Bo, who often ended up on my hip after being passed from person to person like a football. Maya carried him around plenty as well. He was handled a great deal. He was also kissed relentlessly. As an infant, Bo was ruddy and hot. In the presence of strangers, he was an angry howler. Maya and I thought he was the cutest thing to ever have graced the earth and marveled endlessly about his darling chin, his fat lips, his dark curly hair. He was a more willing prop for our living room plays than Lavander was at that point, and so he became the center of every set piece. He was the boy Prince, boy Superman, or boy whatever we could find a costume and a concept for. He was happy to participate in his own way, most of which involved his tearing off whatever outfit we put him in and when he got older, trashing whatever other props we'd constructed. Destruction was always forgivable when he did it. He was a boy, after all.

While Maya and I cuddled and coddled, it was Lavander, only nineteen months old when he was born, who totally co-opted our brother. Bo was the second half of the set that made up him and Lavander, just as Maya was the second half of the set that made up the two of us. As soon as he was old enough to stand, she taught him to bang his crib against the wall and hurl his bottle across the room just as she did. We could always tell when naptime was over for the two of them by the rhythmic Doppler thumping of cribs, the slosh of milk as it hit the floor, and Bo's gleeful chuckle. From the time he formed his first smile, Bo thought Lavander was a laugh riot and he followed her lead in every way.

I never felt as protective of my sisters as I did with my brother. He always seemed so much more vulnerable. Perhaps this was because I'd already discovered that the girls could take care of themselves. Perhaps it was because the boy brought out more maternal instincts than they did. Whatever the reason, it was easy to baby him and to lavish on him the kind of attention I didn't think my sisters needed. Unfortunately, my protectiveness had limits, beyond which lay a maddening helplessness. I discovered these limits when I was twelve years old and he was about two.

He was a sweet little toddler in a light blue jacket and yellow galoshes. He had beautiful curls that my parents didn't want to cut (my father, especially, has always had a thing about hair and always discouraged us from cutting our own) and they hung around his shoulders. We'd moved twice since he'd been born and were living in Upstate New York on the edge of what seemed like a perpetually frozen lake. There was a playground in our town-house complex and I'd taken Bo out to play. We were at the tail end of a particularly frigid winter and hadn't been able to sit outside for months. As we walked down to the playground, I told him a story that I made up as we went along. This was a habit of mine when we went walking. I took the imagery from the fairy tales I'd read and pasted them into my own stories for him. I don't know if he ever really listened to me, let alone understood what I was talking about, but he was always very quiet while I rambled on and he never let go of my hand. I sat on a swing while he poked around in the cold dirt and fallen leaves with a stick he'd found on the ground.

There were a group of older boys, maybe ten or eleven years old, hanging out on the periphery of the playground, chasing each other and throwing clods of dirt and rocks at each other. Up to no good, I thought, and kept an eye on my brother, who was jumping up and down with glee over some particularly interesting leaf or stone he'd discovered. I heard the shouts of the boys come a little closer to us, but I didn't pay it much attention. I was in a state of semi–self-hypnosis, rethinking the story I had told Bo on the way down and watching the way the grays and browns of the trees blended into the grays and blues of the chilly sky.

The rock came so fast, I didn't even see it until after it hit Bo in the face and fell at his feet. He was screaming in pain and shock by the time I ran over to him. There was a large, deep scrape on his cheek, just under his eye. The rock had hit him hard and he was bleeding. I looked up only long enough to see the perpetrators pointing in our direction and laughing. I was filled with a com-bination of blinding rage and utter panic. Bo was crying in that heartbreaking, uncomprehending way that children have when they have no idea what caused the sudden pain they are feeling. Large teardrops fell from his big blue eyes. I wanted to kill.

"Hey! Hey, you!" I yelled at the boys. "Hey, look what you did!"

"Yeah, so what? What are you going to do about it? You can't do nothing, *girl*," I heard come back in my direction. And it was true, there was nothing I could do about it, just as there was nothing I had done to prevent it. I was a girl—a little, timid girl at that. My fury was completely impotent. I couldn't go chasing after them any more than I could a pack of wild animals. I had to pick up my bleeding, crying baby brother, carry him home, and tend to his wounded face. I felt like crying myself over my own lack of power.

My parents were livid when I got Bo home and, ultimately, it was my father who went out in search of the boys who had thrown the rock while my mother wailed about the damage to her son's face. I followed my father as he stalked off to the play-ground, keeping something of a distance between us, both because of my embarrassment over being such a weak girl and because his anger, quiet and cold, was more intimidating when it was directed at someone else. I saw him walk over to the boys, deceptively casual in his approach, and start talking to them. He even smiled. I watched his body language and that of the boys as he continued his speech. I could see when he got to the part about Bo being hit with the rock. The boys lost their tough attitudes, straightened their bodies, and stood at attention. My father leaned in closer to them. I could tell that he'd lowered his voice, even though I couldn't hear either him or the boys. I saw a flurry of finger pointing. "*He* did it," I imagined all of them saying. I saw my father pick up a rock in his hand and weigh it out. I saw him lean over and palm the air about three feet above the ground. My brother's height. Look what you did. Consider the rock. Consider how big the baby is that you hit with it. The boys' eyes rounded with fear. I could see them making fiercely apologetic motions. I could see them leaning, poised to run, as soon as they were released. I could see the strain in their bodies, how difficult it was to stay in that place.

When my father finally walked away, they scattered like dry seeds on the ground. He'd taken care of everything, my father had, in a way that was completely unavailable to me. My brother forgot about his injury almost instantly. His scrape healed soon after that. But I never quite got over the sense of impotence I felt that day. It was the first time I'd ever felt the fundamental disadvantage of being a girl in a world that belonged to boys.

The world certainly belonged to my brother as he grew older, although nobody in our family ever held this against him. He had free reign, as he was growing up, to tease and torture, to practice using his wiles and charm, to be a contemporary (of Lavander's), a baby (to me and Maya), and a protector and defender (to Déja). He was able to discover what worked and what didn't in the realm of women. All the while, he had the impunity that came with being the only boy. I think it's safe to say that if my brother has any self-esteem issues at this point in his life, it has nothing to do with a lack of acceptance and adoration in his childhood.

Nor have we ever given him a hard time about his romantic choices. In this respect, my brother has had the easiest ride of all. His sisters have always been so concerned about his happiness and emotional well-being that we have all striven to make his girlfriends feel welcome and included. We are less critical of the women he dates than we are of each other's boyfriends and *much* less critical than we are of each other's women friends. Perhaps this is because of the protectiveness we still, and will always, feel toward Bo. Then again, perhaps my brother has simply made better choices than we have over the years. With very few exceptions, his relationships have been calmer and happier than ours and when they have ended, my brother and his exes always remain friendly. We are almost always on our best behavior when one of Bo's girlfriends is in the house. Unlike his sisters, Bo doesn't conduct his relationships in the spotlight of the family eye. We respect his need for privacy in this regard, whereas we often ignore it with each other. But we also want his girlfriends to like us. I'd even say this has been more important than whether or not we like *them*. The one exception to this rule has been Lavander, who seldom feels that any woman is good enough for Bo. Nevertheless, she has always tried harder than the rest of us combined to befriend the women in his life. Her loyalty to him is intense and unshakable.

Lavander was more distraught than any of us when, about three years ago, Bo started seeing a woman who was at first guarded around our family, then uncomfortable, and, finally, just flat out rejecting. My family is not oblivious to the fact that, as a group, we can be overwhelming. We are loud and we carry on. We tend to fall into usual patterns of communication when we are together. At the same time, though, everything is always out in the open. There are few smoldering resentments in this family because the demand to deal with it *now* is always present. What you see with us is usually what you get. There is not one of us who is capable of putting on a false face with each other. With each other, we can't help but be genuine, which is why we were stunned when Bo's girlfriend, Hannah, seemed to like us less as their relationship progressed. If she had been a man, she would have been out, off the list, with every one of us, but because she was his girlfriend, we actually tried to modify our behavior around her; we tried, in fact, to be different people, people she might like. There was nothing for it, though, she wasn't having it. She didn't want to come to family dinners, ever. She didn't want to spend time with any of us, individually or together. And, as time went on, she didn't want Bo to, either. For the better part of two years, we didn't see or hear from him at all.

After a while, Maya and I gave up trying, hoping that, ultimately, it would all work itself out. Déja reckoned that if Bo was happy, that was more important than whether or not Hannah liked us (of course, we all suspected that he wasn't, but we weren't about to interfere—*yet*). But Lavander really grieved.

"He's my best friend," she said, "and I never see him anymore. It's not fair. I've tried to be a friend to that bitch. I've told her that we are always open to having another sister. She doesn't care about him. If she did, she wouldn't be doing this to him."

Gradually, Bo started voicing his doubts about his relationship with his sisters. We were very careful never to pass judgment on Hannah herself. Yet each one of us pointed out that he didn't seem to be happy and, from what he related, it didn't seem as if she was happy either. He was young, we told him. Why not put off this misery until later?

I want to believe that this helped him, that he was able to draw on the female wisdom of his sisters when the relationship finally came to an end. I like to think that his unlimited access to the collective womanhood of his siblings has been something of value in his development as a man.

I ponder this as I walk home. I'm wondering if I'd trade places with my brother if I had the chance. I wonder what it would've been like to grow up surrounded by brothers. Would I understand the workings of the male mind any better? Bo's had four entirely different women against whom to judge female behavior. And we've just had him. There's something quite humorous in this. To know my brother is to know that he's not really a quantity against which to measure anything except himself. Although I have to admit, I've gathered a perspective from him that I wouldn't have been able to find any other way. He's gone into some places that neither I nor my sisters would have dared to venture.

My sisters and I all worked for many years as waitresses. Déja, in fact, is still working in a restaurant—the last waitress among us. We've had varying success in this sector of the service industry. If I had to qualify, I'd say that Maya was the most competent (and certainly the friendliest) waitress among us, even though I hold the record for the greatest number of years logged at the table. Lavander was never the world's greatest waitress (and she'll be the first to admit this), although she managed to work in several different restaurants over the course of her brief, checkered career. My brother, however, could never tolerate any aspect of the business. After a short and painful stint as a busboy, he swore off the restaurant business forever. He opted, rather, for another area of the service industry—one that none of us would ever have contemplated—the hotel business. He was the night auditor in a series of midscale hotels and even tried a couple of seedy motels. The weird hours and even weirder clientele suited him perfectly. Soon, he was calling regularly with tales from the dark side, each more twisted and darkly funny than the one before.

"This dude calls me from his room," Bo related one night. "Wants me to send up *two* bottles of Dom Perignon. Tells me 'I'm having a big night up here, dude, I need some alcohol.' So

I tell him, 'Sorry, dude, we don't stock Dom and the bar's closed. I don't know what to tell you, but there's a lovely ice machine on seven.' I mean, I think maybe he thought he was in Vegas or something. So he calls down a little later, says, 'Dude, I've got a couple of ladies coming up here. Make sure you tell them where to go. They've got the room number, but make sure you tell them where it is, okay? There's *two* of them, okay?' Like he's really trying to impress me. He's such a player, right? So I say, "Yeah, dude, whatever.' Then he keeps calling, says he got hold of some booze, wants to know if I can score him some coke. I mean, *come on*. The chicks must have snuck in the back way, if they came at all. And they're almost certainly hookers anyway. He calls me again, says, 'I'm chilling the Champagne right now.' I tell him, 'Have a great time,' and I think that's it, right? Wrong. He calls down again, says, 'Dude, I'm in the *hot tub* with two beautiful naked women. I'm getting it on with two women.' And I can't stand it anymore. I wanted to tell him, 'Dude, you are such a *loser*. You're up there with two women, why the hell do you keep calling me—the night auditor?' Then he says, 'Hey, dude, you want in on this?' And I tell him, 'Yeah, you know that would be great, but I really can't leave the desk, you know?' He says, 'You don't know what you're missing.' I was afraid that he was going to call again and ask me for help. Guess he finally got it together. What a loser."

A week or so later, there was this:

"Guy calls me at the desk, says there's a strange buzzing sound in his room and thinks maybe it's the TV, can I come fix it? I asked him if the TV was coming in okay and he said it was, so I said, 'Well, it's probably not the TV then, is it?' So he says he can't hear it right now, he'll call again if it comes back. Sure enough, ring, ring, and it's him again. The buzzing sound is back and he can't stand it, it's really driving him crazy. I've got to come up and see to it. I tell him I'm not really a repairman, but he doesn't care, wants me up there. So I go up, check out the TV, the bathroom, the lamps, everything's fine, right? I don't hear anything. He says it's been going on and on, just stopped the minute I walked in. Okay, sure. I go back downstairs and, again, there he is. I tell him I can move him to a different room and he wants to know can't I just fix it? Can't I just get rid of this buzzing noise that's driving him crazy? I'm starting to think that the buzzing noise is in his head, but I ask him again if he wants to move to another room. Okay, he says, can I come up and help him move? Up I go again and move him into another room. We get him settled and then I hear the noise. 'See? See?' he shouts. 'There it is! The whole place has that noise. I demand a refund.' I look over at the table next to the bed and see it. 'Sir,' I tell him, 'it's your *pager*. It's vibrating on the table.' He looks over at the pager, picks it up, says, 'Hmm, looks like I missed a couple of calls. Okay, you can go now.' Not 'Thank you' or 'I'm such an idiot.' 'You can go now.' Thanks, buddy."

Almost every week there was a story about how various clients tried to get him to arrange hookers to be sent to their rooms and how annoyed they were when he wouldn't comply. Of course, he did nothing to stop the hookers once they found their way into the hotel and turned a (somewhat) blind eye when they disappeared into the elevator and reappeared an hour or two later, sometimes dropping business cards off with him on their way out, asking him to call cabs for them, and promising large "tips" if he would consider calling them the next time a client wanted some company. "I worry about them," he said more than once. "I want to make sure they get home safely."

"Don't you worry that something will happen to them up there in those rooms?" I asked him. "It's not exactly safe, you know. It could be on your head."

"What am I going to do?" he said. "Everyone's got to make a living, right? They know what they're doing."

"They may know what they're doing, but they don't always know what they're getting into," I told him.

"I keep an eye out," he said. "They know that when they come in. They kind of smile and nod at me. I've got their backs. I'm very popular with the ladies, don't worry."

I was sure that he was.

Although he was offered changes in shift and upgrades in position, Bo chose to remain on the night shift, watching the dark eddies of human behavior ebb and flow around his desk. Although the argument could be made that he chose graveyard because it entailed a great deal less actual work (how many people check in at three in the morning?), there was more to it than that. Bo found it comfortable down there in the middle of the night in his personal little heart of darkness. He also found it very entertaining. Until the night he checked in a suicide.

He was called in to work early the next day to answer questions about the man whom the maid had found hanging in the bathroom earlier in the day.

"The guy seemed perfectly normal," he told us later. "He was friendly. He didn't even check in very late. Just an average guy. Why would a guy do that? Why would you go to a hotel to kill yourself?"

"Maybe he didn't want anyone in his family to find him," Maya said. "He was trying to be considerate."

"Somebody found him," Bo said. "And it doesn't matter that it's not a family member. I checked him in. And now he's dead. They had to call his family. He's got a daughter or something."

"It's not your fault, you know. All you did was check him in," I told him. "You couldn't have known what he was going to do."

"It was my shift," Bo said. "I was sitting there at the desk and the guy was upstairs killing himself. I'm going to have that in my mind forever."

Bo never really got over the suicide. There was dark and then there was sheer blackness. That night signaled the beginning of the end of his illustrious hotel career. It was also the end of his love affair with the late shift. It was a pity only in that we no longer got the stories he so elegantly told. My brother is nothing if not an excellent storyteller. Just don't try to solicit information from him. And certainly don't ask him what his motivations are. Like this brunch, for example. I'm still not sure why he's doing it, but I'm sure there's a reason apart from what he told me in the supermarket. And that's what he wants me to think, I'm sure. My brother is a person, after all, who seldom calls my house as himself. He's always adopting one persona or another, making himself sound like a telemarketer, an old friend we've forgotten about, or a bill collector. A talented mimic, he waits until he's really got us going and then announces himself to a chorus of, "Omigod! I can't believe you did that *again*! Can't you just call like a normal person?" There's never an answer to this question, just hysterical laughing on the other end of the phone.

When Maya, Blaze, and I arrive for the birthday brunch, we find we are the last to get there. It takes me a minute to realize that this is because the people who usually arrive the latest live here and are therefore de facto on time. There is a pile of birthday presents on the kitchen counter and Lavander sits next to them on a bar stool. We wish Lavander a happy birthday and place our gifts on the pile. Déja and Danny are milling about the living room and my parents are already sitting at the table in front of a bowl of apples and bananas. The artful fruit bowl is one of the things that each one of my mother's children have inherited from her. There was always an inviting one in the house when we were growing up. For my mother, there was nothing sadder than an empty fruit bowl. Now, no matter where we have lived as adults, each one of us has always had a bowl of fruit on the kitchen table or somewhere near by. The fruits in the bowl vary, of course, according to which one of my siblings is involved, but there is fruit nonetheless. Lavander sometimes opts for wax fruit. Déja is partial to oranges and apples. I like to have at least one mango hanging around. So it goes.

Bo is standing in the kitchen, frying potatoes and slicing bagels. There is the usual low roar of voices that accompanies all of our family gatherings, but he isn't speaking, just performing his culinary duties with a small, enigmatic smile on his face as if he's the only one in on a joke.

"Would you like some coffee?" he says brightly, waving the pot at me when I walk into the kitchen.

"Nice spread," Maya says, looking around at the pastries, bagels, and fruit juices.

"Yes," Bo says, "isn't it? Jealous?"

"I know you think I'm envious of your masterful abilities here," Maya says, "but you couldn't be more wrong. I'm perfectly happy to have you make *every* meal here, you know. I don't have a problem with that at all."

"Uh-huh," Bo says. "We'll just see about that."

"Whatever," Maya says.

We gather around the table (there are even fewer chairs here than in our house and some of us have to perch on barstools next to the counter, while others sort of hang around the fringes, grabbing a seat if someone vacates it to refill the coffee or something similar) and begin eating. Bo runs back and forth from the kitchen, serving and grinning.

"This is divine," my mother says. "Who knew he was such a good cook?"

"Bo, is there any particular way you'd like us to eat this?" my father says and, although everybody else seems to miss his implication, it really makes me laugh. Even though Maya hasn't made this meal, my father's still found a way to tease her about it.

"What do you mean?" Bo says.

"Debra knows what I mean," my father says, nodding at me.

"Oh, I see," Maya says. "Is that supposed to be some sort of jab at me? Because I don't like it when people take all the cheese off the top of the macaroni or eat all the crust from the pot pie? Is that it?"

"Come on, it's funny," my father says.

"I'm not cooking for you people anymore," Maya says. "You don't appreciate it."

As if to punctuate the conversation further, the smoke alarm starts squealing. Since it's directly over the table, we all cover our ears and turn in the direction of the sound.

"Goddamn it!" Bo says. Danny runs over to the alarm with a T-shirt and starts waving it at the alarm, which continues to shriek.

"Piece of shit!" Bo exclaims.

"What's the problem?" my mother asks. "I don't even smell any smoke. Is something burning?"

"It goes off when you've got something in the oven," Déja says. "It's very sensitive."

"That could be a problem," Maya says.

"Happens all the time," Bo says as Danny continues to fan. "You can hear people's alarms going off all the time and you can't even rip the damn thing out of the wall. I can't stand this place. It's a ghetto."

"Sure, a ghetto," Déja pipes in. "What are you talking about? I'm sick of you always trashing this place."

To be sure, this apartment complex is anything but a ghetto. Like so many of the new developments around here, it sprang up practically overnight, complete with swimming pools, hot tubs, weight rooms, and spaces to host events. The colors are predominantly variations on beige and the shape is square so everything is relentlessly uniform. It's heavy on amenities, very light on character, but character isn't what the denizens, mostly young, unmarried, childless professionals, are looking for. Déja, Danny, and Bo got in here when the paint on the walls was barely dry and management was offering big breaks on the rent as move-in incentives, so it's not a bad deal for the three of them, seeing as how each one of them was having tremendous difficulty finding a place to live before they moved in here.

Lavander, Bo, and Déja have spent the last few years revolving through my parents' house on their way in and out of various other places. They've all moved in and out several times. Lavander and Bo attempted to live together at one point, which was short-lived but disastrous. It turned out to be the kind of situation one often sees in those TV courtrooms where family members sue each other over unreturned cable boxes and unpaid phone bills.

Bo spent a couple of years staying with his girlfriend, but when they broke up, he was unable to find an apartment he could afford by himself. He went through a series of potential roommates— friends and friends of friends—each one less responsible than the one before. One disappeared the day he and Bo were scheduled to move into an apartment they'd found. One flashed lots of cash and offered to pay the lion's share of the rent. Bo thought he'd found a sweet deal until he found out that the source of his new roommate's wealth was his lucrative marijuana crop, which he planned to continue growing in the new house. Another showed up to an interview with a potential landlady covered in cat hair and told her about how he was planning to break his previous lease. Bo was forced back into my parents' spare room.

When Déja started seeing Danny, she began spending most of her time at his house. Unfortunately, Danny was living with a couple of guys who redefined the word *squalor* as a mode of existence. There weren't many surfaces in the house that weren't either sticky or punched with holes and Déja refused to take a shower in a bathroom that sported several as-yet undiscovered forms of mold and bacteria. She and Lavander made a plan to move in together, but Lavander was set on living in the condo she'd found within spitting distance of our parents. "What's the point of moving out," Déja said, "if you're going to be living that close to them?"

Bo made a halfhearted attempt to coerce Danny (who had become one of his best friends) to "kick Déja to the curb" and move in with him, but Déja wasn't having any of that. That they all move in together seemed a logical option, but the three of them took some convincing.

"How am I supposed to live with my brother and my boyfriend?" Déja said. "What kind of situation is that?"

Bo played on her insecurity about the whole thing by threatening to walk around in his underwear and stating that Danny would have to keep his "hands off my little sister," which sent Déja into mild hysterics. Danny remained mum (which he'd found to be a good course of action) and let the two of them hammer it out. Variously, the remaining members of my family advised them to make the leap, because, we reasoned, at least they could trust each other, and if, ultimately, it wasn't a tenable situation, it wasn't as if they couldn't all go their separate ways again after a year.

That was six months ago. It hasn't been the smoothest of sailing since then, although it's Déja who's had the roughest waters to navigate. It's turned out that the men in her house are moodier than the woman. Déja is forever settling ridiculous squabbles between the two of them over who will or should take out the trash, who should be paying the phone bill and why there are so many extra charges on the cable bill. Equal division of labor is a concept that doesn't go over too well in their house.

"You don't know what it's like living with two guys," Déja says. "It's impossible. Especially if one of them is your big baby brother."

In a sense, Déja has been uprooted from her position as the

baby of the family since she does a fair amount of mothering for the two men she now lives with. This has been an interesting transformation to watch. Of course, when she tires of her new role (which happens often enough), there is always Maya to turn to. The two of them have lately become each other's staunchest defenders, even when defending isn't necessary. Like now, for example, I can see Maya getting ready to agree with Déja. I can see the words, "This is not a ghetto!" forming on her lips, but the smoke alarm stops abruptly and so does she.

It can't be easy for Bo, either, I think. I don't think he really believes what he is saying about the apartment. The problem has more to do with the fact that, for the last six months, his intense need for privacy has been compromised by living with his sister and her boyfriend, no matter how close he is to the two of them. I have a moment of sympathy for him and then it passes. In the end, what's easy about this life we live? He's got it better than most, I reckon.

"Time for presents!" Lavander exclaims, breaking the potential argument between Déja and Bo. The gift giving begins. Lavander unwraps a handbag, a pair of earrings, and a bag of beauty products. There are no big surprises. The wow factor is a little low. Then again, Lavander has been absent for many big days this year, including several birthdays, and this is a possible explanation for the lack of fanfare. Still, she seems happy with what she gets until the last present is unwrapped and the last card read. She turns to Bo, who is still tossing plates and cups in the kitchen, and says, "Nothing from you? Why isn't there a present from you?"

Bo looks at her, genuinely perplexed, and says, "I made this party for you."

"And that's it? I don't deserve a gift?"

Bo folds his arms and glowers at her. "Why do you have to be that way?" he says.

"Hey," I tell Lavander. "I didn't get a gift on my birthday, either. And I definitely didn't get a brunch." I'm trying to lighten it up, but my words go over like a lead balloon. It's gotten very quiet in here, which is actually more alarming than if the room were filled with shouts and yells. Even the smoke alarm would be welcome right about now.

"I think I have a right to ask why my brother doesn't feel that I'm worthy of a gift on my birthday," Lavander says, and, for Bo, that's just the last straw.

"Fuck this," he says and drops whatever he's holding, some sort of utensil by the sound of it, into the sink. "I've had enough. I've got to get ready for work." With a huff, he disappears into his room, closing and locking the door behind him. There is a moment of utter silence and then all the air in the room seems to shift as everybody gets up at once and starts moving.

"Well, I guess the party's over," my father says.

"What? What did I do?" Lavander says. "Why are you all looking at me like that? I mean, is it wrong to think that he might have given me enough thought to get me a present on my birthday?"

"You know, he took a lot of trouble getting this all together," Déja says, gesturing at the table and its mostly eaten contents. Nobody else, it seems, wants in on this debate. For once, my family is uncharacteristically free of opinion. My mother confers with Maya about her plans for the day. Déja and Danny start clearing the table. Lavander stands in the middle of it all, and says, "But it's hurtful, you know?"

"I think you hurt *his* feelings," my mother says.

"Fine," Lavander says, and walks over to Bo's closed door. "Open this door!" she shouts. "I'm sorry, okay?" There's some sort of muffled growling from behind the door, but nothing intelligible enough to make out.

"Leave him alone," my mother says. "He's got to get ready for work. Let him be now."

About My Sisters 201

"Why am *I* sorry?" Lavander asks herself as she gathers her gifts and prepares to leave. "It's *my* birthday."

"Get over it," my father tells her.

"I don't think you understand," Lavander says to all of us. "My brother is the most important man in my life. The most. He's my best friend. I spend more time with him than anybody else. It didn't have to be a big thing, you know. It could have been just a token. Just something to tell me he knows how I feel."

There is a brief silence and then somebody says, "Well, that *is* true."

"Let's get this cleaned up," Maya says, and so that's what we do. We bag the leftover bagels, put the juices in the fridge, clean the pots and pans, and load up the dishwasher. By the time Bo reemerges from his room, the kitchen and dining room are spotless.

"Thanks for brunch," Lavander says as he walks to the front door.

"You're welcome," he says. "See you." And with that, he's out. Lavander stands still for a moment, as if hesitating between two courses of action. Conflict flickers briefly across her face and then she makes a decision.

"I'm going to go talk to him," she says, and follows in his wake.

"On the other hand, he doesn't have to be such a baby," Déja whispers to Maya. There is a collective shrug in the room. We gather our things and get ready to go.

"So I guess the next one's back at your house?" my father says to Maya as we leave. "Maybe you want to make dinner tonight?"

"Funny," Maya says. "You're so funny."

We walk down the stairs to the parking lot. Below us, we can see Lavander and Bo standing near his car, talking. They are too far away for us to overhear what they are saying, but their body language implies shared secrets and experience. And laughter.

All is forgiven.

Blaze and Aunties.

8

Aunties

october

I'm on a plane, headed home after a short trip to Albuquerque for some book business. I've only been gone for twenty-four hours, but last night was a school night and Blaze had science homework to do. Maya promised me that she'd try to help him with it, but she wasn't very optimistic.

"Atomic structure isn't really my specialty," she said when I called to check in yesterday. "I'll give it a go, but we might just bake a cake instead."

My money's on the cake. Maya and Blaze have a special assortment of things they like to do together when I go away. Homework isn't one of them.

A flight attendant drops a tiny bag of nuts on my tray table next to the equally tiny cup of coffee I've got sitting there. I inspect the nuts for a minute (it can't be my imagination, these bags are definitely getting smaller) and smile to myself. In my family, especially among my sisters and me, the phrase "nuts from the plane" is fraught with meaning. The first part of that statement, "I brought you some," is most often left off for the purposes of conversational efficiency. Everybody knows what it means, anyway.

The phrase originated with my mother's sister, Auntie, who died in February. Auntie was my mother's only sibling and the two of them were as dissimilar as it was possible for two sisters to be. My own sisters share this view. In the past, Lavander and Déja have gone so far as to ask my mother whether she was sure that she and her sister had the same parents. They had the same parents, all right. Any glance at the old family photos proves that much. It's how differently the two of them developed from those parents that really poses the conundrum.

Both my mother and her sister were born in South Africa to Russian immigrant parents who had lost many of their own family members to pogroms. Both were raised in the long shadow of this tragedy and both grew up under the specter of apartheid. From a very early age, my mother felt an acute sense of displacement and knew that she would have to leave South Africa, which, of course, is exactly what she did. Her sister, on the other hand, never felt the need to make a permanent move from her birthplace, although she traveled often and extensively.

I can never know exactly how my mother felt as a young woman, nor will I ever understand, fully, the relationship she had with her sister or her parents growing up. The dynamic of her family of origin is lost to me because she broke free from it before I was even born. What I do know about my mother, however, is that she is one of the most forward-moving individuals I have ever met. By this I mean that she has always been on a quest to evolve and, because of this, has been able to break from old patterns of thinking and behavior and move on. For me, her willingness to accept change and to modify her way of thinking is one of her best qualities. She is *hip*, for lack of a better word. And herein lies what was always the essential difference between my mother and her sister.

Auntie was only seven years older than my mother, yet the two of them might as well have been born in different centuries. Auntie was . . . well, *colonial* seems a fitting word. She married young and had four children over a seven-year period. Her husband became very wealthy through the garment business and, in time, she opened her own upscale boutique. They had a big, beautiful house, drivers, gardeners, and maids. Auntie's youngest child was born a few months after me, my mother's first. By the time I was old enough to understand what an "auntie" was, she and her family were already quite affluent. The flip side was that my mother and her family were, as far back as I can remember, the poor relatives. It's a cliché to say that money distorts relationships, yet clichés exist for the truth within them. In this case, the disparity between the net worth of my mother and her sister was a constant source of stress that fluctuated in intensity over the years but never, ever went away. Then, of course, there was the distance. For almost all of their lives, my mother and her sister had an average of five thousand miles between them.

My mother's relationship with her sister was a complicated one. They shared a powerful connection, but there was always a great and unyielding strain between them. By contrast, the relationship my siblings and I had with our aunt was fairly simple. We were never particularly close to her, geographically or temperamentally. When she came to visit, which was fairly often considering the distance, we morphed from people with individual personalities to "the children," amusing objects in my mother's virtual curio cabinet to be paraded out, clucked over, and put back away. For a long time, my mother went along with this dog and pony show, which pissed us off no end:

"Darling, can you go make us some tea, please?"

"Aren't they sweet? Like little miniature helpers."

"Maya, bring out your violin and play us something, darling. A little concert."

"Doesn't Debbie look lovely in those jeans? Do a little modeling for us, sweetheart. Let's see your figure."

This was only part of the show, however. A large portion of the theater that was a visit from my aunt involved the distribution of gifts. This is where the nuts came in. My aunt often brought clothing, which was hauled out and tried on and fashioned. But the special gifts, the ones she presented with the greatest ceremony, were things like nuts from the plane. It wasn't just the nuts, of course, because my aunt always flew first class. There were also slippers, headphones, chocolates, and blankets from the plane.

If I had to choose the precept that was most important for my parents to teach their children it would have to be the act of giving and receiving. Naturally, I am not talking about material gifts here. My father has always said that "money is the easiest thing to give," a sentiment echoed at various points by every one of his children. Time, attention, and love are the gifts that count, the gifts that should be graciously and generously given *and* received. It is here that I see the greatest gap between my mother and her sister because "nuts from the plane" has become the symbol of who our aunt was to us—what she gave and what we received. *My* sisters, her nieces, all became aunts themselves fifteen years ago. What they give, and receive, in that capacity marks the ultimate contrast in the two versions of "auntie."

As Blaze has grown older, his individual relationships with my sisters have become layered, intricate, and unique. Each one of them adores my child and loves him unconditionally. Yet each one holds him to a slightly different personal standard. Each one has different expectations for him. Blaze, in turn, modifies his behavior, even his personality, depending on which one of my sisters he's spending time with. His ability to morph into individual versions of Maya's nephew, Lavander's nephew, or Déja's nephew is fascinating to me. It is as if he is able to find and connect with the essence of my sisters and this is why he relates to each one differently. Through him, I am able to learn about my sisters on a level I wouldn't have access to any other way.

Blaze and Déja, for example, are only nine years apart, a much smaller age difference than the one between Déja and me. In a sense, she is more like an older sister to him than an aunt. And, of course, Déja was more like my baby than my sister before Blaze came along, so it all makes one of those perfect life loops.

Blaze has had a special kind of affection for Déja since he was a baby. Out of every member in my family, Déja has always been the one that Blaze has associated with pure fun and simple joy. Blaze always had unlimited access to Déja and to her many friends. He never got the kind of parental discipline from her that he got, in varying amounts, from everyone else. What he did get, aside from tremendous love, was a fierce protector and companion. For many years, Déja was also Blaze's primary baby-sitter. When Maya and I were both working nights, Déja came to my house, most often with friends in tow, and spent the evening there. Before she started driving, Déja gave up many of her weekend nights to stay with Blaze. Of course, there was something in this for her, too. Déja and her friends could hang out in our house without fear of parental interference or judgment. Maya and I always encouraged them to do this. We liked her crew and trusted them implicitly.

Almost all of Déja's friends, a bunch of slightly bent thespians like herself, were involved in the theater with her and well invested in the drama of life. Déja has formed more close friendships outside of our family than any one of us and many of her friends have become like extended family members, always welcome at any one of our houses. Part of this must have to do with the fact that, of all of us, Déja has moved around the least. She is the only sibling to have gone through elementary, middle, and high school in the same place. It's conceivable that she will maintain friendships forever with some of the people she first met in sixth grade. I find this astonishing. I have met several adults in my life who have these kind of long-term relationships and it always seemed somewhat exotic to me. For me, friends have always been transitory; gradually fading icons frozen in whatever part of my past they represented. I have very few close friends for this reason and, of those, only a couple I've known for longer than a decade. It has been much the same for Maya, although she has long been the more social of the two of us.

It was always important to Déja that her family liked her friends and that her friends liked her family. There was never a problem in either direction. Déja's friends were a diverse and unconventional group. Many of them were drawn to the theater because that was the social niche where they best fit: a minisociety where differences and alternative lifestyle choices were not only accepted but encouraged. And of course there was the constant drama, a very important component. For me, at least, unusual has always been more intriguing than usual and so Déja's friends of both sexes were always interesting and fun to have around. More than being interesting or unusual, however, almost all of

Déja's friends had one very important thing in common and that was a genuine kindness. I saw it often in the way they treated Déja and always in the way they treated Blaze.

Because they were at our house baby-sitting so often and because he adored everything about her, Blaze became close to Déja's friends, especially her posse of beautiful girlfriends. Emily and Meagan played games with him, Starkey took him trick-or-treating on Halloween, and Jessie cuddled him. All of them had long talks with him and were genuinely interested in what he had to say. Although they could hardly be considered his peer group, Blaze got along famously with this set of Bohemian teenagers.

Although I am loath to admit it, there were periods when I took Déja's devotion to Blaze for granted. Fortunately, there have also been times when I was reminded just what I had. One of those times happened on Blaze's eleventh birthday.

It was a Saturday and the height of the summer season in the restaurant where Maya and I were waitresses. I'd long since given up trying to create birthday parties for Blaze after a couple of spectacular failures, settling instead for small family affairs. Blaze never demanded much on this score anyway. If there was cake and a couple of gifts, he was generally content. That year, we had a muted celebration in the afternoon and at the end of the day, Déja arrived to baby-sit and Maya and I went off to work.

It was an exceptionally long night where it seemed that everyone who walked through the door wanted an extra dessert, another drink, more coffee, and no, were not yet ready for the check, thank you. I called Déja frequently throughout the shift, apologizing for being so late and promising to be back as soon as possible.

"It's no problem," she said. "A few of my friends came over and they're just waiting with me until you get back. Is that okay? You don't mind, do you?"

"Of course not," I told her.

It was almost midnight by the time Maya and I dragged our worn-out, garlic-scented selves home. I felt terrible about making Déja wait for so long as I was sure she had some kind of plan for a Saturday night that involved something a bit more stimulating than hanging out at my house. When I walked in, I saw my living room festooned with balloons and wrapping paper— none of which had been there when I left eight hours before. Also decorating the floor and couches were several of Déja's friends, drinking tea and eating popcorn. Déja herself was in the kitchen cleaning up the remains of what looked like a chocolate-chip-cookie-baking bonanza.

"We had a little party for Blaze," she said. "He just went to bed a little while ago. He was so excited. Look, everyone brought him something."

It was true, there were gifts everywhere. They had bought him board games and videos and a set of walkie-talkies. They had spent all night playing with him.

"I don't know what to say," I told the room at large. "You're all so sweet. This was such a nice thing for you to do for him."

"It was no big deal," Jessie said. "We love Blaze. He's so much fun."

I went into Blaze's room to say good night and found him sleeping, several gifts scattered on his bed. He stirred when I bent down to kiss his cheek.

"Hi, Mom. I had a good time tonight. We made cookies."

"I know. I saw all your presents."

"Yeah," he said, and drifted back to sleep in total contentment.

Of course, it wasn't the presents that made him so happy because Blaze has never been a very acquisitive kid. It was the time he got—time I didn't always have and couldn't always give him—that meant so much to him. Time and love were what he always got in abundance from Déja and what he—and I—could always count on.

In the comfort and warmth of all this freely given time, Blaze developed a complete trust in Déja and would often share feelings with her that I never got to hear. This started somewhat slowly and built as Blaze became more expressive in general. When I stopped waiting on tables and started working at home, there was no longer a need for Déja to baby-sit. The two of them started scheduling specific times to go out together. Together, they went on Blaze's favorite kind of adventure, an aimless drive. He'd tell her, "I don't want to ruin our time together with a destination," so they'd head out wherever the road would take them (as long as it passed some sort of convenience store so that he could get a Coke, a drink he and Déja shared a passion for).

They'd park at the beach train station with their Cokes in hand, watch the sunset, and wait for trains to go by. Later, Déja would tell me some of Blaze's stories. He complained to her that school was tough, that his teachers were mean, and that he was generally oppressed. There was substantial embellishment in these tales of woe, and Blaze usually made himself out to be very much the victim. Déja was alarmed at first and asked me if I knew what a terrible time the poor kid was having and what was I doing about it? She was even more alarmed when I laughed it off. He wouldn't get the kind of sympathy from me that he got from her, I told her. My line was always to tell him to do his job at school, to go with the flow and stop complaining. Other family members would tell him more or less the same thing. But with her, Blaze could vent without the possibility of censure. With her, his feelings were validated in a way they couldn't be with me or anyone else. Déja understood this and settled into the position of sounding board. She took his complaints with a grain of salt, but didn't lecture him.

Most likely inspired by his attendance at almost every one of Déja's performances over the years, Blaze started writing short plays a couple of years ago. His favorite subjects are fairy tales, reinterpreted. Casting these plays with family members is as much fun for him as actually writing them. Every one of his plays turns out to be a star vehicle for Déja. She is Dorothy, Cinderella, and Snow White. The part of the princess never goes to anyone else. Maya, Lavander, and I are most often relegated to the roles of ugly stepsisters or wicked stepmothers (so much for honoring thy mother) and my mother usually gets a fairy godmother or good witch role to play. With protestations, he'll sometimes change the parts a little (like when I refused to play Aunt Em and insisted on Glinda the Good Witch *at least*), but the shining beacon is always Déja, and the prince (a necessary character, but never one with too many lines) is Danny. In Blaze's metaphorically inclined mind, Déja will always be the fairest one of all, a fun-loving, Coke-drinking, peerless princess. Through Blaze's eyes, it's no stretch at all to see Déja this way.

A few years ago, I took Blaze to one of Déja's plays, although I can't remember which now because there have been so many. There was a whole scene before Déja's entrance and so some waiting for the main event as far as Blaze was concerned, but my sidelong glances in the darkened theater showed that he was, if not rapt, at least paying attention. My own attention was fixed half on him and half on the play. It was usually like this when I took him to Déja's performances—I could never be entirely focused on her or the play while Blaze was sitting next to me since I was always anticipating that he'd speak out loudly by accident or demand to go to the bathroom or something similar. With very few exceptions, however, he was remarkably well behaved at Déja's events. Still, my eyes kept sliding over to his face, just to make sure. This is how I managed to see his expression when Déja made her entrance on the stage. He took a short indrawn breath. The light of adoration came shining through his eyes, brightening his entire face.

"Déja," he whispered, looking at her, not me, and with that, he said it all: *Look at her. Isn't she beautiful? Isn't she wonderful? Isn't she just the best thing ever?*

And yes, she was.

Of all of us, only Lavander has expressed some disappointment that Déja is always the princess in Blaze's mental fairy tales. She came out with it a few weeks ago when we were all gathered at a family dinner at her house. Blaze was upstairs in her bedroom, watching one of the DVDs she keeps on hand for him. The rest of us were gathered around her dining room table. We were talking about how comfortable her house was and how neat and clean. Lavander is the only person in our family to have a candy dish in her living room and guest towels in her bathroom. She is also the only person in whose house one has to search for the trash since it's always so well hidden away.

"I don't know why we don't come here more often," Maya said. "It's so nice here."

"And Lavander's such a good hostess," my mother added.

"Mmm," I said. "This is what my house would look like if I didn't live with people who don't notice when the floors or windows are dirty. And Blaze doesn't make a mess in your house, I see. He loves it here."

"Yes, but he wouldn't want to come if Déja wasn't here," Lavander said. "Déja, the princess. Who can compete with that?" Her tone was playful, but there was an element of seriousness in her comment.

"Please," I said, "you're hardly alone there. I have to play the wicked stepsister. And I'm his *mother*."

"Hmm," Lavander said, unconvinced.

"It's not true, you know," Maya told Lavander. "He's crazy about you. As we were pulling up, Blaze said, 'I can't *wait* to see Lavander.' He was so excited. Didn't he?" Maya looked over at me.

"He did," I nodded, wishing I'd remembered a fraction of a second earlier so that I could have told her that. It was the kind of thing one couldn't hear too often and the kind of thing that didn't get said often enough.

"Did he?" Lavander said, her eyes filling with quick tears. "Did he really?"

"Yes," I said. "He loves spending time with you."

I think about the truth of this now. Blaze does relish his time with Lavander, but the quality of it and his relationship with her is very different from what he has with Déja. Occasionally, Blaze and Déja get into minor skirmishes over plans (Blaze insists on a free-form approach with Déja and gets bent out of shape when she has specific errands to run or places to be), but, as a rule, the time they spend together is about *fun*, pure and simple. Déja keys into whatever mood Blaze is in and lets him set the tone. She doesn't demand specific behavior from him and is always fiercely protective of his right to express himself in any way he wants. She wouldn't dream of asking him to accompany her on a trip to the mall, for example (retail clothing stores are Blaze's equivalent of hell's inner circle) or even taking a route that he doesn't like. She indulges him, in other words, and this suits Blaze just fine. Lavander, on the other hand, presents another kettle of fish altogether. In a way, I feel that the time he spends with her is the most important for him in terms of how well he presents himself to the world outside the protective shell of his family.

For a variety of reasons, Lavander was never a designated
baby-sitter for Blaze when he was little. Most of these had to do
with the fact that there were several other family members willing to pick up this particular slack when needed. Lavander has
never been the stay-at-home type anyway and, by the time Blaze
was born, she'd gotten her driver's license and was out all the
time. This is not to say that she didn't see him often, but when
she did, there were always plenty of other people around. Only
in the last few years have the two of them started spending time
alone together. As a result, Lavander has never perceived Blaze
as a baby and has never offered the same kinds of indulgences
that Déja, Maya, or I do. She expects a certain level of maturity
from him as well. The funny thing is that she, and only she, gets
that level consistently. In her case, Blaze is the protective one
and he wants to rise to her expectations.

Early on, Blaze started doing things with Lavander that he
wouldn't consider doing with anyone else. He's been known to
take out her trash and help her clean her house, for example.
When Lavander first got her real estate license and was trying to
drum up business, Blaze went with her door to door as she
dropped off business cards. This wasn't a chore for him, it was
an activity he actually looked forward to and he'd call her asking
when they could go "carding" together. And then there is the
shopping. With Lavander, Blaze will spend an entire afternoon
running errands, rifling though linens and kitchen supplies
without a complaint. He'll go with her to Target, a store so far off
his list I can't even mention it without a hue and cry from him
about how I am never to even entertain the possibility that he
will darken its door. I want to stress here that if there were *any*
other family members involved in these activities, Blaze would
revert to his usual pattern of refusal, but with Lavander alone, he
is always willing—and happy—to go.

I've wondered about why Blaze is so willing to modify his routines with Lavander and it's true that she simply expects it from him, but there's more to it than that. I've held up the same kinds of expectations and he just ignores them. Lavander has always treated Blaze like a young adult and that is something that none of the rest of us can claim. So, during the time he spends with Lavander, Blaze becomes that young adult.

Blaze has never been an indicator of what is "in" or trendy with his peers and so I've been constantly out of touch with what's happening in his social milieu. He's never wanted to dress a certain way, participate in sports, or requested the kinds of video games that have been popular at any given point. As a result, I don't know what's in or out or even what is considered "normal" out there.

But Lavander does.

Lavander has always had an innate sense of what's in fashion in every social arena. Perhaps even more important, she knows what's out, when it went out, and why. This a real and very valuable talent. It's as if she holds a set of blueprints to the maze that is social interaction. Of course, what one does when one is actually wandering around in that maze is a matter of individual style and personality. Still, I've always thought that knowing the shape and color of the social structure offers an important leg up to understanding how to *be* in the world, without compromising one's individuality. In other words, *in* it but not *of* it. Lavander is way ahead of the rest of us in this respect. And this is why what she gives to Blaze is so significant.

There are the little things:

"Debra, how can you let him wear those swim trunks? He looks like an old man."

"But there's nothing wrong with them."

"They're awful. Here, I bought some new ones for him. All the surfers wear these and he's going to look great in them."

"Okay."

"And I can't believe he's still wearing those shoes. Those things haven't been in style for, like, ten years. Kids get picked on for things like this, you know."

"He doesn't get picked on."

"How do you know?"

"I'd know."

"But how do you know what people are *saying*?"

After taking his considerations into account, I consult Lavander on almost all the clothes I buy for Blaze. If she approves, I know I've gotten it right. And it's not just the clothes. Lavander was the one who bought Blaze a handheld Nintendo and then a Playstation and introduced him to video games—something that "every other kid his age is into."

Then there are the bigger things. It was Lavander who took Blaze to the go-cart track so he could practice driving, something he obviously wasn't going to get from me. The go-cart "experience," as I like to call it now, happened just recently and gave me much insight into the nature of their relationship. The two of them went off, happily enough, with a friend of Lavander's who has two small boys of her own. A couple of hours later, Lavander called me from her car.

"Look, there was a small accident," she said.

"What do you mean?"

"Well, I didn't know that Blaze wouldn't be able to handle the go-carts," she said. "I mean, nobody told me or anything."

"What are you talking about?" I asked, starting to get worried.

"He doesn't know how to handle those things. He was going way too fast and then he couldn't steer. People were yelling and he crashed into the side. He hurt his knee—but it's okay, we bandaged it up—I'm sorry, okay? Don't be angry at me—I didn't know. . . ."

I could hear Blaze muttering something in the background. "No, I'm not going to tell her that," Lavander said to him in response.

"I don't care if he banged his knee," I said. "Big deal. He's not bleeding or unconscious or in the emergency room, right? So he got a scrape—why are you so upset?"

"Because I'm worried you're going to be pissed at me for taking him somewhere dangerous."

"It's a *go-cart*," I said. "That's not dangerous. Skydiving is dangerous."

"Well, I . . . Look, I'm pulling into your driveway now. Don't freak out when you see his knee."

I hung up the phone just as Blaze was walking in the front door. "Look at my knee!" he shouted by way of greeting. I inspected the damage, which was really quite minor and had already been well dressed and bandaged.

"Looks okay," I told him. "What's the big fuss about?"

"Aren't you mad at Lavander?" he asked me.

"No, of course not. I'm not mad at anyone. So you hurt your knee. Next time you'll do better, right?"

"Next time?" He was puzzled. "You'll let me go again?"

"Yes, that's how you learn," I told him. I went out to find Lavander, who hadn't even come into the house. She was sitting in her car, ready to leave and visibly upset.

"I don't understand why you're so freaked out about this," I told her. "I really don't care that he banged his knee a little, you know. It's good for him. Next time, he'll be more careful."

"Next time?" she said, incredulous. "Oh no, I'm not taking him back there again. Are you kidding?"

"But why not?" I asked her. "Who better to take him driving? Or practice driving anyway?"

"I'm really worried about him," she said then. "How's he ever going to be able to drive? He was so uncoordinated. He had no idea what he was doing. I mean, this should just come naturally, you know. If you could have seen him . . ."

I still couldn't understand why she seemed so agitated. I

would have been extremely surprised if Blaze had just hopped into a go-cart and driven around like he'd been born to the road. He's never been a particularly well coordinated kid. Then it finally made sense to me. This was nothing new for me, but for Lavander, who hadn't experienced it directly and who had the highest expectations for Blaze to be just like everybody else, it must have been like a shock of cold water.

"You can't give up," I said. "He'll be able to do this and he'll be able to drive someday. He just needs more practice than most people. I don't want him to be afraid or to think that he can't do it because you think he can't do it. If that happens, he really won't be able to."

"I wouldn't have thought you'd want me to take him again after this," she said.

"A scraped knee is really not a big deal," I said.

"Oh, but you don't know what he said to me when it happened," she said. "He told me, 'You are a terrible aunt. I've injured myself and my mother will never let me go out with you again.'"

"What!?!"

"Oh yes," she said. "He went *off* on how much trouble I was going to be in."

"What a manipulator, to deflect blame onto you! Why would I be angry at you? If anything, I'd be annoyed at him for not being more careful. And he probably feels like he let you down. I can't believe this child. You've been played."

"Hmm," she said, but she was unconvinced. I stood out there for several more minutes, leaning into her car, stressing again how it didn't matter at all to me that he'd gotten into a collision, how important it was that he try it again, and how vital it was that she be the one to take him. And he definitely needed to apologize to her for being such a jerk, I told her. Most definitely.

"I don't know, Deb," she said finally. "I just don't know."

The following weekend, she took him again. This time he drove extraordinarily slowly, prompting Lavander to laugh. But he didn't crash and he was ever so slightly more coordinated.

It was because Blaze intuitively understood Lavander that he knew which buttons to press that day at the go-cart track and he pressed them because he hates the thought that she might be disappointed in him. Most often, he is extremely careful with her. More careful, in fact, than he is with anyone else. "Lavander is a very sensitive person," he told me once. "It's important to be nice to her."

"It's important to be nice to everybody," I responded.

"But it's especially important for Lavander," he said.

In the last year, Lavander and Blaze have become much closer than they were before. She tells me that Blaze is "good company," one of her most important criteria. "I really enjoy spending time with him," she says. "I can talk to him about anything." I don't ask her or Blaze what the two of them talk about when they are together. I consider it both private and precious. All I need is what I already know, that Lavander will always challenge Blaze to be the best person he can be in terms of his awareness of himself in the world, and along with that, will always be there, believing in him.

I see the two of them in my mind's eye now, Blaze with his long arm swung around Lavander's little shoulders, and smile to myself. One of the flight attendants is walking by my seat and takes my grin as a silent request for another complimentary beverage.

"No, thank you," I tell her. "I'm fine." This is a short flight and it's almost over. I'll be home soon. Maya and Blaze will be there to pick me up.

I've done quite a bit of traveling to promote my books over the last couple of years. Whenever possible, I've taken Maya and Blaze with me, but most often I go solo. I always miss them when I am on the road alone. The three of us have been a unit for a long time and, with the two of them, I can always find my center. This level of comfort notwithstanding, taking them on the road for a book tour wasn't the best idea for any of us. Still, there was never a shortage of hilarious moments and I wouldn't have traded one second of those adventures.

The first time, in August of 2000, the three of us flew to San Francisco together, where I had a few appearances scheduled to promote *Waiting*. To start, I gave a lunchtime reading in a bookstore in the middle of the city. The crowd was a decent size but totally unenthusiastic and I started to sweat. Blaze and Maya were seated exactly in front of me, a few rows back so that whenever I looked up from the page to make eye contact, they were who I saw first. Thus, it was impossible not to notice the scuffle over my mother's new digital camera that broke out between the two of them while I was in the middle of my reading. Maya held fast to the camera while Blaze attempted to tear it from her hand. Back and forth they went. Their chairs started to rock with the effort. Any second, I thought, one of them is going to scream and then I'm going to have to die right here. I looked back down at the page, still reading (albeit a bit louder), and could smell the stink of fear coming off me in waves.

When I opened the floor to questions, Blaze's hand was the first to pop up. I refused to call on him because I was almost positive that he had some sort of non sequitur cued up ("When do we get to ride on BART?" for example) that would further estrange this already apathetic crowd.

"Why didn't you take Blaze's question?" Maya asked me when it was all over. I rolled my eyes as if that would be answer enough. "He had a good question," she said. "He wanted to know if you ever served old bread."

"With bites taken out of it," Blaze added.

"Well, how would I have known that?" I asked Maya, sotto voce.

"You know I wouldn't have let him ask it if it wasn't a good question" she said. "Don't you?"

"I don't know," I said, "it seemed like you were too busy fighting over the camera to be discussing the questions."

Maya shook her head. "You should have called on him," she said.

There was a similar scene the next day when I had a radio interview at one of San Francisco's biggest stations. To begin with, we arrived late, having run twenty minutes from the BART station without any clue as to where we were going. I left the two of them in the waiting room when I went into the studio and assumed they were settled. Well into my hour-long interview, I turned slightly to look into the control booth behind me and saw a frantic struggle between my son and my sister over what looked suspiciously like the kill switch for the whole broadcast. From the corner of my eye, it seemed very much like one of those cartoon fights where all you see is a rolling ball of arms, legs, dust, and feathers. I turned my head back to face the host and finished the show, expecting, at any minute, to hear the glass breaking behind me and the two of them to come crashing through. I was surprised, then, when I saw the two of them smiling broadly when I was reunited with them after the show. Blaze flashed a cassette with great pride. He and Maya had been invited into the recording studio where he'd recorded a long monologue about his adventures on BART.

"What the hell was going on back there?" I asked Maya. "I almost had a heart attack when I saw the two of you."

"Why would you worry?" she said. "Don't you think I've got it under control?"

Despite the madness of that jaunt to San Francisco, we decided to try it again the following summer. This time, the three of us flew to Portland where I was starting a West Coast loop. I scheduled a couple of free days before the tour began in earnest so that we could walk around the city and visit all the places we used to live. I thought I'd take advantage of Blaze's constant desire to revisit the past and show him where he was born and where he spent the first year of his life. I hadn't been to Portland since we'd moved to California thirteen years before. Maya and I christened the trip the Memory Lane Tour.

Again, it wasn't the smoothest of visits. Blaze had an almost total lack of interest in seeing where we used to live, work, or go to school. He didn't want to see old friends or visit any of the three homes my family had lived in. What he did want was to ride on every form of public transportation Portland had to offer (including buses, trolleys, and trains). But this was minor. The most pressing problem was that Blaze couldn't find a single thing in the entire city that appealed to his palate.

"I don't eat in other states," he announced after gagging over a plate of restaurant pasta. Maya was on me like white on rice after this pronouncement. How could we stay for two more days if he wasn't going to eat anything, she wanted to know. Why wasn't I doing anything about this? What was wrong with me—didn't I care?

Well, of course I *cared*, I told her, but to myself I had to admit that I relaxed in my motherhood when Maya was with me, especially when we were all away from home. In Maya, I felt as if I had a partner who could pick up the slack where

Blaze was concerned. After all, aside from me, who knew him better? Who else had been as close to him since the day of his birth?

It is nearly impossible to give a name to who Maya is for Blaze. For example, although she's been very much like his parent, she has never been a surrogate mother to him. Maya doesn't play the role of father for Blaze, either. She is his aunt, yes, but to give that as her title is to understate their relationship. Blaze has never called her Aunt Maya or Auntie Maya. Occasionally, he accidentally calls her Mom and then follows it hastily with "No, Maya. I meant *Maya*." He used to get very embarrassed when this happened, as if he'd made a grave mistake, but these days he just corrects himself and moves on to call her what she is, simply Maya, an entity to herself. In a way, this echoes the way Maya and I refer to each other. When Maya mentions our sisters in conversations with others, they are "my sister, Lavander," or "my sister, Déja." When she refers to me, it is always just as "my sister." I never even put "sister" before her name when I talk about her. She is the part of me who is Maya. This, too, is the closest I can come to a definition for who she is to Blaze. And this is why I had the luxury of relaxing somewhat when it started to look as if Blaze was going on a three-day hunger strike in Portland. Maya was there, after all. It would work out.

This past summer, the logistics of my travel made it impossible for Maya and Blaze to come with me, as I was scheduled for a two-week tour covering both coasts. Long before I left, Maya and Blaze went into planning mode, discussing everything they'd like to do while I was gone. Eventually, Maya told Blaze to type up a list and post it on the fridge so that they could check off each item as they went. By the time I packed my suitcase, the list was already up, taped discreetly to the side of the fridge.

Things to do when Mom is gone:

1. Go to Disneyland
2. Make curried lentils
3. Karaoke
4. Explore the places you went to do concerts and see where
   you go for orchestra
5. Go in the pool with clothes on
6. Get the video camera fixed
7. Make bagels
8. Sing the songs that you and Mom wrote

The list made me laugh and it almost made me cry. It occurred to me that it could just as easily be titled "Things I could do with Mom but are *so much better* with Maya." "These are great," Maya told Blaze when she read his list. "We can do all of these. If you want, we can even add some more."

When my sisters are asked whether or not they plan to have children of their own (and they are all at an age where this kind of question tends to come up fairly frequently), they have some interesting responses. Déja says she wants to have children *for sure*. Someday. Lavander is realizing that she doesn't and is in the process of reconciling this choice with what she feels (and I agree) is a societal imperative to reproduce. And Maya? Maya says that she doesn't need to have children. She's had Blaze, she says, and that is enough for her.

I am holding this thought in my head as the pilot announces our imminent arrival in America's Finest City and we start our descent. The nuts on my tray table remain unopened and so I grab them and stuff them into my bag. The plane lands and I walk outside into the warm California sun. I stand with my bag at my feet for five minutes or so before I spy Maya and Blaze pulling up to the airport curb. Blaze gets out of the car, surrendering his coveted spot in the front seat for me.

"Hi, Mom," he says without coming in for a kiss or a hug. It's always like this when I come back from a trip. He likes to check me out for a second or two, make sure I haven't grown a second head or a third arm in my absence and am still the mom he knows.

"Hi, honey," I say, and give him a big, squeezing hug. "Missed you."

I settle into the front seat and Maya looks over at me with a small smile. "Hiya," she says. "How was the flight?"

"Fine," I tell her.

Nobody speaks for the next few minutes. We shift and readjust to each other as I move into the space that Blaze and Maya create around themselves when I am gone. Maya hits the play button for the CD and the song that's been going through my head since I woke up this morning comes ringing through the speakers. I turn my head and smile at Blaze.

"You guys have a good time while I was gone?" I ask him.

"Yeah," he says. "We made an excellent cake. We made *white* frosting, Mom, because, as you know, I don't like chocolate."

"So, I guess you didn't get to your science homework then?"

Blaze and Maya give each other a quick, guilty glance.

"You know, that's really not our thing," Maya says.

I do know and I'm glad it's not their thing. What they have is so much better. I have a sudden, unexpected wave of sadness for my mother. Her sister was never to us what mine are to Blaze. A big part of the joy I have in my sisters is tied to the love they have for my son and the roles they play in his life. My mother never got to experience that particular form of joy and for that I am sorry in so many ways. I can only hope that she gains some of what she missed through her daughters, my sisters, three exceptional aunties.

"I brought you something," I tell Maya as we turn onto the freeway.

"Nuts from the plane?" she says. "I really hope it's nuts from the plane."

"How did you know?" I ask her, and pull them out of my bag.

Déja and Lavander.

9

Separate Realities

november

This year, Lavander hosted Thanksgiving at her place. It is usually held at my parents' house. This was the second Thanksgiving in a row at her house and, despite some reticence on her part ("Um, are we going to do this here every year now? How did this get to be the location?"), I think this might be a new tradition. Part of the reason for the switch in scene is that there is more space in Lavander's house than any of our other homes. She had just moved in when we gathered for Thanksgiving last year and was eager to get her house broken in and comfortable and so she offered to host. It turned out to be one of the best holidays we'd ever spent together as a group.

Thanksgiving is an important day in my family. Every year, my father goes around the table questioning all of us as to what we are all truly thankful for in this life. Despite the fact that all of us take the opportunity to give at least one flippant answer, we always take some time to reflect on what is really important to all of us, and family is usually uppermost on the list.

Unfortunately, Thanksgiving is also a time for at least one argument (or, as Blaze has taken to calling it, a family conflict). After thanks are given, the food is consumed, and we're playing any one of a variety of board games, the disagreements start, the competition for attention heats up, and, presto, there's a fight. There's no real reason this has to happen every year, but I believe that all families operate along the lines of conditioned responses (especially at the holidays) and ours is no different. Last year, however, there were two key changes in the pattern. The first was the new venue. The second, although I hate to admit it, was the karaoke machine. Don't get me wrong, I love music and enjoy singing as much as the next person, but karaoke is, in my opinion, just plain geeky. Or, if you prefer, *dorky*. It was Maya, self-proclaimed queen of the dorks, who bought the karaoke machine and then turned everyone into a believer. She brought the machine, along with an astonishing variety of tunes (Motley Crüe on karaoke—who knew?) to Lavander's house last year and it was an immediate hit. Instead of playing games (or even speaking to each other) after we ate dinner, the whole family gathered in Lavander's living room and we made unabashed fools of ourselves singing karaoke. Although Maya is the only one who would admit to having the heart of a lounge singer, once the microphone was in our hands, the rest of us had no trouble adopting that persona as well. The highlight of the evening was my parents' duet of "I Got You Babe" with my father doing vocals that sounded like Sonny Bono via Bob Dylan. We laughed until we were breathless and weeping. Despite some jockeying for the microphone and Blaze's insistence on listening to feedback every time he had a turn, there was nary a single argument the whole night.

Because the combination of karaoke and Lavander's peerless abilities as hostess was such a success last year, we attempted to re-create it again this year. Maya spent a great deal of money (so much, in fact, that she wouldn't even disclose the exact sum) on karaoke CDs this year in an effort to find something to please every taste. She hit the karaoke store hard, coming home for at least two weeks with this greeting: "Look what I found! Gershwin! Tom Petty! Snoop Dogg! Frank Sinatra!"

She stayed up all night creating and printing out multiple listings of her collection, cross-referenced by artist and song title.

"You need help," I told her.

"Don't be such a wet blanket about the karaoke," she said. "I want to make sure everybody gets something they like. Everybody must sing!"

What she meant by "everybody," I knew, included some of the more reserved participants (Danny and Bo) and Tony, who Lavander had told us was also going to be joining us for Thanksgiving. To this end, Maya's list included plenty of hip-hop for Danny and Bo and a collection of heavy metal ballads for Tony.

In retrospect, it was perhaps predictable that karaoke lightning wouldn't strike twice. This is not to say that sparks weren't generated, but Thanksgiving this year turned out to be a largely subdued event. For one thing, it was the first family dinner for almost a year that included Tony and it seemed to me that there was a concerted effort on our parts to be pleasant and low-key for Lavander's sake. For *his* part, Tony was fairly jovial and kept up his end of the rotating conversations. He seemed well-informed as to what was going on in everybody's lives. He seemed, in fact, very *familiar* and I found it disconcerting. On Thanksgiving, I realized that he was in possession of some personal information (certain items about Blaze and about my love life) that had certainly come from Lavander, the only person with whom I'd chosen to share these things. What's more, he was talking to me as if *I'd* told him all of this, as if . . . well, as if he *knew* me. I tried as well as I could to shrug it off, but I found it perturbing. Adding to this mild but persistent vexation was the fact that Lavander seemed to be watching me when I talked to him, as if she were waiting for something to happen. I was clueless as to what that something was, but I felt as if I should, somehow, be on my best behavior.

The place I felt the most comfortable at that point was at Lavander's kitchen counter, parked in front of a tray of mozzarella caprese, so that was where I stayed until we all sat down for dinner. The food was something else that distinguished this Thanksgiving from all the others. For the first time ever, there was actually too much of it. Lavander made a giant version of her appetizer platter (a dish she appropriated from my father) and it was impossible not to pick away at her marinated mushrooms, cheeses, and olives until well past the point of satiety. My father made two large trays of baked ziti and lasagna and Maya prepared a huge pot pie. There were groans of discomfort well before dessert landed on the table.

Dessert was my course this year and I made the mistake of introducing something new and different for this crowd of pedestrian eaters. Having recently discovered an affinity for baking cheesecake, I made three of them: pumpkin, rum raisin, and pashka. The boring, standard pumpkin went over just fine, but I got into trouble with the other two. The rum raisin was made with cottage cheese, among other ingredients, which was apparently some sort of affront to nature. "Cottage cheese is *food*," Danny protested, "not dessert." I protested that he wouldn't even have detected the cottage cheese if I hadn't told him that it was there, but it was to no avail—he got plenty of support on his position from others at the table. At least the rum raisin cheese-cake was sampled. The pashka (a cheesecake made with ricotta, glacé fruits, and molded overnight in a flower pot) was too exotic for anyone to even try.

"Weird texture," Déja said.

"Smells funny," Lavander said.

"What *is* that?" Danny said.

"Bunch of ingrates," I countered.

"You know how it is," my mother said, and repeated an oft-quoted Yiddish expression that translates, roughly, into "When the mouse is full, even the grain tastes bitter."

Tony was the only one who didn't offer an opinion on the cheesecake. He couldn't eat any, he said, because he had a sec-ond dinner to attend somewhere else. Family obligations, he said. Lavander seemed disappointed. Her table was spread with uneaten cheesecakes and her kitchen was full of leftovers. Nobody seemed to know what to do about this and, for a while, we just stared at it all, stunned.

"Where did all this food come from?" Déja asked. "Seems like we really overdid it this year."

"Is it time for karaoke?" Maya asked, and got a lukewarm response along the lines of "Maybe later." Undaunted, she pro-ceeded to hand out copies of her cross-referenced song list.

"Could you be a bigger dork?" Déja asked, laughing over her copy.

"No," Maya said. "Not really."

While everybody was shuffling through the lists, picking out songs that they maybe, possibly, might sing, I went in search of Lavander, who had drifted away from the table. I was on a mis-sion, actually, and I was hoping she could help me.

I've recently lost enough weight so that none of my clothes fit properly anymore. Like many women I know, I have clothing that falls into two categories: "fat" and "thin." When pants or skirts get too tight, I've got other, more forgiving clothes to replace them and for those happy times when there are loose folds of fabric, I've got slimmer backups. These days, though, even my "thin" clothes are too big and nothing looks right. Shopping for clothes has never been particularly fun for me and the thought of searching through endless stores looking for a pair of pants that wasn't too long, so high it hugged my ribcage, or so low it required thong jewelry, was totally repugnant. I was hoping that Lavander would have a pair or two of blue jeans that she didn't wear anymore and wouldn't mind passing on to me. It was a risk because my sister is a tiny thing (Lavander also has two categories of clothing: "thin" and "thinner") and I'd just eaten a full Thanksgiving dinner, but I was willing to take it for the possibility of a pair of jeans that fit me.

I found her upstairs in her bedroom, tidying.

"What are you up to?" I asked her.

"I had a phone call," she said. "And then I just saw some stuff that needed to be put away."

"Maya's got all her karaoke stuff ready down there, rarin' to go," I told her.

"Yeah, I saw," Lavander said. "I was going to come down in a second."

"I was wondering if you had any old jeans that are maybe too big for you," I said. "I really need a pair of jeans and I think I might actually be able to fit into one of yours."

"I'm sure I've got something," she said, and marched into her walk-in closet, one side of which looked very much like a department store since dozens of the garments there still had their sales tags attached. Unlike me, Lavander loves to shop and has no problem finding clothes that fit. I rarely go shopping with her for this reason. For example, I'll be standing on my side of the dressing room, agonizing over whether to buy a pair of boring black pants that might look okay if I have them hemmed and Lavander will stand next to me, tossing around bell bottoms that lace up the side and tops trimmed in fake fur that all look great on her as is.

"You should get some of these," she'll say.

"I can't wear that."

"Why not? You know, you ought to *live* a little, Deb."

Come to think of it, I can't really go shopping with any of my sisters. Maya is what my mother calls a "depressed shopper." For her, nothing ever looks good and everything is overpriced. This attitude usually extends to me as well when I am with her:

"Do you like this?" I'll ask her.

"No."

"What about this?"

"No."

"This?"

"No."

Déja hates shopping as much as I do and would much rather go the vintage or resale route than to a department store. She has little patience when it comes to trying on clothes and can never find anything in her price range. My mother calls her "an irritated shopper." Lavander, on the other hand, is a "frantic shopper." While the rest of us will at least look through the sale racks for bargains, Lavander never buys on sale what she can get for full price. In fact, Lavander overspends on just about everything she buys. For her, "cheap" is an ugly concept on every level and in her quest to avoid looking, acting, or being cheap, Lavander often goes to extremes. In our family, Lavander is the top earner by far and always the person with the least cash on hand. As I peered into her closet, I had a clear view of where some of that money had gone.

"Okay," she said, emerging from the folds of her wardrobe. "Here are three pair. I haven't worn these forever. See if they work."

I held the jeans in front of me, becoming a little frightened when I saw how small they looked.

"Are these your *big* jeans?" I asked her. "I can't believe I'm going to try these on after eating a Thanksgiving dinner. Could there be a worse time to do this?"

"Just try them," she said. "You always think you look bigger than you do. You've got a great body. I've always thought so."

"What do you mean?"

"When I was little, I thought you were hot. I always wanted to look like you."

"When was that?" I asked her, baffled.

"I don't know. When you were about sixteen, I guess, and you were going out with that guy. What was his name?"

"Never mind him," I said, "when I was sixteen you were *seven*. You thought I was hot when you were seven? You noticed things like that? You were so little."

Lavander shrugged and pulled a black jacket from her closet. The sleeves and collar were trimmed with faux leopard.

"Did you hear about this jacket?" she asked me.

"Is that the one you paid a million dollars for that Mom found for thirty bucks at Marshall's?"

"I can't believe it," she said. "It's the *same* jacket. I bought it at this boutique and they *swore* it was one of a kind."

"And I suppose you can't return it."

"No, I can't," she wailed.

"How much did you pay for it, really?"

"I can't tell you." She bit her lip. "Three hundred dollars."

"What!?!?"

Déja walked in as I was sputtering and smiled at the two of us.

"What's going on?" she said.

"Lavander's jacket," I said, as if this would explain it all.

"Ooh," Déja said. "Is that the one you paid all that money for?" She looked at the jacket. "It *is* nice. Can I try it on?"

"Go ahead," Lavander sighed. While Déja tried it on, I squeezed myself into Lavander's jeans. They were on the tight side, but, to my grateful astonishment, they all fit.

"Look, look!" I said. "I fit into Lavander's jeans. I'm so excited about this."

"That jacket looks great on you, Déj," Lavander said, ignoring my happy outburst.

"It does, doesn't it?" Déja said. "You know, I really need a jacket."

"You can't have it," Lavander said. "The tag is still on it. I've never even worn it. And you know how much I paid for it."

"Are you sure?" Déja said. "I really, really need a jacket."

"Déja!"

"Okay," Déja said, and took it off. "Pity. We'd better go downstairs now. They're all gearing up for the karaoke." She handed the jacket off to Lavander and left the room.

I'd finished putting the jeans on and off by then and stacked them all in a neat pile on Lavander's bed. "Thank you so much for these," I told her. "I can't tell you how much time and trouble you've saved me."

"You're welcome," Lavander said. She stood looking at the overpriced jacket in her hand for a second or two as if she were solving a puzzle in her head. "Déja!" she called, and, in a moment, Déja popped her head back in the door.

"Here," Lavander said, handing her the jacket, "you can have it."

"What? Really?"

"It looks better on you anyway," Lavander sighed.

Déja enveloped Lavander in a hug and squealed with delight. "That was quick," she said to me. "Usually she waits a day or two before she gives it to me. Thank you, Lavy. You're the best sister in the world." She winked at me. "But don't tell the others," she said.

The three of us headed downstairs then, Déja and I laden with our gifts and crowing about how happy we were. It was like going to a store, we told the gathered crowd, and finding everything you want for free. Even better, I said, was discovering that I was small enough to fit into Lavander's jeans. I considered it a personal best. I held my stack of jeans up in a victory salute.

"Looks like you scored, huh?" Tony said to me, and there it was again, that note of familiarity and my ensuing discomfort. What was it that was bothering me, I wondered, and why didn't I know?

Maya had set up the karaoke machine in the middle of the living room and was no longer accepting refusals to sing from anyone. My mother offered to go first, but Maya offered the microphone to Tony and pointed out the songs she thought he might like. Tony begged off, saying that he had to leave and go to his second dinner. Lavander asked him if he would come back afterward and he said he didn't think so. She asked him why not and he said he thought it might be too late. He said good-bye to all of us and Lavander went outside to see him off. She shut the door behind her and a brief ripple and murmur went through the room. Would have been nice if he'd stayed, somebody said. He's got family to see, someone else countered. Still, the consensus went, for Lavander's sake he could have stayed a little longer.

When she came back inside, Lavander took her place on the couch and even did a rousing karaoke rendition of "Baby Got Back" which made everybody laugh, but her heart wasn't really in it. Nor, it turned out, was anyone else's. Déja refused to sing anything and Danny complained the songs were scripted incorrectly on the screen. After a couple of tunes, people started criticizing each other's ability to follow the music, read the lyrics, and pick songs that were in an appropriate range. Bo and Lavander got into it over one of these items and then he left in a huff, signaling the beginning of the end of the party. Maya and I decided that, rather than waiting for the little smoldering disagreements to ignite into a major conflagration, we should leave while the going was still relatively good. Knowing when to leave, in my opinion, is as much an art as anything else.

It's been pretty quiet around here over the last few days since our Thanksgiving dinner. Maya got some sort of stomach ailment right afterward and spent the next day in bed. My feeling was that her disorder was psychosomatic, spurred by karaoke disappointment, but I would never have mentioned that. As always, she accused me of being cold and unfeeling while she was sick.

"How is it you don't even come in and offer me a cup of tea?" she said.

"You hide out in your room with the door closed," I told her. "If you were out in the living room, I'd be happy to make you some tea."

"So I should lie on the couch in my sickness and bring everyone else down?"

"Yes," I said. "I can't come running into your room."

"As usual," she said, "you're the very soul of compassion."

She's back on her feet now and off rehearsing with her orchestra. Blaze is in his room, watching a movie, finished with me for the evening. I decide to call Lavander to say hello and see how she's feeling.

"What's the matter?" she says when she answers the phone and finds out I'm on the other end.

"Nothing's the matter," I tell her. "I just called to see how you were doing. To see what's up. Why does something have to be the matter?"

"Well, it's just that you never call," she says. "So I figured something's got to be wrong."

"Come on, Lavander, that's not true. I do call, you just don't ever answer your phone. Anyway, I'm calling you *now*, so let's get on with it, okay? How's it going?"

She tells me that things are fine, but that she's starting to get busy now. There all kinds of Christmas parties coming up through work, she says, and she has to go to every one of them whether she wants to or not. And then there are the gifts she has to buy and they have to be *nice*; she can't buy anything cheap for her managers. Do I have any ideas, she wants to know. I suggest gift baskets and she laughs. Gift baskets are nothing special, she says. She gives a gift basket practically every day. I tell her I can't think of anything else because I'm so out of the loop. I have no idea what goes on the business world that she's in and I don't know how she does it. Then she tells me she's glad that I called, actually, because she's been thinking that she wants to do something creative on the side. She's been thinking about writing something, she says, but she doesn't know how or where to start.

"You know I get all these magazines," she says, referring to her subscriptions to *Glamour, Cosmo, Elle,* and a host of others, "and I read these articles and think I could write them just as well if not better."

"You probably could," I tell her. "You know those women's magazine issues better than anyone I know."

"But I wouldn't want to write anything *personal*," she says. "That's the real problem, I guess. When I think about writing, I get so self-conscious. Like, who cares what *I* think?"

"You can't let that stop you if you want to write," I tell her. "It's not like you're under contract to write an article or a book that somebody's going to critique. If you want to write, you should just do it. Nobody has to see it, anyway. Write for yourself. Sometimes writing is the best way to work things out."

She's not convinced. She tells me that she doesn't want to write a journal, that she's not into that touchy-feely kind of thing.

She needs an assignment, she says, and can I give her one? Then she can write it and maybe I could look at it for her and tell her what I think. She knows how busy I am writing my own stuff, she says, but maybe I could take a little time and help her. I tell her I'd never be too busy to help her and I think it's a great idea and, of course, I'd be more than happy to look at anything she writes. I tell her that she should write an article about waxing.

"Waxing?" she says. "What is there to say about that?"

"Plenty," I tell her. "This is something you really know about. Remember when you told me that women *my age* don't go for the same kinds of extreme waxing as women your age? I think you should write about how the standards of beauty are always changing. Waxing is just a part of that, but it makes a good lead-in to the rest."

"Hmm," she says. "I could do that. That's a good idea. So if I write something tonight and e-mail it to you, will you look at it?"

"Of course," I tell her.

"I'm going to do it," she says, "as soon as we get off the phone." There is a small pause and I swear I can hear a shift in her tone before she even speaks again. "I need to ask you something," she says.

"Yes?"

"Why don't you like Tony?"

"What? Who said I didn't like Tony? Where did that come from?"

"Come on, Debra, it was totally obvious at Thanksgiving. Everybody could tell. Everybody. Except Tony. He didn't notice, thank goodness, but it was plain to everybody else."

"I don't know what you mean," I tell her, scrambling frantically through possible responses to her impossible question, wondering if there's any way I'll get out of this conversation without making her angry. She's halfway there already as it is, that note of stridency I know so well insinuating itself into her voice. "I was perfectly nice to Tony at Thanksgiving," I tell her.

"Well, you weren't outright *rude*, if that's what you mean," she says, "but you were definitely not nice. It was all over your face. And I don't know why. Why don't you like him?"

"Why do you care whether or not I like him?" I ask her, avoiding the question and knowing that she'll be right there to call me on it. "It doesn't matter whether or not I like him. It only matters if you like him."

"Bullshit," she says. "I want to know what he's ever done to you."

"He hasn't done anything to me. I don't even know the guy, Lavander. Which is why it makes me a little uncomfortable that he seems to know a lot about me."

Now it's her turn to ask me what I mean, so I tell her that, if she must know, it's slightly upsetting to me that she shares information with Tony that I've given her in confidence. She is a little startled by this and tells me that she really didn't think it was that big of a deal, that there wasn't any malice in it, and that I'm so open and out there about everything in the first place.

"Not everything," I tell her.

"Well, I'm sorry," she says, her tone clearly indicating that she isn't, "but that doesn't excuse your behavior."

"What behavior are you talking about?"

"Just ask Déja."

"What's Déja got to do with this?"

"After you left, she told me that you didn't like Tony. She told me that it was really obvious."

"I don't believe that. She wouldn't say a thing like that, she's got no reason to."

"I wish she was on the phone right now," Lavander says. "She'd tell you."

"Don't worry, I plan to ask her myself!"

I realize that I've raised my voice to match the pitch of hers and that this is as good an indicator as any that we are no longer having a conversation but a full-blown argument. I tell her to calm down, that we need to talk about this like adults, and that means lowering our voices. I reiterate that what I think of Tony is irrelevant, that what matters is that she's happy in her relationship. *If* she's happy, I stress. Because as everybody knows, I tell her, she hasn't exactly been happy in this relationship most of the time.

"How do you know?" she says. "How do you know whether or not I'm happy or what goes on between the two of us?"

I know I should let this go. I should just shine it on, tell her she's right, and move on. But I can't. I just can't let it go.

"Lavander, how many times have you been miserable during this relationship? Think about it."

"I had one breakdown," she counters. "So what? Everything's been fine. Everything is fine now."

"Look, all I know about Tony is what *you've* told me. And if you tell me you're unhappy, if you're crying on the phone—"

"Crying on the phone? How about you? How about when you called me hysterically weeping when you were—"

"First of all, I wasn't hysterically weeping. Second of all, this isn't about me! This is about you and what you tell me. You can't expect everybody else to bounce back like you do. Your relationship with Tony, for whatever reasons—and no, I don't know what they all are—has been tempestuous, and everyone's been there to share that with you."

"Tempestuous? Do you even know what you're talking about? This is the way I am. I'm an emotional person, I have highs and lows. We can't all be as *cold* as you, you know. I have *tempestuous* relationships with everybody in my life. I have a tempestuous relationship with my boss, okay? That's just who I am."

"All I know is what you tell me, Lavander. If you complain

about Tony, if you're upset with the way things are going, why wouldn't I take that to heart? Why would I like him in the face of that?"

"Well, why do you have to listen to me all the time? Why do you have to take everything I say so seriously?"

"You're going to make me nuts," I tell her. "Listen to you, don't listen to you. What you're saying now doesn't make any sense."

"Well, I'm telling you that this is the way it is. I love him."

"Fine, I'm glad you're happy now and I'm glad everything's okay."

"You've got no reason not to like him," she goes on. "If you knew him, if you'd spent some time with him, you'd have a right to an opinion."

"Listen, Lavander, I liked him fine when I first met him. In fact, I liked him more than you did. You didn't even like him that much when you first started seeing him. He was a second-best for you. Don't you remember?"

"You're crazy, do you know that?" she spits. "Where do you get this from? *Do you just make this shit up as you go along or what*? I don't know what reality you're living in, Debra, but it's got nothing to do with mine. It's all in your own head. It's your creation."

This, finally, is what stops me short, what deflates me instantly, and leaves me with a sense of total futility. Because maybe she's right, maybe I do make it all up. Maybe all my perceptions about who we are and what we're doing here are completely false—figments of my own imagination twisted and shaped so that, I hate to think now, they *look good on paper*. With that one sentence, Lavander has managed to make me question what I think and what I do and I've come up short. I feel, for lack of a better word, invalidated.

"I'm not getting this from nowhere," I tell her now. "I can't." I don't sound convincing, even to myself, and Lavander knows it.

"I can't talk about this anymore," she says. "I have to go."

"Don't hang up on me," I tell her.

"I'm not hanging up on you. I've got a lot of things to do. I have to go. I'll call you tomorrow." She hangs up and we both know she won't call me tomorrow or the next day or the day after that. I won't speak to her again unless I call her first. Even then, there's a good possibility she won't answer her phone. I resist the urge to hurl my phone against the wall and sit on my couch in a state of vibrating frustration for several minutes until I can come up with another course of action. Déja, I think to myself. What was she thinking? I dial Déja's number and wait impatiently for her to answer the phone.

"What?" she says. "I'm on my way out the door. Can I call you later?"

"No," I say. "I need to know right now why you told Lavander that I don't like Tony. Why, Déja? What good did you think could come of that?"

Déja is furious. "I never said that!" she barks. "And I'm sick of being caught in the middle of your thing with Lavander. She— both of you are always making trouble and being mean to each other. I don't want any part of it."

"You made yourself part of it," I shout. "What did you tell her?"

"I CAN'T TALK ABOUT THIS RIGHT NOW!" she bellows in my ear. "I'm late and I've got to go. I'll call you later or tomorrow."

"Don't bother!" I scream into the phone, but she's already gone.

As I predicted it would, my argument with Lavander has turned into a long, cold silence. This is not at all of my choosing. After my initial anger passed, I started to think again about what she said and convinced myself that her points were all valid and that

I assumed too much about what went on between her and Tony. As she said, I was so caught up in my own version of reality that I couldn't see hers. I didn't feel that I had anything to apologize for, but I wanted to keep our lines open. I wanted to talk to her without it turning into a battle. It seemed as if we'd been conflicted for so long and I couldn't understand it. She didn't fight like this with Maya or Déja, I told myself, even if those relationships weren't discord free. Why, I wondered, did she always take target practice on me? I wanted this to stop and I was determined to transform our quarrel into something positive, the beginning of a better understanding between the two of us. This, like so many best laid plans, was not to be.

She came to my house a few days after our phone call, but not to see me. She came to pick Maya up so that the two of them could go holiday shopping for her office parties. I was not invited. She breezed into the house, nodding in my direction.

"Hi, Lavander," I said as brightly as I could.

"Debra," she murmured, acknowledging me, but leaving off any kind of salutation. "Maya, are you ready to go?"

I'd gotten some family photographs developed and I had them spread out on my desk. There was one of the two of us (in happier times, I thought) that I wanted her to see.

"Hey, Lav," I said, "do you want to see these photos? There are some really good ones of you here." I smiled at her, beckoning.

"I'm really in kind of a hurry," she said, shutting me down completely. "I just need to get going." She didn't bother to say good-bye on her way out.

I gave up then, at the very moment she turned on her high heels and click-clicked out my door. I couldn't do it anymore, I decided. I couldn't keep feeling bad about myself and I was sick of being hurt by her. To hell with it, I thought. What she said was true; I'd made everything up as I went along. I'd made up our whole connection. Obviously, the notion that we could be close in spite of our differences was a complete illusion.

"Don't tell me that it's my fault," I told Maya and Déja a few days later as the two of them were lamenting the sad state of my relationship with Lavander. "I try with her, I really do, but she doesn't want to hear it."

"You say such mean things to each other," Déja said.

"Stop with the 'mean things' argument, Déja. I am not mean to her and it's not even that she's mean to me. She's just always so angry at me."

"Maybe she thinks you judge her," Maya said.

"No, she thinks *you* judge her," I said. "That's not it. She disagrees with my whole version of reality. She thinks that I live a fabricated life."

My sisters shook their heads. "You know Lavander," Déja said. "She's just like that. She's like that with everybody."

"Did it ever occur to you," I asked them, "that she just doesn't like me?"

"Oh, come on," Maya said.

"I mean it," I said. "And I believe it. She doesn't like me. What can I do about that?"

"You should tell her how you feel," Déja said.

"I don't think so," I said. "I'm tired of getting bitten."

And that's where the two of us are now, frozen in our separate realities with no sign of a thaw. All three of my sisters have gone out together today. Another shopping adventure that I've not been invited to participate in. I believe that the destination this time was to the great temple of Ikea. I tell myself that I don't care and remind myself that I can't stand shopping, but it's a weak argument and I'm not buying it. I'm realizing now that I've been depressed and exhausted since Lavander and I had our falling out. I don't know how many days ago it was, but right now it seems like years. Who knows, perhaps we've been falling out since the day she was born. I can't tell anymore.

Blaze is out doing "guy things" with Bo today (most of which involve eating candy and slurping frozen Cokes) and the house is quiet. I'm debating whether or not to take a walk before he comes home when the door opens and my three sisters come marching in bearing batteries, bedspreads, and lightbulbs.

"We've come for tea!" Déja announces.

"All right, then," I smile at her. "Did you have a successful outing?"

"All kinds of wondrous items," Maya answers, turning on the kettle.

"Hey, Deb, can I see those photos now?" Lavander asks me. She sits down next to me on the couch, smiling and conciliatory. I look away from her for a moment only, but it's long enough to see a look pass between Déja and Maya, telegraphing a wealth of silent information. So that's it, I think. They talked to Lavander. They told her how I felt and they tried to make it right. I turn my eyes back to Lavander, looking for a sign that she's trying to pacify me because she promised the other two that she wouldn't fight with me anymore. I search her face for a clue that she's faking it, that she'd rather be somewhere else, but I don't find it. She looks open and interested. If I weren't feeling so tentative about it, I might even say that she looks loving.

"Okay," I tell her, "I'll get the photos."

We spread them out on the coffee table and Lavander picks them up one by one, studying them. "These are great," she says. "Especially this one." She points to the photo that shows the two of us turned to each other and laughing as if we are sharing a particularly juicy secret.

"That's my favorite, too," I tell her. Lavander throws her arm around my shoulders as we shuffle through the rest of the photos and I realize that this brief touch is all it takes to change my mind about her. I can't give up and neither can she. I'm ready to get up and give it another go. I don't believe it will ever be easy between the two of us. She will keep challenging me and I will keep questioning my version of reality as long as she's there to call me on it. This is who she is and this is what we do. She doesn't always like me, of this I am certain—just as certain, in fact, that she will always love me.

Out of the corner of my eye, I see Déja and Maya steal another glance at each other. They are smiling. Mission accomplished.

Déja and Debra.

10

Driving Forces

december

I'm on my couch and Déja is on the phone. "I'm not going to be able to go with you tomorrow morning," she says. "We're going to have to reschedule."

"Okay," I say.

"It's just that I've got rehearsals now for this new play. And I've been working these double shifts. And Danny's mother's coming to town. She's staying with us. You knew that, right?"

"It's no problem, Déja."

"I mean, it's just that this is the worst possible week for me to do this. I'm sorry."

"Déja, I said it's fine, don't worry about it. We'll reschedule. Why don't you call me tomorrow when you know what's going on and we'll make another plan?"

"I know, but I really want to do this. I just can't—"

"Déja, call me tomorrow."

"Okay, I'll call you tomorrow. Love you."

"Love you, too."

I hang up the phone. Déja was going to take me driving tomorrow and this is at least the fifth time we've rescheduled it. I'm off the hook again and I'm glad. I shouldn't be, but I am.

I don't drive. Four decades here on earth and I've never driven myself anywhere. I am perpetually in need of a ride. It's not even that I don't know how, because I do, and over the years I've taken the wheel several times in vain attempts to become a driver. I'm great in an empty parking lot. I know what needs to be done and I am able to handle a car. I know the rules of the road. I've taken the written test for a driver's permit at least a half dozen times and each time I've missed no more than two questions. But that's always as far as it gets. Although I've made the decision that I *must* do it now and Déja is more than willing to help me, I still don't want to. This is the truth of it.

Driving (or *not* driving, as it were) is my Achilles heel, my bête noire, my weakness, and my curse. This sounds extreme, I know, but it's really not an overstatement. I don't have the slightest difficulty being *in* a car as a passenger, but as soon as I get behind the wheel myself, I start to sweat and tremble. My heart rate goes into the hundreds and I become short of breath. I lose depth perception and the space around me twists into a totally unfamiliar shape. Crash, my brain shouts. You are going to crash, crash, CRASH!

Over the years, it's been very difficult to explain the intensity of this fear to anyone who isn't a family member. Driving isn't high on the list of common phobias in this day and age. When I tell people I don't drive, I get a variety of responses. I once had a boss who was sure I just wanted to be driven like some kind of princess my whole life and that was why I claimed I couldn't drive myself. Acquaintances and co-workers have been convinced that I didn't drive because I'd had my license revoked for drunk driving and didn't want to admit to it. My insistence that I'd never had a license to lose fell on disbelieving ears. I dated a man for a while who took comfort in the notion that I was some kind of throwback.

"It's okay," he said. "My grandmother never drove either. I loved my grandmother."

A woman I was friendly with for a while, who had spent many years in analysis, commented that, "I think it's great that you've come to a place where you're cool with the fact that you don't drive. Some people might, you know, want to do some work on that, but you're just totally okay with it. Aren't you?"

Over the years, I've had many friends who have offered to teach me to drive, each one convinced that he (because they've almost all been men) would be the perfect instructor. I respond by saying that if it were only a matter of learning, it would be easy. It's the crippling fear that's the problem.

"But," they say, "can't you just get over it?"

As I said, I've made some attempts over the last twenty-odd years to do just that. When I turned seventeen, I asked my father to teach me to drive. My father is still the best driver I've ever known. He has driven taxis and vans for a living and even spent some time as a driving instructor. None of that meant anything, unfortunately, when it came to helping me behind the wheel. I'd start the car and he'd yell, "Mirrors!" right off the bat. Then there were a series of omigods as I headed down the street. "Too slow!" he'd say. Then, "Too fast! Did you even *see* that car? This is somebody's driveway—what are you doing?" His favorite trick was to quickly cover the rearview mirror with his hand, and say, "What's behind you?"

"You know, I just don't think I'm ready," I told him after a few abortive lessons.

"Fine," he said.

I didn't really need to drive for the next few years. I lived in Portland, a city with excellent public transportation and, all through college, very few of my friends had cars anyway. Then, suddenly, I was twenty-two and a license seemed way overdue. I made the mistake then of buying a used car and asking the man I was in love with to teach me to drive it. I'll skip the ugly details. Let's just say it all ended with a bent front axle, waiting for AAA in the rain, and a big bottle of gin.

When I was thirty years old and had been living in California, the land of cars, for almost four years, I tried a driving school. My instructor was morbidly obese and showed up at my house for every lesson reeking of the fast-food burgers he'd consumed on his way over. He hardly ever spoke, except to say, "Doncha worry, I got an extra set of pedals right here." My hands slipped from two and ten to five and seven because the steering wheel was consistently covered in grease. After the first set of lessons, the instructor asked me if I wanted to pony up two hundred dollars more to continue and I declined.

A few years after that, I tried driving with a girlfriend of mine who hadn't gotten her own license until she was thirty years old. She understood my fear and I felt very comfortable with her. But we were living quite a distance from each other and had opposing schedules. It became very easy to just let it slide.

Finally, a year ago, I went to a therapist. "This driving issue," I told her, "is the only thing that's wrong. Everything else is fine. Perfect, actually. In fact," I joked, "if I drove I'd be perfect."

"Ha," she said. "Wish I could say the same for myself."

Our sessions turned into the exact opposite of what I was looking for. We started talking about my family, my relationships, and my work. I began thinking that there were problems in each one of these areas. I started getting depressed. And I still wasn't driving. My therapist insisted that I obtain a car somehow and just enlist people to go driving with me.

"You have to do this," she said. "We only have an hour a week together and that's not enough. You have to make the effort and if you keep resisting, I can't help you."

Well, it was true, she couldn't.

My father, however, took a particular interest in my therapy.

"What do you talk about?" he asked.

"Oh, like I'm going to tell *you*," I said.

"No, really," he said. "Do you talk about me? You must. One always talks about one's father in therapy."

"Dad, please."

"I mean maybe it's my fault that you don't drive. Has that come up?"

After a good laugh over this statement, I told him, "Okay, Dad, yes. It's your fault. It's all your fault. You get full blame."

That fact is, it would be easy to blame my father and make someone else responsible for my own inadequacy, but I can't pin this one on him. Even if I could, it would be high time to get the hell over it. Unfortunately, there is nobody to blame here, no fault to be assigned. A few months after I canceled my visits to the therapist, however, I finally came to an understanding of what is probably the genesis of my driving phobia. It was my mother who brought it up first as a possibility.

"I think you're afraid to drive because of what happened that day," she said. "Do you remember? When we were living in the Catskills. Bo was a baby and you were all in the car."

I knew exactly what she was referring to, but I dismissed her. "It wasn't such a big deal," I said. But then I took the memory out, looked at it, and relived it in full color.

It was early 1974 and I was eleven years old. Bo was barely a year old, only beginning to walk. Maya had just turned nine and

Lavander was two. There was no Déja yet. She wouldn't be born for almost four years. I'd been invited to a birthday party and my mother took us all out in our big green Pontiac to buy a gift and drop me off at the party. Car seats were unheard of in those days. Not one of my siblings came home from the hospital in a car seat. Each was nestled in my mother's arms, which everyone always assumed was the safest place for a newborn. We didn't even wear seat belts. I don't know if that car even had any attached to its long vinyl bench seats. I never saw any. When we went out for drives, my parents would sit in the front with Bo. The three girls sat in the back seat, Lavander wedged in between me and Maya.

When my father was driving, we played the three, five, ten game from the backseat. My father would come up with a question worth one of those point values and Maya and I would take turns answering. We watched his eyes in the rearview mirror for a clue as to whether or not we were on the right track. Three-point questions were the easiest and tens were particularly tough. The questions covered a wide range. There were math questions (I always picked the three-pointers there), current-event questions, logic questions, and general trivia (Maya's perennial favorite). We were allowed to choose which point-value question we wanted. My questions were slightly more difficult because I had the age advantage. Nevertheless, Maya and I were in competition. Not that we really cared who *won*. We were more invested in being able to answer my father correctly. Occasionally, my father would throw in an impossible question and add a couple of points if it was answered correctly. I still remember the one that impressed him the most. "Who is Patty Hearst's lawyer?" he asked me, and I knew. I dined out on that victory for a long time.

When my mother was driving, though, there was no game and one of us got to sit up in front. My position as the eldest usually got me that privilege and that was where I was perched that day. We bought a birthday present that was standard for us at the time, which was a sketch pad and colored markers. At the drugstore where we purchased the gift, there were several nickel gumball-style machines offering plastic rings and bracelets. Maya and I got five cents each and tested our luck. My prize, encased in its bright blue plastic bubble, seemed unusually heavy. When I opened it, I saw that it contained a ring, but a ring unlike I'd ever seen in one of those machines before. This one was a real prize and I showed it to my mother and Maya with a great show of excitement. For starters, it was made out of metal instead of plastic, but I couldn't tell if it was silver because it was dull and gray. The center was cut out in the shape of a lightning bolt and there was a tiny cut-out moon on the left side. I slipped it on my finger and it fit perfectly.

"Wow," my mother said. "That's a special one, isn't it?"

I felt pretty smug with my special ring on my hand and I kept staring at it. Perhaps, I thought, it was a magic ring placed in that machine especially for me. Maybe it would give me secret powers that I would discover only when I turned it a certain number of times. I experimented with that, twisting the ring back and forth, wishing for things like invisibility and the ability to control the weather. The only thing that happened, though, was that my mother said she had to stop for gas before we could go to the party.

The gas station was directly off the freeway, perched on the top of a steep incline. One could drive in, get gas, and merge right back into traffic at the bottom of the hill. My mother left the motor running and the driver's-side door open when she got out of the car to pay for the gas. Bo stood up and bounced up and down on the seat, inching away from me and over to the driver's side, where he leaned against the steering wheel, banging and twisting it and singing some baby song of his own creation.

I admired my new ring and let him play. In the backseat, Maya and Lavander were starting to make noise, which I also ignored.

I didn't notice that Bo had grabbed hold of the gear shift. I wasn't watching when he dragged it from park into drive. And then, suddenly, we were rolling. It took a fraction of a second for me to realize that my mother was not in the car and, for that reason, it shouldn't be moving at all. My brother was laughing, delighted that we were in motion. I looked at him jumping with glee, leaning onto the steering wheel for support. Unbelievably to me, the car kept going. After what seemed like a long time, I finally comprehended that we were not going to stop, that we were going to keep rolling down the hill until we rolled right into oncoming traffic. I turned my head to see my mother at the top of the hill, growing smaller as we picked up speed and moved away from her. I could see the look of stark terror on her face as she saw what was happening. Her mouth dropped open and she was shouting something I couldn't hear. I couldn't hear anything. The world had contracted into the silence of fear. I froze in that position, utterly disabled and helpless. I didn't make a move over to the driver's side. I didn't grab my brother. I didn't try to slide my leg over to put my foot on the brake. If the car had been at a stop and I'd been asked to point out which pedal belonged to the gas and which to the brake, I could have done it because I knew which was which. But at that moment, I knew nothing. The car had become a huge unknowable monster that had sucked all of my power into its own. I did nothing at all.

My mother hesitated for a second (perhaps she also expected the car to just stop moving, or perhaps she felt, somehow, that I'd be able to stop it) and then she started running toward us, faster than I've ever seen anyone move. She was in four-inch platform shoes and she ran like a hurricane down that hill. I knew that she wasn't going to make it. I knew that she would miss us and that we'd go hurtling onto the freeway. We'd be hit

instantly in the rush of oncoming cars and we'd all be killed. I
knew this. I knew that we were all going to die. And I knew that
it was going to be my fault, because, even in possession of this
knowledge, I did nothing.

My mother reached the car just as it was turning at the bottom of the hill, a few feet before it would have hit the freeway.
She grabbed the door with one hand and slid halfway in, slamming one foot on the brake while her other scraped the concrete
outside the car. And, like that, we came to a stop. My brother fell
across the seat into my lap and starting squalling. All the sound
in the world came rushing back into my ears. My brother crying,
Lavander and Maya shouting from the back, my mother saying,
"Oh my God, oh my God," over and over again.

The gas station attendant reached the car a couple of seconds
later.

"You okay?" he asked my mother.

"Yes, we're okay," she said, and he broke into a grin.

"You ran pretty fast," he said.

"I've got my kids here," she said by way of explanation. "My
whole life is in this car."

"Are you all right?" she asked me, but it was a question for all
of us.

My mother didn't ask me why the car started moving. She
didn't ask me why I did nothing to stop it. I'd seen my mother
cry, heard her shout, even scream. But I had never seen her like
this—too shocked to do any of those things. A post-disaster quiet
settled inside the car. Even my brother stopped crying and sat
still next to me as my mother slowly navigated her way back onto
the freeway.

"I don't want to go to the party," I told her.

My mother didn't argue, didn't ask me why not. The day was
ruined; she understood that. "Let's go home," she said. She
looked into the backseat for the first time. "You all right?" she

asked Maya, who nodded, mute. Lavander's little lips were pursed tight and she held the fringes of her purple poncho in her hands. I thought she looked incredibly small. My mother looked over at me once more and I forced myself not to cry by digging my fingernails into my palm. As far as I was concerned, I'd almost killed my whole family with my inaction and I didn't deserve the luxury and release of tears.

When I thought about that horrible afternoon in all its particulars, I realized that the feelings I had then—paralysis, helplessness, impending doom—are exactly the same as the ones I feel every time I sit in the driver's seat. So there it was, the reason *why*, and my problem solved. Well, not exactly. As I learned a long time ago, understanding the antecedent of an undesirable behavior pattern doesn't necessarily eliminate it. For me, it was only a start to getting myself, literally, on the road.

I turned forty six months ago and had to go to the Department of Motor Vehicles to get a new identification card. While I was there, I decided to take the driver's permit written test one more time—for the last time, I told myself.

"Hey, great job," the woman correcting my test told me. This time, I missed only one question.

"Thanks," I said. "I've had quite a bit of practice with these tests. I'm going to see if I can actually make this one turn into a license."

She glanced at my birth date on the form. "Why now?" she asked me.

"Well, I'm forty," I told her. "Seems like the thing to do."

It's taken six months for me to actually get into a car with somebody and start driving. There was the question of who I was going to go with to settle first, as well as quite a bit of backpedaling on my end. To be honest, the thought of driving is still immensely unappealing to me. Enlisting the aid of nonfamily members was out as a possibility. I've taken that route before and it's been totally ineffective. It's too difficult, at this point, to try to make someone else understand what is at the root of my problem with driving and, besides, I feel like a complete idiot trying to explain it. Even among my family, there are few possibilities. I can't drive with my mother. She dislikes driving herself and is convinced that my fear of crashing will end up causing an accident. I can't drive with my father because, well, I've tried that already. Besides, his advice is this:

"I told you, the only way for you to drive is to get yourself a little car, get in it, and just drive."

"I can't do that, Dad."

"Yes, you can. It's the only way."

"Who knows better, Dad, me, who doesn't drive, or you?"

"I do."

My siblings have never known me to drive and have accepted it as part of who I am. They don't all understand it, to be sure, but it is familiar to them. Most of them have difficulty visualizing me as a driver at all. Still, when I asked for their help, they all seemed willing. Déja actually seemed excited about helping me and looked on it as an adventure as opposed to a chore. She was also the only one who wasn't worried about what I might do to her car. After pondering the situation for way too long, I decided that Déja was the only choice, the only person who I could feel truly comfortable with. Déja is open and ultimately accepting. She is sometimes moody, sometimes overly blunt, and perpetually late, but she is, and has always been, the sweetest person I've ever known. Perhaps more important than this, though, is that Déja was the only person who *wasn't* in that Pontiac the day it rolled out of control down the hill. I feel safe with her.

————

On the fifth reschedule, my day of reckoning finally arrives. Déja shows up at my house after her yoga class and hands me her keys. "Let's go," she says. "This is going to be so much *fun*."

"Not likely," I grumble, climbing into the driver's seat and wondering if I really have to do this. Déja's legs are at least six inches longer than mine, so I have to adjust the seat and the mirrors. Before I can even turn the key in the ignition, my stomach takes a familiar lurch and my depth perception wavers. Objects in the mirror are nearer, farther, bigger, and smaller than they appear.

"I hate this," I tell Déja.

"Look, it's fine," she says. "I'm fully insured and I have airbags."

"Great," I sigh. "A real vote of confidence." I turn the key, place my foot on the brake, and put the car in drive. "Okay," I say, "we're off."

"Um, Deb," Déja says with slight hesitation, "you're going to want to put the car in reverse so that we can back out of the driveway."

"Right," I say. "Reverse." I glance over at her. Her eyebrows are raised into the same zigzag of puzzlement she's had since she was a tiny baby. She's struggling to hide it, I can tell, but she's a bit worried. For some reason, this makes me laugh. She giggles with me.

"You sure you want to do this?" I ask her.

"Let's just go," she says.

I pull out of the driveway, out of my street, and we're on the road. I'm relieved to find that I'm not sweating yet and my heart is only beating double time instead of triple. Both good signs.

"Okay," Déja says. "Now, I just want you to remember that you *own* this space, this car. You are in control."

"I don't own anything," I tell her. "Believe me. Just watch what I'm doing, okay?"

"Let's go around the neighborhood," she says. "I'll show you where I go with Blaze on our aimless drives."

So this is what we do, drive aimlessly through adjoining neighborhoods, through intersections, cul-de-sacs, and school zones. We turn left, turn right, change lanes, and yield. Déja starts to get excited. "You're doing so well," she says. "I'm so impressed."

"That's because there aren't any other cars around," I say. "Other cars are the problem." This isn't entirely true. Speed is also a problem. As soon as I get over forty-five miles an hour, I start feeling like I'm losing control, like the car is developing a mind of its own. I wonder if I'll ever be comfortable in this position and start feeling that maybe it's all for naught, maybe I just don't have the capacity to get over this mountain. Then Déja reminds me that this is only my first day out.

"Well, you've got a point," I tell her. "But I'm definitely not ready for the freeway."

"Don't worry, we'll take it slow," she says. "Look, we've already been driving for almost an hour. Seems like no time, doesn't it?" I have to admit she's right and that, even though my hands grip the steering wheel, my knuckles aren't white and I am able to talk to her and drive at the same time. I'm not paralyzed. I haven't crashed.

Déja starts talking about her nails. Lavander bought Déja a set of acrylic nails for her birthday, and Déja, who's never before taken an interest in her nails unless it was for a character she had to play, is thrilled. Lavander, on the other hand, is in the nail salon at least twice a month. I can't remember what her hands look like without a manicure.

"Lavander's so funny," Déja says. "You should see her at the nail place. She's on the phone, making deals, and talking to me, loudly, across the salon."

"How do you talk on the phone when you're having your nails done?" I ask.

"I don't know, but she manages to do it," Déja says. "It kinda scares me." She lowers her voice. "You know, they don't like her at the nail place. Don't tell her I said that."

"What do you mean, they don't like her?"

Déja stifles a nervous giggle. "She's always telling them what to do and that they're not getting it right. She's been through, like, ten nail places. They won't wait on her after a while."

"Why do you suppose she does that?"

"Well, if you ask her, she says that they're just no good and she should get what she pays for. She always tips big, but she's just, I don't know, *rude*. She doesn't think so, though." Déja sighs. "Please don't tell her I said that. Maybe she's not rude. Maybe it's just what I see, because I'm just so not like that."

"Or maybe it's just a game she plays with herself. And you."

"Maybe. But I'm going in by myself next time. Less stress. You've got a stop sign here, by the way. You're going to stop, right?"

"I see the stop sign, Déja."

"You know, Bo's thinking about moving in with Lavander again," she says.

"Really? I suggested that to him a while ago, but he said he needed to live alone."

Déja, Bo, and Danny have been living together in that apartment for almost a year now and their lease is about to expire. None of them wants to renew it. The search for affordable housing is on again.

"It's so expensive to live alone around here," Déja says. "And it's lonely. I don't know why anyone would want to live all alone."

"I really liked it," I tell her. "I was perfectly happy living by myself before Blaze was born. Probably could have gone on that way for quite a while. Then I had him, of course. You're never alone after you have children. Once you share your body with another person for nine months that privacy thing is pretty much over for good."

"But you still spend a lot of time by yourself," Déja says.

"Yes, that's true," I tell her. "Blaze is really good about giving me time to be by myself. He also needs that time. Maya's like that too. We all give each other a lot of space. I hardly speak to Maya at all some days, just watch her coming in and going out, like some kind of time-lapse photograph, while I sit at my desk and work."

"I think Maya gets lonely sometimes," Déja says. "I get the same kind of lonely feeling from her that I get from Bo sometimes."

"Don't take it so much to heart," I tell her. "They're okay. We're all okay. I'm a little sad that you're moving out, though. I thought it was nice that you were all living together. I've gotten used to having you around the corner, too." I sigh. "Listen to me," I say. "I'm turning into our parents, wanting to keep everybody close. I'm telling you, Déja, it's a scary thing when you start hearing your parents come out of your mouth."

What I am hearing right now is a recent conversation between me, my parents, and Maya. My parents were talking about how Danny was feeling pressure from his family to move back to New York. He is the only member of his close-knit family to be living so far away. Before he met Déja, his intention was to finish school in California and then move back home. He misses them and they miss him. Because she is so close to her own family, Déja understands this and feels great empathy for him. The two of them have discussed the possibility of Déja moving to New York for a short period of time, but Déja is hesitant.

"Of course Déja can't move to New York," my mother said. "Déja could never live that far away from her family."

"But Danny's living that far away from *his* family," I said.

"That's what you have to do, though," my mother said. "You have to go where your mate is. And where your mate's family is."

"But wouldn't that apply to Déja?" I asked her. "Why wouldn't she go where *her* mate's family is?"

"No, no, no," my father said.

"Why not?" Maya asked.

"Because Déja's *here*," my father said. "And so is he."

I don't tell Déja about this conversation. Nor do I tell her that, despite my devil's advocate position with my parents, I feel very much as they do. I can't imagine what we'd do without Déja. Nor she without us. She herself has said, "I never opted to leave my family for any length of time like he did. I don't know how long I have to spend with my parents. They aren't going to be around forever and I don't want to miss any of that time. Besides, my family are my best friends. They are my people."

And, although I give Danny enormous credit for integrating our family into his life so seamlessly, I also believe that he's getting a pretty good deal. His own mother confirmed this when she came out to visit recently and we all met her.

"Thank you for taking such good care of my son," she said. "I was worried about him being out here all by himself, but I see now that he has not just Déja but her whole loving family around him."

"Where do you want to go next?" Déja says, interrupting my thoughts and making me realize that, for the last few seconds, I have been able to drive and think about something other than how afraid I am at the same time.

"Let's go home," I tell her. "I think that's enough for today."

"Okay," she says. "You've done really well. Honestly, I thought you were going to be all over the place, really sketchy, but you aren't. You really *can* drive. Let's go again on Friday."

On Friday, I'm marginally more comfortable as I drive us down to the market to buy some tea. I park in front of the store and we get out.

"Look at that!" Déja exclaims. "That's a perfect parking job. I wish I could take a picture of that."

"I love parking," I tell her.

"Why?"

"Because it means I get to stop moving."

"You've got to get over this anxiety," she says as we take the same aimless drive we took a couple of days ago, "because you really can drive."

"Slowly," I tell her. "There are many years of conditioning here I've got to get over."

"Well, what is it?" she wants to know. "Accidents you had?"

I tell her about all the times I tried to get beyond my fear and how those attempts ended up in failure. She knows some of these stories, but has never heard them all in detail before. Then I tell her about that day we hurtled down the hill and I did nothing to stop it.

"Oh, but you were so little," she says. "How could you have known? It wasn't your fault. What were you, like, eight years old?"

"Eleven," I tell her. "Really old enough to know. I just froze and did nothing. And that's what I feel like every time I drive now."

"Well, that's terrible," she says. "But it was such a long time ago and you're really not responsible."

"I know that intellectually," I tell her, "but that doesn't mean it hasn't lodged itself in my subconscious like a worm. Anyway, that's why you're the only person I can do this with. You weren't in that car. I didn't nearly kill *you*."

"You're not going to drive with Lavander?" she asks.

"I asked her," I say, "but I don't think so. She's really busy and anyway, I don't think I'll ever be able to drive with Lavander. Driving is so natural to her, it's like an autonomic nervous-system function. I don't think she can understand how anyone else wouldn't be able to drive like that too. I mean, for her, this is incredibly lame. She doesn't know why I can't just drive."

"That's true," Déja says. "Lavander's been driving since she was, like, two years old or something. I drove with her a little when I was first learning and she laughed at me."

"Yes, see, that really wouldn't work for me right now," I say.

"What about Maya?" Déja asks.

"I don't know," I say. "She's also got ideas about who I am and what I should do. She's kind of gotten used to me this way, you know? How am I doing with the center line, by the way, Déja? I always feel like I'm too close to oncoming traffic."

"You're fine," she says. "Try loosening your grip on the wheel a little. And how does Blaze feel about your driving?"

I laugh. "It makes him uncomfortable because it's so far out of his range of reality. But I think he'll probably get used to it pretty quickly. He wants to drive himself. It's funny, he's the one person I can't imagine ever driving *me*."

"Who's going to teach Blaze to drive?" Déja wonders out loud.

"I don't know," I say. "Definitely not me. Daddy would be the best person, although he probably won't want the job. Blaze loves Daddy's style of teaching—eats it up. It's the same style that terrified me as a kid. Go figure."

"It's true," Déja says. "Daddy's not easy." She covers the rearview mirror with her hand. "Quick, what's behind you?"

"Déja, please!" Then I answer her. "A FedEx truck."

Déja removes her hand and looks at the mirror. "Hey, pretty good," she says. "It works! Who knew?"

Déja rolls down her window and puts her arm out, hand up on the roof.

"Why are you hanging on to the roof, Déja? What am I doing wrong?"

"Nothing. Relax. I always sit like this, I'm not hanging on to anything. I'm totally comfortable."

I look over at her and realize that, yes, unbelievably, she is.

"Deb, you have no idea how your world is going to change once you start driving," she says. "You're just going to be so . . . *free*. Do you know that? Have you thought about it?"

"I can't get past this right now," I tell her, taking one hand off the wheel long enough to gesture at the road in front of me. I don't mention that I'm still a little queasy over forty miles per hour and I feel as if the measure of comfort I do have is borrowed.

"I can't wait for you to get there," she says. "You're not going to know how you even managed before."

"I'll take your word for it," I tell her.

By the time Déja and I get into her car again two days later, word of the miracle has spread. Maya has decided that she'd like to take me out driving, too. She's got it all planned out how I'll learn to shift on her Echo, which is surprising because she's very protective of that car. I tell her no, I'm not ready to add shifting to my repertoire. I haven't even taken on the freeway yet, thank you very much. "Well, whatever," Maya says, "but shifting is easy. You'll see."

After putting me off for weeks, Lavander calls and wants to know when I want to go driving with her and why haven't I called her to ask. I tell her not to worry, that I know how busy she is and that Déja's got the time. "We can still go if you want," Lavander says. "Okay, maybe when you have time," I tell her, knowing that this happens about as often as a hailstorm in summer. I know, perhaps better than she does, that she does not want to take me driving anytime in the near future.

I hear from my mother as well and it is her take that pleases me the most. "Déja's so excited about this," she says. "She's really proud of herself."

"As she should be," I say. I've felt a little selfish asking so much from Déja in this respect, I tell my mother. She's giving me so much more than the use of her car and her time. I am happy to know that she is getting something out of this too, that I am able to give her something in return.

For a while, I am lulled into believing that I *will* become a driver and that it is going to be as easy as Déja predicted. On our third time out, Déja takes me to pump gas. On the fourth drive, I manage to get the car over fifty miles an hour for at least ten minutes. It's all going swimmingly, in fact, until our fifth outing when we finally hit the snag I've been waiting for.

We've pumped gas for the second time and I'm exiting the gas station, turning onto a busy stretch of road.

"You need to change lanes," Déja instructs, "or we're going to end up on the freeway."

"Okay," I tell her.

"Okay, so do it," she says sharply. "Change lanes."

I steer casually to the left and Déja yells, "NO! There's a car—oh, shit!" A horn shrieks behind me and my hands go into a death grip on the wheel. My first instinct is to slam on the brakes, but I catch myself and manage to avoid paralysis. Déja is shouting—actually *shouting*—at me.

"NO GOOD, DEBRA! You have to move faster. You can't hesitate—there was a car coming up behind you."

"You told me to change lanes," I say.

"Yes, but *you've* got to look and then *move fast*."

I can't respond to this until I maneuver the two of us onto a quiet, single-lane road. I'm sweating and jangled and any ease I felt at the start of this drive has evaporated. I tell her, "I don't think I can do this. It's not going to work."

"What? You want to give up? Is it because I yelled? I'm sorry, I just got nervous."

"It's not the yelling," I tell her. "Although you've never yelled at me before. Like this, anyway. It's just that I don't think I have the instincts for this. I can't do it."

"This is just one little thing," she says. "You can't give up so easily."

"It's not little," I tell her. "I'm going to get us killed."

Déja sighs. "Do you want to go home?" she questions. Yes, I think, I'd like to go home and forget about driving forever, but I don't tell her this because I don't want to let her down. I don't want *her* to feel as if she's failed. These two desires battle it out in my brain where I can feel the beginnings of a major tension headache.

"Let's just stop for a minute," I tell her, "and then we can talk about the next move."

We've reached the ocean's edge and so I pull over into a beachfront parking spot, turn off the car, and roll down the windows. Déja sighs again and it blends with the sound of the waves breaking in front of us.

"I need a cigarette," I tell her.

"What?"

"Come on, I know you've got one in here somewhere."

"Well, Danny usually leaves one. . . ."

"Yes, Danny smokes. I know." I look at her, leaving the rest unsaid. Déja, always our family's loudest voice against all vices, also smokes sometimes, and now she knows that I know.

"Do you think it will make you feel better?" she asks, but she's not waiting for my answer, she's already reaching for the secret stash and she's got a book of matches in her pocket.

I light the cigarette she hands me and blow smoke out the window. Then I go one step further and give it back to her. "Want some?" I ask her, and she takes it.

"I can't believe I'm doing this," she says, turning away from me so that I won't see her inhale.

"Why? Because you don't smoke?" I laugh. "Or because I don't?"

"Well, *you know* . . ." she begins.

"It doesn't matter, Déja. Do we really need to lecture each other?"

Déja exhales in response and I feel a subtle but important shift between the two of us. I made a bad lane change, she yelled at me, and now we're sharing a cigarette. On the surface these seem like little things, but on a deeper level, we've broken down a barrier I'd always believed was immovable. In this moment, the fifteen years between us have disappeared and we've transcended our first/last positions in the birth order.

I think that as the eldest and youngest, Déja and I have faced the greatest challenge in breaking out of our established patterns of behavior. Among my sisters, it seems to me, Déja and I have always felt more of a need to set an example for each other. We need, in other words, to be *good* when we are around each other. The result is that we shield each other and often hide our vulnerabilities and weaknesses, the aspects of ourselves that aren't up to the standard we've set.

Now, as we sit in the car sharing a forbidden cigarette, those shields are down. There is nothing hidden and no need to hide. Within the hurricane of my insecurity (of which driving is only the most prominent aspect), this is an eye of total comfort.

"Feel better?" Déja asks me.

"Much."

"Well, if I'd known that's all it would take, I would have offered you one sooner."

"Yes, but of course one wouldn't want to make a *habit* of it," I tell her.

"Funny," she says. "So what do you want to do now? Shall we go home?"

I think about it for a second and then I tell her, "No, let's keep going. Might as well. If you're okay."

"Me? I'm fine, really. It's you . . ."

"I'm all right," I tell her. "It's just hard, you know? This is hard for me."

"I shouldn't have yelled at you." She giggles. "I'm sorry."

"Don't be. I'm glad you yelled at me. You *have* to."

"But, really," she says as I start the car, "I want you to know that I *am* comfortable with you driving. Do you believe me? You *are* a driver, you just don't realize it yet."

"I know," I tell her. And I do. I believe her.

Sisters and Bo, 1978.

11

Presence

christmas

Maya stands in our kitchen surrounded by sugar and vanilla.

"God, I'm good," she sighs as she pulls the last batch of cinnamon rolls from the oven. "Look at these. They're perfect, even with this stupid, half-assed oven of ours."

I should mention that our oven has been broken for exactly a year. Only the small top half of this ancient double oven unit is functional. In our house, I am always the one who organizes the repairs, appliance replacements, and carpet cleanings. If it were left up to Maya, queen of procrastination, nothing would get done. When the oven finally gave up the ghost, however, I made a stand. "I don't want to do this one," I told Maya. "You deal with the oven." The result is that we have spent the last twelve months baking everything in an area only marginally bigger

than a toaster oven. Somehow, it hasn't stopped Maya from making any of her specialties. In an amazing show of versatility, she
has managed to work around the problem without actually solving it. Her cinnamon rolls, the hands-down family favorite, are a
perfect example. She packs the last of them into a large plastic
container now, dropping plump sticky raisins onto the linoleum.
I'm going to have to mop later.

"Okay," she says. "I just have to take a shower and then we
can go."

"Better hurry," I tell her, "or we're not going to make it there
by ten."

"Well, nobody else is ever on time anyway," she says.

I wait until I hear the water running to sneak a warm cinnamon roll and then I turn my attention to the giant heap of gifts
sitting near the fireplace. There are dozens of shiny wrapped
boxes here, and these are just from me and Maya. I'm going to
need at least three large shopping bags to pack all of these up
and transport them. I can't imagine what the pile is going to look
like when all of us add our individual stacks together under the
tree—and there is a Christmas tree this year. It's at Déja's apartment and that is where we are all headed for an extended
brunch and gift exchange.

What to do for Christmas this year was the source of much
family discussion and it started way back at the beginning of
November. That was when Maya first informed me that "We've
all been talking about it and we've decided to have gifts this
year."

"What?" I said. "Who's been talking? Who decided? I suppose
I don't get a say in this at all, right?"

"You know, if you don't want to participate, you don't have
to," she said. "You don't have to get anything for anybody and
nobody will get anything for you."

"Oh sure, like that's going to work," I said. "I'll be Scrooge, sitting off in the corner. Sounds great. Don't make it sound like I have a choice about this, okay?"

"We knew you were going to object," Maya said, which irritated me even more. "And, just so you know, there's a price limit. Twenty-five dollars per gift."

"Thank you. I'm so glad that this has all been decided for me," I told her.

I felt as if my annoyance, which had its roots in the ghosts of family Christmases past, was well justified. Both my parents are Jewish. My mother was brought up in a religiously observant household. My father's upbringing was culturally observant as opposed to religious. Neither one of their families would have ever considered celebrating Christmas. My parents, however, had rejected organized religion altogether by the time I was born. I have been in a synagogue exactly once and that was for my brother's *Miami Vice*–style bar mitzvah, which my parents put together more for the sake of their families (most of whom were still alive then) than anything else.

When I was about eleven or twelve and we were living in the Catskills, my parents started "doing" Christmas. These were specifically nondenominational events. We had lights, a tree, and gifts to go under it. We did not have eggnog, Santa Clauses, or nativity scenes. I don't know how or why this started, but it was extremely popular with all of us. I loved decorating the tree and arranging the presents beneath it. I loved the smell of pine, coffee, and wrapping paper on Christmas morning. And December 25 was the only day of the entire year that I loved snow. When we went back to school after the holidays, we were able, like everybody else, to exchange stories about what we wanted and what we got for Christmas.

As the years rolled on, though, the trees began to get progressively smaller and menorahs started making an appearance as part of the decoration. By the time we all moved to California when Blaze was a year old, we had what my parents described as a Hanukkah bush. Despite the shifting icons, however, the size and number of gifts never diminished. As my brother and sisters got older and started working, Christmas became a time of frantic shopping and overspending. We started buying multiple gifts for each other. The number of presents started multiplying exponentially, as did the collective debt. It took hours to unwrap everything and there was invariably a skirmish or two when this one felt that one hadn't put as much thought into the gift that she bought for the other one. It finally got so out of control that we started drawing names from a hat so that each person would only be responsible for one gift. This didn't last too long. People cheated, buying side gifts on the sly and trading names. There was a big disparity between the amounts spent on gifts depending on who was flush and who wasn't. Christmas wasn't merry, it was stressful.

Finally, about five years ago, we were all exhausted and threw in the towel on the gift exchange. Christmas, we decided, should be more like Thanksgiving. In other words, a day of family and food. The Christmas brunch was born and, like most family events, was held at my house. As a bonus, we added going to the movies and whatever Chinese restaurant was open for dinner. There hasn't been a complete ban on gifts since then, however. Blaze always gets something from everyone and there are girlfriends and boyfriends passing through who give and receive gifts as well. But there has been an absence of that frenzied shopping mania for the last few years and I can't say that I miss it. This year, my reluctance to dive back into all of that has earned me the title of Scrooge.

I discovered that Déja and Maya (betrayer!) were the main architects of this year's switchback. Maya claimed that she saw "little things for people" all the time that she wanted to buy and she thought it would be nice to have a gift exchange again. Déja was the one who wanted the trimmings. "That's right," she said, "I'm getting a *big* tree. We've never had a tree with all the lights and everything."

"Oh no," I told her, "we used to have a tree every year, but you missed that. Born too late." Danny will be here for Christmas this year, instead of with his family in New York, and this is another reason why Déja wants to have a big event. She is trying her best to alleviate his homesickness as much as possible. The strain between his desire to stay and wish to be near his family is growing and Déja doesn't have a solution at the ready.

So, for the last few weeks, we've all joined the ranks of hapless holiday shoppers out there, listening to endless loops of "Jingle Bells" in stores while the bright California sun renders the very notion of snow impossible. I started my shopping with Maya but quickly gave that up after she kept saying, "No, she doesn't want that. No, he wouldn't like that. No, what she really needs is . . ."

"We need to do this separately," I told her.

"Fine," she said. "Since you don't want my help."

Blaze and I argued for at least two weeks about what gifts he should give. His part of the argument involved telling me that I should give him money to buy the (expensive) items he had picked out for each family member. I told him that nobody expected him to buy gifts since he didn't have a job and didn't earn any money. He should make something, I said. We went back and forth on this for a long time until he finally conceded to my mother's idea, which was that he make a mixed CD with a song picked out for each person. I helped him with this and we made a game out of it. "Let's see if everybody can guess which song is theirs," I told him. His pile of CDs sits wrapped and ready on the fireplace now, a nice addition to the rest.

I got into it briefly with Lavander over the gift issue as well. (Actually, every member of my family has had a crack at me over my initial resistance to the Currier & Ives Christmas that everyone seems to have in mind. Even my brother weighed in with this statement: "I've got a title for your next book, Deb, *The Christmas I Never Had.* What do you think?" I told him, "I think I prefer *The Birthday I Never Had.* Smart-ass."). Lavander requested that everyone submit to her a list of gifts that they'd like. In turn, she had designated items that she wanted each person to buy for her.

"No," I told her. "I'm not doing that. What's the point of getting gifts at all, then? Might as well just give you cash."

"You are so difficult," she said.

"I am not difficult. A list defeats the whole spirit of the thing."

"No, it doesn't," she argued. "I don't want people to get me things I don't want or need. This way, you know what to get."

"So, basically you're saying that you don't trust your family to give you things that you'll like?"

"No, that is *not* what I'm saying! Listen, don't you want me to get you something you want?"

"I'll like whatever you get me," I told her, "because it will have come from *you.*"

"Well, fine, we'll just see," she said.

It turned out that Lavander's gift was the first one I bought. I got her four aromatherapy candles and a set of wishing stones in a small leather bag. When I saw them, the stones reminded me of the tiny worry dolls that Lavander gave me for my birthday a few years ago. There were three of them in a soft cloth box. "I only got you three," Lavander said then, "because you're not allowed to have more than three major worries at a time."

Wishes and worries. Between us, Lavander and I have so many.

I think about this as I put the last of the gifts in bags for transport. Maya emerges from her room, ready to go, and gathers the baked goods from the kitchen.

"You've been eating the cinnamon rolls, haven't you?" she says.

"Let's just go," I tell her, and summon Blaze to come help me load up the car.

There is a wreath on Déja's door and a sea of gifts on her living room floor that extends several feet past the Christmas tree.

"Wow," is all I can think to say as we walk in and survey the scene. My parents have already taken their places at the table and are waiting for breakfast. Déja hustles frantically between the tree and the kitchen, arranging gifts and pouring coffee. She seems a little wound up, not her usual state of being. Behind Bo's closed door, we can hear the frantic crunch and taping of last-minute wrapping. Lavander comes out of his room holding ruined ribbon and tissue.

"He's beyond help at this point," she says. She's come by herself today. Tony is with his family in northern California. I remember now that he spent last Christmas with us and that she's been seeing him for a year. Seems both longer and shorter than that, I think.

Blaze wants to dive bodily into the gift pile but my father stops him. "Food first," he says. "Then presents."

I suggest that we listen to Blaze's CD while we eat brunch and see if we can identify whom each song belongs to. There is a total of sixteen songs, I tell them, two for each person, and there is no particular order. This gives Blaze something to do while he waits for the ceremonies to begin and provokes much commentary. "Yes!" my mother says as the initial strains of "The Girl from Ipanema" fill the air. "This one's mine."

"I can't wait to see what he picked for me," Lavander says.

Bo emerges from his room and places what is clearly a bowl, albeit hastily wrapped, on the pile. "Mystery gift!" he exclaims, and, with that, the party is under way.

"So, Debra," my father says, as he selects a cinnamon roll

from the rapidly diminishing stack, "I read somewhere that the next *Harry Potter* book is going to be something like eight hundred pages long."

I take a sip of coffee to fortify myself. I know what's coming next. "Yes?" I say.

"I'm just saying, that's a lot of pages," he says. "And she just keeps writing them."

"And?"

"Can't you come up with something like that?"

"Like *Harry Potter*? Books that sell in the gazillions of copies, you mean? I'll just whip some of those up. No problem."

"I mean, there has to be a formula," my father says.

"Dad, you can't compare me to J. K. Rowling."

"Why not? We're talking about books, right?"

I'm getting ready to embark on what I know will be a useless argument, but Déja interrupts me, throwing up her arms and exclaiming, "Yes, this is *my* song! Woohoo!" as Stevie Wonder starts singing "You and I." Blaze goes rushing over to Déja to give her a hug.

"How are the cinnamon rolls, Dad?" Maya asks.

"So good," he says, distracted, thankfully, from the topic of best-sellerdom. "I'm telling you, Maya, if you could package these . . ."

I'm reminded of something my father told my mother recently (which my mother then repeated to me). He said that of all his daughters, it was the most surprising that Maya wasn't married. He just couldn't understand how she hadn't been snatched up. Sure, all his daughters were beautiful and talented and intelligent, but Maya could *cook*. She could bake amazing, delectable treats. What else could a man ask for, really? My mother accused him of being Fred Flintstone and asked him what century he thought he was living in. Exactly, he told her. Men haven't evolved much. They're simple creatures. It's everything else that's gotten complicated. I look around the room at my father, Bo, Danny, and Blaze, our four "simple creatures," and wonder if he's right.

"Does anyone want more potatoes?" Déja asks. "Because I'm just about done in the kitchen now."

"Enough food," my mother says. "It's definitely time for presents. Let the festivities begin."

We all straggle toward the living room, climbing over the boxes on the floor, and trying to find a place to sit. This apartment is clearly too small for a gift exchange of this magnitude.

"Okay," Déja says. "I'm going to hand them out one at a time."

Predictably, this sparks a debate. Some of the opinions offered are that it will take too long that way, Déja should let Blaze help her, everybody should get a pile of his or her gifts and then unwrap them one at a time, and that it should just be a giant free-for-all.

"No!" Déja says. "This is the way I'm going to do it. And I *am* doing it, so everybody just be quiet."

Déja seems as if she is on the verge of a major meltdown, so we all capitulate. Blaze eyes her warily. In this group, Blaze is the only one who gets really rattled when Déja gets upset. This is not to say that we don't care, but Déja's breakdowns, when they happen, are usually caused by physical concerns. When she's overtired, hungry, or has cramps (the biggest culprit), she gets weepy and starts slamming doors. Her outbursts are dramatic but short-lived, and almost always mitigated by food, sleep, or analgesics. It's when she gets quiet and doesn't talk, rare occurrences, that we worry about her. Blaze, however, can't stand it when she's distressed in any way for any reason and always rushes to her aid. Danny doesn't deal with Déja's tears too well, either, come to think of it. He's hovering around the edge of the living room now, looking a little edgy himself.

Déja gives Blaze the first gift, a DVD he's been wanting from her and Danny. Maya insists that Blaze gets her gift next, which is a set of movie-watching accoutrements (red-and-white-striped containers, soda glasses, and microwave popcorn) and a six-pack of Coca-Cola (a forbidden beverage in our house). Blaze is surprised, but very happy.

"Well," he says, and casts a loving gaze at the Coke, "*this* is unusual, isn't it?"

Déja hands out more gifts. Lavander gets, and likes, her wishing stones. Maya receives a heated massaging seat cover for her car. Danny gets a Buddha-in-a-box and a travel mug. My mother gets a yoga mat and a bracelet. Bo gets skin cream and an herbal dietary supplement. My father gets a fleece vest. This is only the first round. It's going smoothly until Déja opens my father's gift to her which is a pair of silver hoop earrings.

"I could just see those on you," my father tells her.

"How could you see these on me?" Déja says. "I don't wear earrings. I've never worn earrings, I don't even have pierced ears."

"You wear earrings," my father says.

"I don't wear earrings, Daddy!" And that's it, the tears start flowing. "I need a break," Déja sobs, and heads to her room. Blaze follows her with a Coke in hand.

"You can take them back," my father calls after her. My mother sighs. Maya looks over at Danny.

"What's the matter with your girlfriend today, Danny?" she asks him.

Danny shrugs in that gesture universal to all men who are asked what ails their women. "I don't fuckin' know," he sighs.

"These would look good on me," Lavander says, holding the hoops next to her ears. "I'll take them."

"Dad," I say, "I find it interesting that you got Déja earrings considering that you wouldn't even let me get my ears pierced back in the day."

"What?" he says. "Oh yes, but that was different, you were a little girl then."

"Eighteen," I tell him. "I had to wait until I moved out to get my ears pierced."

"That's not true," he says.

"It's just interesting," I say, "how things change."

"Go get her," my mother tells my father. Dutifully, my father gets up and goes into Déja's room. "And don't make it worse!" my mother calls after him. The sound of Blaze's CD fills the brief silence that follows, with Anita Baker singing "Just Because."

"This one's for me," Maya says.

"This CD was such a good idea," my mother says. "Wasn't it, Debra? Well, wasn't it?"

"Yes, Mom. Yes, it was."

My father comes back out and resumes his seat. "She has cramps," he announces to the group at large and gets a collective "Aah" in response. This is another great divide between me and my sisters. I'd rather eat dirt than discuss the state of my uterus with my family, but Déja and Lavander aren't at all hesitant to broadcast this kind of information in all its particulars. Maya is somewhere in the middle of those two extremes. As for my father, he's spent a lifetime picking up feminine hygiene products on the way home and delivering Midol to the various workplaces of his daughters. In my entire life, I've never met a man who was as comfortable discussing PMS and sanitary napkins.

Déja comes out of her room sniffling. "Let's get on with this," she says, and starts tossing gifts around. When we get to the gifts from my parents, there is much confusion. It seems they misla-beled several gifts. They start arguing over who gets what and accusing each other of being incompetent. In the meantime, Lavander gives me her gift.

"I just want you to know that I put the most thought into

yours," she says. And it's true, this is the most thoughtful gift she's ever given me. It's a framed enlargement of a photograph my father took of the two of us at Disneyland thirteen years ago. We are sitting side by side with Blaze's stroller between us, legs crossed, chins in hands, staring in opposite directions. Captured in a moment of complete synchronicity, our body language and the expressions on our faces are identical. How much longer? What's next? This is what I hear the two of us thinking when I look at the photo.

"I love this," I tell her, and show it around.

"A thousand words," my father says.

"This one's worth two thousand," I tell him.

Despite the fact that everyone has opened at least three gifts each at this point, the pile on the floor has hardly receded at all. Déja is starting to tire again. Instead of opening our gifts in an orderly fashion, we've now started trying things on and asking each other, "Do you *really* like what I got you or are you just saying you do?"

"He*llo*," Déja says. "We've got a way to go here. Pay attention." She speeds it up, handing out packages two at a time and not waiting for reactions before redistributing.

"You *are* a wee bit ratty today," my mother tells her. "You know that, right?"

"Excuse me, I'm in pain," Déja says, opening her gift from Danny, which is an electric back massager. "Oh, good," she says, "I think I'm going to try this out right now."

"Um, while you're all admiring your gifts, I'd like to take a moment and point out what I've received so far," Bo says. "There seems to be a theme." All eyes turn to him. "Yes," he says, "I've got, let's see, a love voodoo doll, some herbal diet formula, and, um, itch cream. Are you all trying to tell me something?"

The room erupts with raucous laughter. Once again, my

brother has rendered us speechless and rolling. Lavander and my mother wipe tears from their eyes.

"Give him ours, please," my mother manages to tell my father when she can take a breath. "Poor thing." My father hands Bo a box and he opens it eagerly to reveal a very handsome gray turtleneck.

"This is great," Bo says. "I've been needing one of these." He holds it against himself and everyone agrees that it looks wonderful.

"Um, there's a bit of a problem with that turtleneck," my mother says.

"No, there isn't, it's terrific," Bo says.

"Well, actually, it's Danny's gift," my mother says. "We put the wrong name on the box."

"We did?" my father asks. "No, you did. I told you—"

"Here you go, Dan," Bo says, handing it over.

"Cool," Danny says. "Thanks a lot."

"Give him mine," I tell Déja. "It's this one."

My gift to Bo is a set of cereal bowls with a milk pitcher and sugar bowl, all decorated with Toucan Sam and Tony the Tiger. I thought it was cute and kitschy when I bought it, but as he opens it now and gives it a look of stunned incomprehension, I just feel bad.

"I think you made a mistake, Debra," my mother says. "What is that?"

"No, *you* made a mistake," I tell her. "At least I didn't give him somebody else's gift."

My mother starts to argue with me, but Bo interrupts us with his laughter. "Jeez, Deb, I just don't know what to make of this," he says. "I think I'll save it for the swinging bachelor pad I'm going to have."

"Well, I'm sorry," I tell him. "I thought it was cute."

Blaze comes back into the room and reaches for another Coke as the last song on his CD begins. It's Sade, singing "By Your Side."

"No more Coke," I tell him. "You'll be bouncing off the walls."

Blaze ignores me, and tells Lavander, "This is your song."

"Oh, is it?" she says, and her eyes fill with tears. "He's so sweet. Always by my side."

Déja scrambles through strewn wrapping paper and tinsel on the floor, searching for more gifts. "I think that's it," she says, finding none. "Somebody else needs to clean this up now."

Bo gets up to make more coffee and the rest of us start cleaning up the apartment. Danny provides several trash bags for the leavings. It's not even one o'clock yet and everyone looks totally exhausted.

"And that's it—over," my mother says as the last piece of gift wrap is thrown out. "Like it never happened. Such is the transitory nature of things."

"Almost time to eat again," my father says.

"I bought stuff for dinner," Maya says, "so we don't have to search around for food like we did last year. So you can all come over to my house to eat later."

"Great," my father says. "What shall we do until then? Maybe we should just hang out here."

"No!" says Déja. "I mean, it's not necessary for us to all stay here. We've done this venue. Time for a shift."

"We don't have to spend every second of the day together, do we?" I ask. "Can't we split up and regroup later?"

"But why?" my father asks.

"Let's go to my house," Lavander says. "We can play some cards or something and then we'll go over to Maya and Debra's for dinner."

"Perfect," Déja says. "And why don't you all head out, like *now*, and then we'll follow, okay?"

As Déja hustles us toward the door, it occurs to me that I like getting kicked out of her house. To state it a little more clearly, I like that she *has* a house to kick me out of. I like the fact that we are visiting her, that she made breakfast, that she's got a tree and a boyfriend she loves. I like that she makes dinner for our brother in her house and worries about him when he comes home late or seems lonely. I like that she goes swimming with Maya in her pool three days a week and brings Blaze here on the weekends. I like that she has a place I could come to anytime for any reason.

And it's not just Déja I feel this way about. I realize that this is the first year that both she and Lavander have had their own places. Lavander's house has been open this year, too. She has been hosting some of these family events instead of leaving them early to go somewhere else, which was always her modus operandi in the past. I am as comfortable in Lavander's house as I am in Déja's.

I suppose what it really comes down to is that I like the fact that my sisters are catching up to where I feel I've always been, in the land of the grown-ups, and I like having the company here as I head into the second half of my life.

"Okay, Blaze is coming with me," Lavander says as she gathers her packages and prepares to leave. "Just give me a minute to get my house together before you all come over, will you? And can you find some poker chips to bring over? I don't have any." She calls out for Blaze. "Honey, come help me carry my stuff to the car, please."

Once again, Blaze obliges.

"How does she do it?" I ask Maya as I watch Blaze lumber down to her car all loaded up with candles and shopping bags. "And he doesn't even drop anything."

Maya and I decide to go home and drop off all our things before we head over to Lavander's house. And there are the poker chips, of course. We're going to have to find some of those, too. I go into Déja's room to say good-bye to her. She's lying facedown on her bed and Danny is running the massager up and down her back.

"See you in a bit," I tell her.

"Mmpf," she says from the folds of her pillow.

"Are you all right?" I ask her.

Déja lifts her head and turns toward me. "You know the voice of the teacher on *Charlie Brown*," she asks me. "You know how it goes 'waa waaa waa waa'? Well, that's how everybody sounds to me today. Just incredibly irritating. Know what I mean?"

"I can dig it," I tell her.

It's quiet in the car without Blaze in the back complaining about how his legs are too long to be squashed into the backseat. Our copy of his CD is playing in here, though, with the song he chose for Danny, Nelly's "Hot in Herre," coming through the speakers.

"This is such a weird collection of songs," I tell Maya. "I mean, one wouldn't really think to put João Gilberto, Tom Petty, and Outkast on the same CD, but somehow it works."

"They actually sound pretty good all together," Maya says. "Even if it is a bit of a wacky combination."

"Well, that's all of us, isn't it?" I ask her. "We're a wacky combination, but one that works. You just wouldn't want to listen to it or be around it all the time."

"That's true," she says. "Did he really choose all of these songs himself?"

"Of course," I tell her. "This is one thing he didn't need any help with."

She turns up the volume on the CD as the song switches to

Bo's selection, Sly and the Family Stone's "If You Want Me to Stay."

"So, part one went okay," I tell her. "Don't you think?"

"Yes, I think it's a good idea to change locations during the day," she says. "That way people don't get antsy and start fighting."

I wait for a moment, and then I ask her, "Do you like your present?" I gave her a violin pin that she saw, coveted, but didn't buy for herself when we were shopping together several months ago. She's wearing it now.

"I love it," she says, touching it lightly.

"Do you remember when we looked at it, you asked me, 'Why doesn't somebody get this for me?' "

"No," she says. "I'd totally forgotten I ever saw this pin."

"Well, I remembered."

"Yes."

"I want to tell you," I say, a conspiratorial tone creeping into my voice, "that I spent more than the allotted sum on your gift. Just so you know. In fact, I spent almost *twice* that amount." I wait a beat or two to let this sink in. "But don't tell the others," I add.

Maya smiles, a little Mona Lisa thing that turns up the corners of her mouth.

"Don't worry," she says. "I won't."

Sisters lounging.

Epilogue

january 2003

It's a new year and raining like mad. It's going to be another El Niño year, they say, and so we should expect more of the same in the months to come. Weather phenomenon or no, southern California rain always seems a bit crazy to me. The drops are fat and heavy, the palm fronds slap and whip with fury, and something, usually the mall parking lot, always floods. Rain falls with a great deal of drama here and so I suppose it's appropriate that I'm going out in it today to meet my sisters for breakfast.

The four of us haven't spent much time together since Christmas. There has been quite a bit of shuffling and readjusting in the last few weeks. Déja's new gender-bending play is about to open and she's fully immersed in her character, a bitter misogynistic *man*. She claims to have come to a whole new realization of what men are all about. "They just don't go very deep," she says. In the middle of this, she and Danny have just moved into another apartment without Bo, who is now staying with Lavander.

Maya's been booked solid lately, either playing, teaching, or rehearsing for concerts. She spends more time out of the house than in it these days. For the first time ever, we've had to start scheduling things like grocery shopping, which we still do together.

Lavander is perennially busy, but even more so now than usual. She's so busy, in fact, that she doesn't even answer her cell phone anymore. At this point, she's operating solely in "I'll return your call as soon as possible" mode. Her relationship with Tony seems to be coming to an end as well, but it's a protracted process. They've broken up a number of times already and now even she seems tired of talking about it.

As for me, I've gone further into my internal space, disappearing, for days at a time it seems, into whatever is on my desk. Unlike my sisters, my radius of activity has gotten smaller. It's a safe bet that, at any point during the day, I can be found at home or very close to it.

There's no event to celebrate today and no passage to mark. But we've been spinning like planets in our own little spaces long enough now for the inevitable pull of gravity to bring us together, to center, for a couple of hours. This is the reason for today's breakfast.

It's just after ten in the morning when Maya and I pick Déja up at her new apartment and the three of us head out to a nearby restaurant that I've chosen for our rendezvous. Maya makes a last-ditch attempt to change the venue to Honey's, a restaurant she knows that makes "great potatoes."

"You can get potatoes anywhere," I tell her.

"Not like Honey's."

"Then think of it this way—I'm doing you a favor. Do you really need those potatoes?"

"Okay, forget it," she says.

In the backseat of the car, Déja just laughs.

We scan the restaurant for Lavander before we seat ourselves, hoping that she's already arrived, but there's no trace of her. A tall pleasant waitress gives us three menus and takes our coffee order. Maya and Déja scan the offerings and Déja wonders out loud if it's too early to order lunch.

"They have potatoes," Maya says.

"Told you," I say.

"What are you having?" Déja asks me.

"I don't know. Just a bagel or something. I'm not really that hungry."

Déja and Maya put down their menus and stare at me accusingly.

"Why did you want to come out to breakfast, then?" Déja says. "You're never hungry. What's the point?"

"It's not about the food," I tell her. "You know that."

"I don't know about that," Maya says. "In a restaurant, it really *is* about the food, wouldn't you say?"

The waitress returns with two cups of coffee and Maya's tea and pulls out her order pad.

"Are you girls ready to order?" she asks.

I look at my watch and then at the empty seat at the table. "Can we hold off for a few minutes?" I ask the waitress. "We're waiting for one more girl."

The waitress gets flustered. "Oh, I'm sorry," she says. "I didn't mean to call you girls. I mean, um, *ladies*, or, er . . ." She seems lost and uncomfortable.

Déja, Maya, and I all start talking at once:

"Oh no, it's okay—"

"Girls, ladies, whatever—"

"We *are* girls—"

"She should be here any minute," I tell the waitress. "But just let us know if you need the table and we'll order if she doesn't get here soon."

The waitress assures us that there's no problem and backs away from our table in a hurry.

"Oh no," Déja says. "I think we offended her."

"I think she thinks she offended us by calling us girls," I say.

"It's so not like that," Déja says. "Can you imagine being one of those women who gets all bent out of shape being called a girl? I wait on those types all the time. It must be such a strain to get upset about things like that."

"Maybe she sensed that we're sisters," I say. "Sisters are always girls, somehow."

"Whatever *that* means," Déja says after a moment. "But it just doesn't sound right to say 'Are you *women* ready to order,' does it?"

"Guess not," Maya says.

After a few more minutes and another coffee refill, Déja says, "Do you think Lavander got stuck in traffic? She knows what time we were supposed to meet, doesn't she?"

"I confirmed with her twice," I tell Déja. "Let's call her and see what's going on."

All three of us pull out our cell phones, but Déja gets to hers first. "Hi, Lavy," she says to Lavander's recorded message. "Where are you? We're waiting for you. Call us on one of our phones. . . ."

By the time Lavander arrives, we've been in the restaurant for an hour. It's no longer raining and the sky has lightened enough to promise sunshine. We've ordered and are almost finished eating. Lavander has called three times, as she passed various exits on the freeway, to make sure we would wait for her. She got caught in a meeting, she said, and the traffic is horrendous, and she's so sorry.

"There she is," Déja says, glancing out the restaurant's window and we all turn to look as Lavander parks her car and hustles inside. She's a vision in beige and taupe today, outfitted in a dress shirt, slacks, and the pointiest snakeskin boots I have ever seen.

"Poor thing," Maya says. "She looks so stressed out."

"She really does remind me of Grandma," Déja says.

"It's true," I say. "Grandma was the only other person in this family who could put herself together like that."

"I am so sorry," Lavander says by way of greeting. "That meeting just took forever." Déja and Maya pat her shoulders affectionately.

"It's okay," Maya says. "We ordered for you."

And it really is all right. We don't care that she's an hour late and that we have little time left before we all have to go our separate ways again today. We're just glad that she's here, that our quartet is complete. In the last half hour, our conversation has been petering out and we've been leaving our sentences unfinished. We've started complaining about everything we have to do today. Now that Lavander is here, though, I can feel the shift in attitude at the table. We've become revitalized and we're all talking at once.

"How's your new roommate?" Maya asks Lavander, referring to Bo.

"He's fine," she says. "I think it's going to work out. He did eat all my food, though."

"You need to watch him," Déja pipes in. "He'll eat everything. And you need to make sure you get money from him for bills, otherwise he won't—"

"Don't tell her that," I chide Déja. "Let them work it out. You're finished living with him now."

Maya rushes to Déja's defense, telling me that I have no idea what she went through living with our brother. Lavander says that Bo is different *with her*. I tell Maya she doesn't know anything firsthand and tell Lavander not to pay attention to either one of our sisters. And, just like that, it happens. Like the angles of a square, we settle immediately into our own familiar corners. We are comfortable, even relaxed, in our positions and the crisscrossing lines of tension and energy between us.

Maya switches topics and asks Lavander why she's wearing so much makeup.

"Do you think it's too much?" Lavander asks. "I keep feeling like I have to cover my skin."

"Way too much," Maya says.

"Get some of it off, will you?" Lavander asks her. Maya picks up an unused napkin and wipes off some of the base coating Lavander's face while I pull a mirror from my purse so that Lavander can study the results.

Déja watches and smiles. "Sometimes I just can't get over it," she says.

"What's that, Déj?"

"You're all just so . . . *beautiful*," she says. "I have the most beautiful sisters in the world."

We all share this feeling, but only Déja could give it voice. In anyone else's mouth, these words would sound syrupy and insincere. Déja manages to convey their real meaning. My sisters *are* lovely, but she's not talking about physical beauty. Together, we illuminate each other. When we reflect off each other, whatever light we possess individually is made that much brighter. It is this brightness that Déja finds beautiful. It is the brilliance and power of sisters.

Acknowledgments

Much love and grateful thanks to Marjorie Braman,
Amy Rennert, Janell, Pat, and Gabe.

And, as always, very special thanks to my extraordinary
family for giving me so much wonderful material
and allowing me to use it.

BOOKS BY DEBRA GINSBERG

ABOUT MY SISTERS
ISBN 0-06-052203-8 (paperback)

In *About My Sisters*, Debra Ginsberg examines the mysterious, fascinating relationship between sisters as seen through the special bond she shares with her own three sisters, Maya, Lavander, and Déja.

"Poignant . . . Debra Ginsberg takes a big-hearted look at the ties that bind and the bonds that break and mend again." —*Elle*

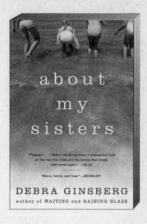

RAISING BLAZE
Bringing Up an Extraordinary Son in an Ordinary World
ISBN 0-06-00433-9 (paperback)

Blaze never crawled; at one he simply stood up and walked. By the time he was four, he knew the complete works of Miles Davis.

"Refutes many common assumptions about single mothers, special-ed kids, "experts" of all kinds and American public schools." —*Publishers Weekly*

WAITING
The True Confessions of a Waitress
ISBN 0-06-093281-3 (paperback)

Debra Ginsberg takes readers on her 20-year journey as a waitress at a soap-operatic Italian restaurant, an exclusive five-star dining club, and the dingiest of diners. A behind-the-scenes look at restaurant life and how most people in this business are in a state of waiting to do something else.

"A lively and insightful look into restaurants. . . . Ginsberg is a charming and talented writer."
—*San Francisco Chronicle*